J'accuse!

The Men Who Betrayed France

by André Simone

INTRODUCTION BY CARLETON BEALS

KENNIKAT PRESS, INC./PORT WASHINGTON, N. Y.

J'ACCUSE!

Copyright 1940 by Andre Simone
Reissued 1969 by Kennikat Press
By arrangement with The Dial Press Inc.

Library of Congress Catalog Card No: 68-26224
Manufactured in the United States of America

ESSAY AND GENERAL LITERATURE INDEX REPRINT SERIES

CONTENTS

	INTRODUCTION	7
1.	SURRENDER	13
2.	FROM HITLER'S RISE TO THE PARIS RIOTS	28
3.	THE REGENTS OF FRANCE	68
4.	PAPA DOUMERGUE—THE SAVIOR WHO FAILED	79
5.	FIFTEEN MONTHS OF LAVAL	105
6.	THE TWO EDOUARDS	144
7.	HITLER MARCHES—FLANDIN WEEPS	155
8.	THE POPULAR FRONT IN ACTION	169
9.	CHAUTEMPS: ANTI-CLIMAX	215
10.	MUNICH	232
11.	MUNICHMEN AND ANTI-MUNICHMEN	273
12.	PRAGUE	281
13.	THE APPROACH OF WAR	301
14.	FROM SITZKRIEG TO BLITZKRIEG	314

INTRODUCTION

THIS book is considerably more than the equivalent of *Washington Merry-Go-Round*, which it somewhat resembles in its sprightly but deadly humor, its lack of reverence for the great so long overpuffed by dutiful headlines, and its knowledge of inner scandals, intrigues, petty ambitions and vanities—all the small trickeries that are part and parcel of the behind-the-scenes maneuvering in any large capital. It is more than *Washington Merry-Go-Round*, because it is written in an hour of defeat and betrayal for France, so that sprightliness and wit are charged with lurking tragedy and deep indignation. Although Simone wields his weapon of rhetoric with that combination of grace and sarcasm which is inimitably French, he gouges it deep into the rotten cancer that had eaten into the moral life of the rulers of France.

André Simone knows better than the palm of his own hand the major actors in the tragi-comedy that saw the French Republic assassinated in the Compiègne Forest. He takes us, so to speak, to the Last Supper before the crucifixion of a great nation, and the characters present are etched before our eyes with all the brilliant fidelity of another Leonardo. This is not a good parallel, for M. Simone leaves little doubt that instead of one Judas there were eleven, and that the price of betrayal was far more than thirty pieces of silver.

The Republic of France was more than a glorious name. Into that name M. Simone breathes the reality of its sturdy peasants, its workers, its shopkeepers, its soldiers, all the love for democracy, the zest for living, and the true meaning of its great enlightened culture that led the world for so many centuries, so that we lay aside his book feeling that not merely has a republic been betrayed, but a whole people and a way of life.

And so intimately does M. Simone know those Frenchmen who connived at that tragic destruction, and so able is he in depicting the rapid onrush of events, that the reader enjoys the same vivid reality, the swift action, and the intimate knowledge of character and human and social motives that light such a blaze of irony, pathos and understanding in the pages of the great Maupassant. Here are the *Ball of Fat* and *The Diamond Necklace* and *Mme. Tellier's Excursion* translated into politics. Not that this volume is in any sense fiction. It is too well informed, too well documented, too frightfully exact to be other than a powerful *J'Accuse*, but one can almost see Laval beaming like Mme. Tellier and saying of the war which broke France to bits, "We don't have a holiday every day," and then, with a sigh of relief from his heaving bosom, getting back to his regular professional and remunerative duties.

John Gunther wrote an *Inside Europe*, and Simone has here written an *Inside France*, except that the details, since the spotlight is thrown on a smaller circle, are still more intimate, the portraiture more exact, and the forces at work, from the activities of the Popular Front to those of the 200 Families, more sharply dissected.

The inescapable conclusion of Simone's book is that France was not so much stabbed in the back by the concerted last-minute entry of Mussolini into the war, as by her own political leaders, who for their brief moment so enjoyed the adulation of even the best American commentators. France was stabbed not once but a hundred times between that day of January 30, 1933—when Hitler took power—and the last bloody gasp and rattle in the improvised government-salons of Bordeaux. One wonders whether Weygand was really brought back from disgraceful retirement in the Near East to fight the already lost Battle of France or to help arrange for the establishment in power of the representatives of the 200 Families and the fascist groups to which, prior to the war, he had sold the rifles and ammunition of the French army that they might riot at the portals of the Ministry of State and shout for Pétain. If he did such things before war finally engulfed the French nation, what hope was to be expected from him after the breakthrough at Sedan?

Simone's book has vital importance for every American. It definitely concerns our own powers of defense and our national integrity. No American who cherishes the honor and safety of his own country can afford to miss reading this book. The lessons are painful. But it is better to learn the truth before it is too late.

CARLETON BEALS

August 26, 1940
New York City

J'ACCUSE!

SURRENDER

IT WAS June 16, 1940. I did not know until late in the afternoon that it would be my last Sunday in France. I will never forget that day. Nobody who has lived through those fateful hours in Bordeaux will ever be able to banish them from his mind.

I had arrived in the lovely old harbor town the previous day, a newspaper man without a paper. A battered old Citroën had carried four of us out of Paris on June 11. Squeezed in a seemingly endless stream of vehicles—cars, buses, trucks, bicycles and carts—our little machine crawled along at the rate of about ten miles an hour. We took no notice of the incessant stops. We had no answer ready when bewildered villagers asked us what was going to happen. We did not know where the Germans were and where the French armies were—or even if they still existed. Like forty million other French men and women, we had not yet grasped the true meaning of what had happened. We were uncertain whether our paper would be published somewhere in the provinces. The only thing we really knew was that the Government of Paul Reynaud had gone to Tours, that charming medieval town along the Loire. So we proceeded to Tours.

It took us sixteen hours to get there. The streets of the new capital were jammed with refugees. No rooms were available in the hotels. There was almost no food to be had. We slept in the car.

When I arrived in Tours, the attack of the Fifth Column inside and outside the Government was in full swing. A Cabinet Minister whom I met in front of the City Hall told me that General Maxime Weygand, the Army chief, insisted that no successful resistance to the onrushing Nazi forces could be offered. He was supported in his plea for an armistice by the two Vice-Premiers, old Marshal Henri Philippe Pétain and wily Camille Chautemps. Today, the Minister informed me, the fate of France was hanging by a thread.

Here was his story: During a Cabinet meeting General Weygand had abruptly risen and left the room. A few minutes later he had rushed back, terribly agitated, and had shouted: "The Communists have taken Paris! There are riots all over the city. Maurice Thorez [the Communist leader] has moved into the Elysée [the Presidential palace]." Weygand demanded that an immediate request for an armistice be forwarded to Hitler. "We cannot leave the country to the Communists. We owe that to France!"

Weygand's declaration, according to my informant, made a profound impression on the council. But Georges Mandel, Minister of the Interior, immediately

Surrender 15

went to the telephone and called the Prefect in Paris. He was told that Paris was calm. No riots, no street-fighting, no Communist rule. Weygand's attempt to ape the technique of the German Reichstag Fire incident had misfired.

"But for how long?" the Minister asked me dolefully.

Yes, for how long? A wave of rumors came from the hotels and cafés where the politicians were congregated. I made the rounds of the cafés on the main street. In the course of an hour I heard that the Germans would be in Tours that night; that the British had sued for an armistice behind the backs of the French; that Winston Churchill had committed suicide; that Paul Reynaud had done so too; that Paris was in flames; that a Communist uprising was due to break out within a few hours; that it had already begun; and last, but not least, that Hitler had offered generous terms to Pétain, as one soldier to another.

In one of the cafés, Pierre Laval, the swarthy former Premier, was speaking to some associates. He asserted that he had seen it all coming. "I was always for an agreement with Hitler and Mussolini," he said. "This insane pro-British policy and those overtures we made to the Soviets have ruined France." Had his advice been followed, he assured his listeners, France would now be a happy country, living at peace.

He was interrupted by an elderly gentleman in a grey suit. "Monsieur le Président Laval?" the man asked. And before Laval could answer, the old man had slapped him in the face, disappearing in the general uproar that followed. Later I learned that his son, an aviator, had been killed in action.

That was the atmosphere in Tours when Winston Churchill, accompanied by Lord Halifax and Lord Beaverbrook, arrived. They went to the City Hall where the French Ministers awaited them. It was a dramatic scene. At any moment the scales might tip in favor of a capitulation by France. Both groups knew that this might be the last time they would meet as Allies. They knew that the campaign in France was lost. They could not stem the tide of events on the Continent. But the question they discussed was whether the Reynaud Government would continue the war from the vast French Empire with its seventy million population; whether part of the French Army could be evacuated; and, most vital to the British, whether the French Fleet would continue to fight on the side of England.

In those days it was more difficult than ever to obtain genuine information. I have heard various versions of that historic meeting. One told of a frightful scene between Weygand and Churchill. Another described Chautemps' maneuvers to swing the French Ministers to accede to an armistice. A third maintained that the

Surrender

British leaders had shown no understanding of the French situation and had thought only of British interests. But all the versions agreed on the main point, that Premier Reynaud had asked England to release France from its obligation not to make a separate armistice or peace. Churchill had rejected this plea. But his rejection had lacked his usual force. He had given the French the impression of a deeply worried man. Finally, the French and British Ministers agreed that Reynaud should make a new appeal for help to the United States.

Journalists crowded around Reynaud when he left the council room. "Are you going to continue?" they asked.

"Of course!" the little Premier answered quickly, very quickly. I can still hear the sound of his words.

Then a strange thing happened. The text of an appeal for help to President Roosevelt, sent by Reynaud a few days before, was released. Reynaud declared that France would continue the fight in Africa, if necessary.

"We have published this appeal," a high official of the Ministry of Information explained to us, "to increase the pressure on the United States."

"But what if the answer isn't satisfactory?" one of my colleagues asked. "It will have a terrific effect on the morale."

The official shrugged his shoulders.

There was something peculiar going on. It was impossible to find out who was responsible for the publication of the appeal, Reynaud or Information Minister Jean Prouvost, who was in favor of an armistice.

The rumors began to fly faster. British colleagues told us that their embassy took a gloomy view of the situation. Churchill was reported to have left the meeting convinced that French surrender was only a matter of days.

This fiendish uncertainty and nerve-racking anxiety lasted for one more day. Then we were again on the move. On to Bordeaux, where once before, in 1914, the French Government had sought refuge from Germany's armies. They had never reached Paris in 1914. Hitler's army did.

When the news came that Paris had fallen, nobody said a word. We got into the car and drove off. The shadow of conquered Paris was with us. Paris, the gay lovely city of pre-war days; the sad and mournful capital during the war, bombarded, attacked, the mutilated symbol of the people's will and their thirst for liberty. It was in Nazi hands.

In Bordeaux the air was even thicker with rumors. The influence of the Pétain-Weygand group was gaining hourly. . . .

The Mayor of Bordeaux, Adrien Marquet, had turned from Socialism to Fascism during his political career.

Surrender

He now championed the theory that the "new France" could collaborate with the Nazis to wipe out Communism, democracy and, of course, the Jews. His friend, Pierre Laval, with a larger crowd of politicians around him than ever, repeated one phrase as if by rote: "Mussolini, whom I know like my pocket, will stop Hitler from being too hard on France."

The Pétain followers were busy all over town asserting that the old marshal was the only one who could get fair terms from Hitler. The "hero of Verdun" would build a new France on the ruins of the defeated France —in the image of Catholic Franco Spain.

Adherents of Pétain, Marquet and Laval agreed that the Popular Front, Soviet Russia and England were responsible for the downfall of France.

The British journalists were warned by their consulate to make ready to leave.

A new appeal from Reynaud to the United States was published. It bore an exceedingly pessimistic undertone. The Premier asked for a "cloud of airplanes" and added, "The very life of France is at stake. Our fight, each day more painful, has no further meaning if, in continuing, we do not even see far off the growing hope of a common victory."

Forerunner of the capitulation? A couple of Ministers emphatically denied this. "Tomorrow," one of them announced, "we're going to decide where the Government will move to continue the war."

Tomorrow—that was the Sunday of which I have spoken. My last in France.

Few people slept that night. Everyone knew that the decision would be made within the next twenty-four hours.

The Cabinet met three times. President Roosevelt's answer was the chief topic of discussion. At the first meeting the partisans of resistance clung to one phrase in his reply: "Every week that goes by will see additional material on the way to the Allies." The Pétain group, represented in this debate mainly by Chautemps, argued that Roosevelt had also declared he would undertake no military commitments. When the meeting ended, it was reported that thirteen Ministers still favored continuing the war, as against eleven of the opposite opinion.

The afternoon council of Ministers was presented with a British offer to form a common Franco-British Government with a joint Franco-British Parliament. At the end the majority of the Cabinet was reported to favor continuing the war. The vote still was thirteen to eleven for resistance. A Minister told me that it had been decided to transfer the Cabinet to Perpignan on the French-Spanish frontier. From there the North African possessions could easily be reached by air.

What happened during the next two hours is still a mystery. All that is known is that several conversations took place which were of momentous importance.

Surrender

The Premier was closeted with General Weygand and Reynaud's lady friend, Countess Hélène de Portes. She was known to favor capitulation.

Air Minister Laurent-Eynac, who had voted in favor of continuing the war, had a long talk with Marshal Pétain.

Camille Chautemps worked on the Minister of Supplies, Henri Queuille. Both saw President Albert Lebrun.

The third Cabinet session started at about ten o'clock in the evening. It did not last long. Vice-Premier Chautemps wasted no time in demanding that an armistice be requested at once. If the terms were impossible, he argued, the French people would continue the war with greater readiness. Georges Mandel opposed him. Once an armistice plea was made, he said, no soldier could be induced to fight again.

Charles Pomaret, Minister of Labor, supported Chautemps with a sharp attack against Great Britain. Ybarnégaray seconded him with a thinly veiled hint about Mandel's Jewish blood. He could understand, he exclaimed, why the Jews wanted to fight Hitler regardless of the odds.

Marshal Pétain and General Weygand raised the old specter of the Communist menace. President Lebrun was on their side.

Reynaud pleaded for acceptance of the British offer. But it seemed to some Ministers that his plea lacked conviction. After he had spoken, Chautemps renewed his proposal. And then the break came. Two Ministers, Laurent-Eynac and Queuille, thus far on the side of resistance, came out in support of Chautemps. The majority was reversed.

There was a quick jump of a Socialist Minister on to Pétain's bandwagon. Then the vote was taken—fourteen to ten for capitulation.

The Reynaud Cabinet was finished. Pétain became Premier of France at the age of eighty-four.

When the decision was announced we took it without a quiver. After a while, somebody remarked: "It seems to be the fate of old marshals to deliver their countries to Hitler. Hindenburg in Germany—Pétain in France."

If such was the destiny of aged marshals, Henri Philippe Pétain had certainly labored strenuously to live up to it. Born in a region of France which produces people of strong physique and stubborn character, he was educated at Saint-Cyr, training school for the élite of the French officer corps. When the war broke out in 1914 he was a colonel fifty-nine years of age, in command of an infantry brigade. At the top of his card in the Army files was the notation: "Do not allow to go beyond Brigadier-General." No outstanding qualities drew the attention of his superiors to him. Like Hindenburg in

Germany before 1914, he was considered to be an average French superior officer.

For years after the World War, legend linked his name with that of Verdun. The oracles are still discussing whether he was the real "hero of Verdun."

The austere general with the clear blue eyes and the typical French mustache became the Commander-in-Chief of the French Army in 1917. At the École de Guerre he had preached incessant offensive "practiced without afterthought." Now he had an opportunity of practicing it on a gigantic scale. He was responsible for several offensives in which French army corps were sent, without sufficient technical coverage, against the Kaiser's machine-gunners.

Costly offensives and the inefficiency of the High Command had caused despair in the French Army. A mutiny broke out. Pétain suppressed it. He had every tenth man of the mutinying regiments shot. Since then, for one section of France, his name has been linked more with these tragic events than with Verdun.

After the war he retired.

But he emerged again in 1925 when he was called upon to subdue the Riff uprising in Morocco. One of the officers on his staff during that campaign was Colonel de la Rocque.

The marshal and the colonel met again a few years later, this time in Paris. De la Rocque was then leader of the "Croix de Feu," an ex-service-men's organization which had been turned into a fascist league. Marshal Pétain, by nature and training in the camp of French reaction, began to lend his prestige to the "Croix de Feu."

Pétain was the organization's hero. When, after the February 1934 riots, he became War Minister in the Doumergue Cabinet, he helped cement the friendship between the "Croix de Feu" movement and the military chiefs.

It was in this Cabinet that the marshal became associated with the men who were to become the leading spirits in the Cabinet he formed in 1940, after the defeat of France: Pierre Laval, Adrien Marquet, François Piétri and Henry Leméry.

His short stay at the War Ministry must have stimulated the marshal's interest in politics. From then on he was in the mêlée of daily political life in France.

He is a fervent Catholic. His thoughts are confined in the strait-jacket of military discipline. Since the days of his youth at Saint-Cyr, he has been in sympathy with the Royalist cause.

His fear of Communism made him take the road which many other high-placed Frenchmen had taken. He who had preached the never-ending offensive, was in his eighties one of the most fervent advocates of a *rapprochement* with Hitler, one of the strongest adversaries of the French-British Alliance, and, of course, an implacable foe of Soviet Russia.

When General Franco emerged in Spain, Marshal Pétain became his most influential lobbyist in Government circles. Franco had sat at the feet of Pétain at the École Militaire. They had fought together in the Riff. Now they were to unite against France.

Pétain was France's first ambassador to Franco Spain. Once when he was distributing bread to the hungry people in the streets of Burgos, crowds of phalangists greeted him with shouts of "Down with France! Long live Pétain!"

In Spain he met the Nazi ambassador, Eberhard von Stohrer. They became good friends. Pétain shocked many people in political circles when, at the end of September 1939, with France already a month at war with Germany, he warmly shook hands with Stohrer at the doors of the historic chapel of the Monastery Real de las Huelgas.

That was not his only contact with the Nazi envoy. During the entire course of the war, Pétain remained in contact with the Nazi ambassador. At least three times the aged marshal forwarded to Paris Hitler's proposals for a separate peace, accompanied with favorable comments in his own hand.

This was the man whom Paul Reynaud made Vice-Premier in May 1940, after the Nazi Army had broken through the French lines at Sedan. With him, other Ministers entered the Reynaud Cabinet who "feared a Hitler defeat more than a Hitler victory." The Trojan Horse had been wheeled inside the Government.

In Bordeaux, after he became Premier, Pétain made two telephone calls to Madrid. One was to Spanish Foreign Minister Colonel Juan Beigbeder; the other to German Ambassador von Stohrer. So during the first twenty-four hours of Pétain's tenure, Hitler was told that the Battle of France was over. As one news-reel shows, Hitler greeted the event with an hysterical outburst of joy. He had every reason to. Pétain's move made Hitler the master of France.

During these first twenty-four hours of Pétain's rule, Georges Mandel was arrested. While he was sitting in a Bordeaux café with a general and a lady, an officer approached him and said, "I have the painful duty to arrest you." A few hours later Mandel was released. When Pétain, who had summoned him, tendered his apologies, Mandel refused to shake hands with the marshal.

The marshal sent emissaries to Hitler to receive the armistice terms.

On June 22 the Third French Republic was officially buried in the old railway carriage in the Forest of Compiègne. The armistice with the Nazis was signed.

Surrender

The era of "Fatherland, Work and the Family" had begun in France: the Hitler-Pétain era.

I had left Bordeaux two days after Pétain's accession to power. As the boat slowly cut through the waves, I was concerned, like many others, with but a single question: What has become of France, and how has it happened?

I have an indomitable faith in the people of France. Whatever was done before, during and after the war, was done without their knowledge. They have been kept in the dark by leaders who had every reason to fear the light. They have been betrayed by men to whom betrayal is second nature. They have been sacrificed for the sake of a small group who hope, with Hitler's help, to preserve their privileges and their power. But I am sure that the day of reckoning will come.

The French people may be misled, duped, betrayed —but they cannot be enslaved. Neither by their countrymen nor by foreign rulers.

To understand what really happened in France, one has to go back to the day Hitler took power in Germany. So my story begins on January 30, 1933.

2

FROM HITLER'S RISE TO THE PARIS RIOTS

FRANCE was without a Government on that fateful January 30, 1933 when Adolf Hitler was nominated Chancellor of the German Reich.

Two days before, the ninety-first Cabinet of the Third French Republic, headed by Joseph Paul-Boncour, had resigned. Wrestling with a plaguing budgetary problem, it had sought to reduce the salaries of civil servants by 5 to 6%. Then, after a spirited debate which lasted almost an entire night, it had suffered the fate of several of its predecessors—it had been "guillotined at dawn."

Well-to-do Paris took the news of Hitler's accession to power with a show of calm. On that chilly wintry day the Parisians went about their affairs as usual. The cafés on the fashionable boulevards were crowded during the *apéritif* hour, buzzing with argument and conversation. But the main topic of the day, overshadowing all others, was business. Times were hard and getting harder. Neither Hitler nor the French ministerial crisis figured very largely in the discussions.

The Paris Stock Exchange paid scant attention to Hitler. Expectantly and with a certain prudent reserve, it awaited the news of the formation of the new French Cabinet. The afternoon newspapers tended to belittle the catapulting of Hitler to power. They played down or glossed over the fact that the Nazi Führer had in *Mein Kampf* preached the isolation and annihilation of France, calling her "the hereditary mortal enemy" of Germany. The French papers hastened to explain that Hitler and his two Nazi Party colleagues in the German Cabinet were, in fact, prisoners of the majority of "good" conservative Ministers who surrounded them. As the semi-official *Le Temps*, the mouthpiece of French high finance and heavy industry, blandly put it: "It is possible that the new Chancellor will be quickly exhausted by his exposure to power, and his reputation as a worker of miracles will vanish."

The lobbies of the French Chamber of Deputies bustled with activity. The deputies lost little time discussing Hitler. The domestic scramble for position was more to the point. The Premier-designate went through the time-honored routine of visiting or telephoning influential politicians who, in turn, eloquently reminded him that they would be delighted to serve under him. Deputies and senators known or rumored to be members of the next Ministry were surrounded in the lobbies by throngs of questioners, well-wishers and petitioners. Everybody zealously sought a place as assistant or secretary for one of his own protégés. On this 30th of January the battle for Cabinet posts was in full swing. Influential politicians vied with one another in extolling the merits of sons, nephews or friends. The competition was brisk—even for minor jobs for underlings.

I remember seeing former Premier André Tardieu standing in a corner, surrounded by a cluster of friends, and smiling sardonically. Since he was the leader of the Opposition, he and his political henchmen had no chance of filling any of the vacancies. Hence they discussed the tactics with which they might best combat the incoming Government. A journalist brought them the news of Hitler's nomination as Chancellor of Germany. "What's your opinion about it, Mr. President?" Tardieu was asked. He rasped a categorical answer: "I expected it. A few weeks ago I read Léon Blum's prediction that Hitler and the Nazis were doomed, definitely on the way out! Whenever Blum makes a prediction—just count on the opposite to happen. You'll never fail to guess right." This was the extent of Tardieu's appraisal of an event which marked a decisive turning point in European history.

In another corner Henri Queuille, a former and future Radical-Socialist Minister of Agriculture, formulated his opinion in the following nugget of wisdom: "Hitler in power? What's the difference? He can't make the Germans drink more wine." For him, as for so many of his colleagues from rural constituencies,

From Hitler's Rise to the Paris Riots 31

wheat and wine were the destiny of France. Consumption of wine was their measuring-rod for the political and social future of Europe.

Dinnertime brought a truce to the "battle of the lobbies." At about the same hour Adolf Hitler, from a balcony in the Wilhelmstrasse, was witnessing a torchlight parade of a hundred thousand frenzied, goose-stepping Storm Troopers. Two moments in the lives of two neighboring peoples!

The next day the new French Cabinet was formed, with Edouard Daladier as its Premier. Reporters and photographers swarmed enterprisingly around the Presidential Elysée Palace, where the Ministers had convened. The stock market closed strong on the news of the formation of the Daladier Ministry. The Bourse brimmed with satisfaction that no Socialists were included on the list. It was particularly pleased with the choice of a new Minister of Finance, Georges Bonnet.

The evening papers carried pictures of the new Premier. The photographs showed a broad, bulky face, rigid and half-scowling. Some papers alluded vaguely—almost wistfully—to a certain resemblance to Benito Mussolini.

Edouard Daladier entered the world scene one day later than Adolf Hitler. The seven years which led from the Nazi leader's assumption of power to the European war were filled with drama and tragedy. During that interval, for almost five years, Daladier played a decisive rôle in French politics—either as Premier or War Minister or both. He was destined to be at the helm of the French Government when Czechoslovakia was murdered, Spain strangled and Poland overrun. He was France's War Minister when Belgium, Holland and Norway were swallowed up. He was War Minister, too, when, in May 1940, the startling Nazi breakthrough at Sedan occurred.

Entering the Chamber of Deputies in 1919, he secured his first Cabinet post in 1924 when his former schoolteacher, Edouard Herriot, gave him his start. Thereafter, he had been in several Cabinet positions, the last as Minister of War. "How do you get along with your new War Minister?" a Radical-Socialist Deputy once asked General Maxime Weygand, then head of the Army. "We never quarrel," Weygand promptly replied, with a meaning smile.

Daladier had achieved a reputation in political and journalistic circles as a strong silent man. Not knowing whether his taciturnity was due to his lack or to his abundance of ideas, he was given the benefit of the doubt.

Daladier himself had been a schoolteacher of history and geography. One of his former pupils, André Stibio, perhaps the cleverest French parliamentary correspondent of our day, described him as "a teacher of geog-

From Hitler's Rise to the Paris Riots 33

raphy without any sense of it." Daladier, the son of a baker, came from a rural district in the South of France. The belief grew that he was eminently a man of the people; that he had a profound feeling for the reactions of the French peasantry. During parliamentary debates and Cabinet meetings, he defended his point of view stubbornly and tenaciously. This gave rise to the legend that he was a strong man. As events will show, his strength was lavished on parliamentary jousts and ministerial tilts. In the face of momentous historic events, it vanished into thin air.

Into his first Cabinet, Daladier took two men whose names are likewise indissolubly linked with France's downfall: his Minister of Finance, Georges Bonnet, and his Minister of Interior, Camille Chautemps. Both men had already occupied ministerial posts, but it remained for Daladier to give the forty-four-year-old Bonnet his first job of major rank in a French Government. Georges Bonnet first entered the limelight in 1919 as the man in charge of France's demobilization. This task brought the ambitious young politician into contact with influential financiers and industrialists. These contacts were never severed, never forgotten. With powerful backing, Bonnet entered Parliament in 1924, where he immediately concentrated on problems of finance and trade. He established himself securely in the important Radical-Socialist Party by marrying the niece of its one-time chief, Camille Pelletan. Many Deputies used to gossip that Odette Bonnet's ambition was even bigger and longer than her husband's nose. Though not an overfriendly description, it conveys an accurate idea of Mme. Bonnet's fierce strivings. Together, the Bonnet pair played a sinister part in the betrayal of France.

Like Daladier, Camille Chautemps received his first Cabinet post from Edouard Herriot, but unlike Daladier he made no pretensions of being a strong man. Nor did he exhibit the ostentatious ambitions of a Bonnet. From his father, who had himself been a Cabinet Minister, he had learned that French politics is largely a matter of compromise. And so Chautemps established himself as an extremely skillful parliamentarian, a wily maneuverer who, in moments of crisis, could iron out differences and deliver speeches calculated to soften wrath and appease the discontented. When, in 1933, he became Minister of the Interior under Daladier, he was extremely well-liked in Parliament. However, a few of his colleagues insisted that they had never seen Chautemps look anybody straight in the face. His eyes seemed to conceal a perpetual secret. Georges Mandel, who had inherited from his old master Georges Clemenceau the talent for making biting remarks, once snapped: "This Camille Chautemps—he has the face of a traitor."

These three individuals—Daladier, Bonnet and Chautemps—were members of the Radical-Socialist Party which for many decades had either directed the parliamentary destiny of France or played a preponderant rôle in it.

The Radical-Socialists pretended to be the genuine inheritors of the energetic Jacobins who had flourished during the great French Revolution of 1789. They also laid claim to Georges Clemenceau, the Tiger of World War fame. Indeed, he had been honorary chairman of the Radical-Socialist Party—but his mantle was sought by practically every party in France except the extreme Left.

As a matter of fact, the name "Radical-Socialist" was more frightening than either the program of the party or the party itself. There was nothing either radical or socialist about it. It was the party of the middle class; the party of a mild liberalism, often watered-down, obscured, or perverted into its opposite. Its strategic strength was based on the fact that few workable or working Cabinets could be formed without its support. It was a fulcral party, in a key position to make or unmake Ministries.

The Daladier Government was the third Radical-Socialist combination since the elections of May 1932, which had brought a considerable victory for the Left cartel (consisting of the Radical-Socialist and the

Socialist parties). But already the rift in the coalition was plain to see. Although it lingered weakly on for a year, parliamentary strategists could foresee the moment when the Radicals would break and veer sharply to the Right.

Having constituted his Cabinet with himself retaining the Ministry of War, Daladier called in the ultra-conservative General Maxime Weygand. The Premier was closeted for several hours with Weygand. No information was divulged concerning this long—and as it now seems, vital—colloquy, but a few days later the editor of the paper for which I worked visited Daladier and had a lengthy talk with him. My editor expressed his anxiety concerning the new situation created in Europe by the Nazi rise to power. To reassure him, Daladier gave him a résumé of his discussion with General Weygand, which had hinged on Hitler's advent to power and the possible consequences for France. On leaving the Premier, my chief immediately wrote down the gist of the conversation. The following gives the essence of his notes: As then expressed to Daladier, it was Weygand's emphatic conviction that even if Nazi Germany harnessed all her energies and exploited all her potentialities in the direction of rearming, it would take her at the very least another ten years to develop a military machine capable of comparison with the Kaiser's. Weygand held the skill, leadership and organization of the Reichswehr in high esteem. However, he believed that Germany's lack of trained officers and trained reserves would make it impossible for the German Army for a very long period ahead to equal, let alone surpass, the striking power of the Kaiser's forces. Moreover, in Weygand's opinion, this menace could not assume any undue proportions because a formidable line of fortifications was already under construction on the Franco-German frontiers. These defences were scheduled to be completed by 1934 and, once finished, they would render France practically impregnable. These same fortifications later became famous under the name of "Maginot Line."

Commenting on the Allies bound to France by a network of alliances, General Weygand attributed only a nuisance value to the Polish Army because of its inadequate technical equipment and its incompetent leadership. As for the Belgian Army, pledged by the Locarno agreement to come to the aid of France in the event of aggression, Weygand did not rate it highly because of the serious differences between the Walloons and the Flemings. He had high praise for the Czech Army. He deemed that the British Army could not be counted on for much, but that the British Fleet would play a decisive rôle.

As for the political aspects of Hitler's rise to power, these, in Weygand's opinion, had their advantages. France, he believed, should certainly welcome a movement directed against the German Communists, who had become a challenging force. The spread of Communism in Germany had already produced repercussions in France where, according to the reports of the military intelligence, the Communists were slowly but surely gaining strength. The repression of Communism in Germany would contribute to the weakening of the French Communist movement as well. Moreover, Nazi Germany's anti-Communist crusade would certainly leave its mark on future Russo-German relations—and that, too, could only redound to the benefit of France.

Summarizing, it was Weygand's opinion that France's position of dominance on the Continent was secure. French policy could be shaped on the assumption that peace would not be disturbed in Europe for at least ten years. Inasmuch as France had just entered the period of the "lean years," when the losses in manpower of the last war were only beginning to make themselves felt in the number of men annually called up for military service, Weygand recommended an eighteen-month extension in conscript service. He also drew Daladier's attention to certain weaknesses in the air force and suggested a plan for strengthening it.

But the situation of the budget was precarious. Difficult days lay ahead for the Cabinet. In view of these facts, Weygand agreed with the War Minister that the introduction of the eighteen months' term of service could be deferred.

Weygand's judgments carried weight with Daladier. The brisk, tight-lipped little General was a symbolic figure. Together with the deceased Marshal Foch and the aging Marshal Pétain, he personified to many Frenchmen the military victory over Germany in the last war. The talk with Weygand must have given Daladier a momentary feeling of exhilaration. He, the baker's son, who had fought as a captain in the World War, was analyzing the chinks in France's military armor on a plane of equality with the renowned warrior-general. Weygand had previously admitted that he never quarreled with Daladier. Nor did he find any reason for quarreling in the future either. The French generals found Daladier a most suitable, compliant War Minister. It was the General Staff which sedulously fostered the legend that Daladier was an extremely able organizer and executive.

Weygand's career had been unusual. At the outbreak of war in 1914 he had been a Lieutenant-Colonel in a regiment of light cavalry. On General Joffre's recommendation, he was made Chief of Staff of General Foch's army, then in formation. He stood at the side of Foch in the famous railway car at Compiègne in 1918, when the marshal received the German delegates suing for an armistice with the stinging query: "What is it all about, gentlemen?" In 1920 Weygand was sent by Foch to Poland when the Polish Army of Pilsudski so narrowly averted being wiped out by the Red Army of the Soviets. A few years later he was dispatched to the French mandated territory of Syria where, with unprecedented cruelty, he crushed a growing revolt. After Foch's death, the story got around that his last words had been: "Whenever France is in danger, call in Weygand."

In 1931, Weygand succeeded Marshal Pétain in the key post of Vice-President of the French Supreme Council of Defence. That same year he was elected to the French Academy. At that time the French Army in Europe numbered about 370,000. It was a political army. Its officers, trained in select military schools of which Saint-Cyr—the French West Point—was the most famous, were educated and indoctrinated with a thoroughly reactionary spirit. Many of the generals—like Foch or Pétain or Weygand—were monarchist-minded. They regarded the Republic as a necessary evil. They tolerated it with a mixture of indulgence and contempt, but never considered it a form of government worth fighting for. Marshal Pétain, Weygand's predecessor, had strong ties with the reactionary Right-wing parties and later with the French fascist groups. Weygand was of an intensely clerical frame of mind—on one occasion Clemenceau asserted that he was "in with the priests up to his neck." He was an influential patron of the "Patriotic Youth," a semi-fascist youth organization. He even went further: as we shall later see, he was one of the guiding spirits of the "Cagoulards," or "hooded men," who plotted to overthrow the democratic government through terrorism and force of arms.

The French military leaders had learned that in order to forge ahead within the framework of the Republic, it was necessary to dissemble their anti-democratic sentiments, or at least to propagate them discreetly. Weygand was a past master at this art. When Daladier was warned by his young Air Minister, Pierre Cot, of the General's anti-democratic reactionary tendencies, he promptly retorted: "Why, you should hear Weygand talk! I'd go through hell for him!"

What was the balance-sheet of France at the moment Daladier became Premier and Hitler Chancellor of the Reich?

An authoritative economist has written that at that time the military, political and monetary strength of France was the greatest in Europe. France possessed a network of alliances which gave her, in the event of attack, the assurance of help from Great Britain, Belgium, Poland and Czechoslovakia. Although no military alliances with Jugoslavia and Rumania existed, there could be no doubt where the sympathies of these two countries lay. Italy, in the throes of the world crisis, was in no position to move against France. The recently proclaimed Spanish Republic was governed by men who during the last war had ardently sympathized with the Allied cause. Relations with the Soviet Union had improved during the past year. In November 1932 Herriot had signed a non-aggression treaty with the U.S.S.R. It dispelled the nightmare of Germany and Russia forming coalition against France.

But the economic picture was not so promising. The world economic crisis, first felt in the Wall Street crash of 1929, had by now spent its fury in the great industrial nations of the West: the United States of America, Great Britain and Germany. By 1933 there were already fitful gleams of light on the horizon for these prostrate industrial giants. The next year saw the beginning of a kind of recovery from the deepest troughs.

The curve of the crisis in France distinctly differs from that in the above-named countries. For a number of reasons specific and peculiar to France, the depression began to make itself felt there later, and reached its lowest point between 1933 and 1935. France weathered the first stages of the storm in a relatively successful fashion. A definite time-lag was at work. Like a delayed illness less virulent at the start, the crisis, when it did come, had a protracted, lingering and paralyzing effect on the body politic.

In 1933 the real crisis began to appear in France from behind the haze of slogans, myths and illusions which had almost succeeded in lulling the French people temporarily to sleep. The nation grew preoccupied with its increasing burdens. The coming disaster threw long shadows before it. The Daladier Cabinet inherited a swollen, unbalanced budget from its predecessors. Estimates of the deficit varied from between twelve to fourteen billion francs. Tax revenues were running far below normal. Exports and imports had dropped by more than one-third. The adverse balance of trade was mounting. Tourist traffic, one of France's most lucrative sources of income, had sagged in the last years from four million visitors to below one million. Unemployment was gnawing at the social structure of the nation. The number of unemployed had quadrupled—two and a half million able-bodied workers were without jobs, and only 275,000 of them were receiving a meager pittance of a dole.

An army of nearly one million government workers had to be paid by the State. Succeeding Cabinets sought to make these civil servants pay the penalty of the crisis by accepting wage cuts. It was the same old shabby plea: balance the budget, enforce strictest government economy, swing the fiscal axe. Incapable of fighting back alone, these civil servants, by the tens of thousands, joined various groups and movements of protest.

The peasants, an army of more than eight million thrifty, hard-working souls, cursed with heightened vociferousness. The price of wheat and wine—there was the rub! They were the two talismans of the French peasant. When he got a good price for them, as was the case until 1931, he was content. But let the world price and, consequently, the domestic price for wheat and wine fall, and Jacques Bonhomme scratches his head and snorts with wrath. Then he blames the fools and crooks and blunderers in Paris for his predicament. Since 1929 the price of wheat had fallen by one-third, with wine suffering an even more drastic decline. A still darker outlook for these two basic commodities faced the peasantry.

The middle class, too, was badly hit by the crisis. Torn between the yearning to enter the ranks of the wealthy and the fear of being shoved down into the ranks of the working class, these people clung to a diminishing hope. Perhaps, after all, their small factories, their modest shops, their little farms would not only afford them a living but also enough savings to ensure them security in old age. In addition to 400,000 *rentiers* (persons living on a regular fixed income, however modest in scope), there were about six million people holding French Government bonds and loans. Anxiously they

From Hitler's Rise to the Paris Riots

followed the fluctuations of their *rentes* on the official quotations of the Exchange. These were falling, falling . . . an average decline of 12% within one year. Gone were the days when the Finance Minister in Clemenceau's Cabinet could glibly assert: "The Boches will pay!" This same Minister, Klotz by name, was later brought to trial for issuing worthless checks. But not only were his checks a fraud, so also were his blatant promises that Germany would foot all the bills; so also the promises of Cabinet after Cabinet that the catastrophic drop in world prices would not affect France. France was to be a fortress, a haven of prosperity, a vacuum of good times. But the middle classes had only to follow the plummet course of the Stock Exchange quotations. Their possessions and property, their *rentes* and farms and shops and factories were in danger. They whined and snarled with discontent.

Of the eleven million employed workers in France in 1933, about six million were engaged in industry. Two compact centers were clearly discernible. The one was concentrated in and around Paris, with metal, armament and automobile factories; the other in the northern section, stemming from Lille, engaged in the coal-mining and textile industries. But it is one of the specific characteristics of France that there is a fairly large working population in practically every section of the country. Nevertheless, it is Paris labor which leads the French workers. The "red girdle" of communities around Paris gives the signal for fight.

Hence it was in Paris that the pulse of the labor movement quickened as the crisis intensified. When Daladier took office, labor had already become restless. This restlessness remained vague and sporadic; it was only gradually crystalizing. But the number of strikes was increasing. A slow shift was under way from the Socialists to the Communists, but the membership figure of neither party was impressive. About one million and a half workers all told were organized in trade unions.

The Socialists, whose pre-electoral pact with the Radical-Socialists had brought about a significant victory for the Left parties in the 1932 elections, were now feeling even stronger pressure from the electorate. At the same time, one section of the leadership of the Socialist Party, the right wing, was preparing to cut loose and join the Radical-Socialists. The men in this group were called the "Neo-Socialists." Their "neo-Socialis" later easily slipped into fascism. Their leader was the dapper Mayor of Bordeaux, Adrien Marquet, a dentist-politician noted for his sartorial elegance.

The critical problems facing the Radical-Socialist triumvirate in power—Daladier, Bonnet and Chautemps —were many: the budgetary deficit, the deepening depression with its inevitable train of mounting unemployment and fermenting social unrest, the disarmament problem and relations with a Nazified Germany. The most crucial issue, of course, was relations with Germany.

As to Hitler's intentions, the Government could not entertain any doubts. He had published the blue-print of his plans in his book *Mein Kampf*. To isolate France in order to be able to annihilate her was his declared program.

It is the ideal of every general staff to know the plans of its potential adversary. The French Government was in this ideal position. It could take the measures it thought necessary with the full knowledge of what the enemy wanted to do.

That the Government did not take *Mein Kampf* seriously became evident to me after a conversation with a member of Daladier's Cabinet. Mentioning Hitler's book, I spoke of the policy and program he had outlined in it. "But do you really think a policy can be made according to a book?" the Minister asked me lightly, visibly amused at this idea. When I answered that I did think so, he chuckled: "You're a newspaper man. You believe in what is written. But I'm a practical politician, and I assure you there is not a chance in the world of Hitler following his book. Reality will teach him." And that was that.

Instead of forming a peace coalition to check Hitler, Daladier sought to come to an understanding with him. He began to handle relations with Germany, with an eye to what was later called "appeasement." Unquestionably, Daladier's appeasement at that time lacked the contours and outlines it later assumed. It underwent many metamorphoses. It passed through many stages and zig-zagged across numerous contradictions. It sloughed off many an old skin before donning the new. It was interrupted by so-called rebursts of energy and resistance. It was hammered out in the course of interminable political fights. Politicians changed sides several times before the two fronts—that of appeasement and that of anti-appeasement—were solidly drawn up on the eve of the Munich Conference of September 1938. But the essential elements of appeasement were already inherent in Daladier's foreign policy in 1933.

In his first radio speech as Chancellor, delivered on February 2, 1933, Hitler had cleverly struck a chord which sounded sympathetic to the democratic world: "We should be happy if the rest of the world, through the reduction of its armaments, relieved us of the necessity of always increasing ours."

For Daladier, Hitler's oratorical flourish was an invitation. He could utilize it to overcome those pressing internal difficulties which threatened to overturn his unstable Cabinet at any moment. If he could come to some kind of an understanding with Germany, his position, especially with the political parties of the Right, would be immeasurably strengthened. Traditionally, the Right in France claimed a monopoly on patriotism, nationalism and love of the fatherland. But now, for the first time since 1918, the Right-wing newspapers and periodicals were quite restrained in their attacks on Germany. They were unable to make up their minds. One part of Hitler's program appealed to them: the relentless struggle against Communism. Another element in it, however, terrified them at first: the pan-German expansionist tendencies of the Nazi Party, its swaggering imperialist aims, its championing of the fight against the *Diktat* of the Treaty of Versailles. But the mere fact that the French Right was already beginning to waver between class interests and national interests marked, if not a victory, at least an initial blow in Hitler's favor. In his *Russian Campaign*, the renowned German military theoretician Clausewitz had written: "A great European country of civilization cannot be conquered without the help of internal disunity." The way to disunity leads through doubt and divided counsels, through the juxtaposition and severing of private and national interests.

The attitude of the French Right was made especially clear on the occasion of the Reichstag Fire, in February 1933. While the entire civilized world was burning with indignation, several of the French reactionary papers took obvious satisfaction in reprinting the Nazi claim that the Communists had set fire to the edifice.

The Reichstag Fire was a "sign from on high" for Hitler to outlaw the German Communist Party and burst the choking bonds of conservative Ministers in his Cabinet. Edouard Daladier picked this very moment to send his first emissary to Berlin. His name was Count Fernand de Brinon. He came from the highest Parisian society, was a skilled journalist and the confidential representative of an important banking firm. He had already carried out undercover missions for former Premier Pierre Laval. The Count was recommended to Daladier by his Minister of Finance, Georges Bonnet, who had intimate ties with the same bank in whose interests de Brinon labored so deftly and so deviously.

Daladier had just seen Ramsay MacDonald, who was on his way to Rome. Chasing the phantom of disarmament, the British Prime Minister hoped to win over Mussolini to a new formula—a pact between the four major powers, Great Britain, Germany, France and Italy. It was after his conversations with MacDonald that Daladier dispatched the Count de Brinon to Berlin. And at the moment the Storm Troopers, unleashed by Hitler after the opportune Reichstag blaze, were trampling across Germany, bringing ever-increasing terror, torturing and killing liberals, Socialists, Communists, Jews, Catholics, trade-unionists, and the flower of Germany's intellectuals—at this same moment the Count was closeted in Berlin with Hitler's henchmen.

When the news about the projected Four Power Pact leaked out, former Premier Edouard Herriot protested energetically against it. He had just been reëlected Chairman of the Radical-Socialist Party. There was scarcely a chance for Daladier to put through the plan in the face of Herriot's robust opposition. So Daladier sent his former schoolmaster packing off to America on a goodwill tour to gauge President Roosevelt's intentions and to allay the bitterness aroused in the United States by France's refusal to make even token war-debt payments. Daladier hoped thus to kill two birds with one stone: he would get rid of Herriot during the period when the foundations of the Four Power Pact were being laid, and he would entrust him with a mission which could accomplish negligible results at best. Against the advice of his closest friends, Herriot fell into the trap. When he returned empty-handed from the United States, he was for many months the favorite butt of French cartoonists and columnists.

In its first draft the Four Power Pact did not so much as mention the Covenant of the League of Nations. It provided for "an effective policy of coöperation among France, England, Germany and Italy in order to maintain peace." It foresaw possible revision of the Treaty of Versailles.

This original draft of the Four Power Pact already

indicated the appeasement trend. It signified a brusque departure by France from its traditional policy of maintaining the Treaty of Versailles through, and by means of, the League of Nations, which alone possessed the power to revise the treaty. It ignored the Soviet Union. It threatened to upset the delicately balanced equilibrium of the small European States, who still saw in the League of Nations a guarantee of their national independence. If the four great powers of Europe, by flouting and overriding the League, could form a "Continental Directorate," the small countries had cause indeed to fear the worst. How well grounded their fears were, was later demonstrated at Munich.

As the negotiations leading to the Four Power Pact demanded more time than was foreseen, Herriot returned opportunely to lead a furious attack against its original provisions. In a turbulent discussion with Daladier lasting several hours, Herriot forced the Premier's hand. He insisted that war would certainly follow, if France entered a Four Power attempt to revise European frontiers. He also released a public statement in which the same points were underlined. So a new draft of the agreement was made. Lawyers and jurists strained meanings and spun a fine web of casuistical phrases. Treaty revision and the disarmament formula were made dependent on the Covenant of the League of Nations.

This pact, which Herriot had called "either useless

From Hitler's Rise to the Paris Riots

and meaningless or else dangerous," was a still-born child when it was signed on June 7, 1933 in Rome. But this abortive Munich already opened new vistas for the policy of appeasement. Although the pact was finally rendered innocuous, even its original draft left a bad taste. For the first time since Versailles, a French Government had accepted in principle the revision of the treaty outside the framework of the League. Such damage could not easily or quickly be repaired.

The worst reactions were forthcoming in Poland. In March 1933 the dictator of the Polish State, Marshal Josef Pilsudski, had informed the Daladier Government of Hitler's secret plans for rearming. Germany had already gone far beyond sketches and plans; she was rearming furiously behind a thick curtain of secrecy. Marshal Pilsudski proposed to France that the Hitler régime be crushed by means of a "preventive war." Daladier demurred, then refused. The offer was repeated in April 1933, buttressed by an *aide-mémoire* of the Polish Ambassador to Paris, which gave a wealth of detail about Hitler's feverish rebuilding of a mighty military machine. This *aide-mémoire* was not even answered. But a few days later the news leaked out that the Four Power Pact was beginning to assume more definite shape. The Polish Ambassador protested to the French Foreign Office. In reply, he was assured that the Franco-Polish alliance would in no wise be affected.

That was not enough to "appease" Warsaw. At this point, a Cabinet Minister informed me, Pilsudski had summoned his counsellors and had charged them to sound out the possibilities for a German-Polish understanding. The Four Power Pact negotiations dragged on. Warned by Polish General Sikorski that a Polish-German pact was in the making, Emile Buré, editor of the nationalist Paris daily *L'ordre*, sounded the alarm: "Poland is betraying us!"

It culminated in a diplomatic bombshell: the German-Polish Non-Aggression Treaty, which pledged the two countries for the next ten years "under no circumstances to proceed to the application of force to settle mutual disputes." Here was the result of Daladier's initial Four Power flirtation. The first breach in the interlocking system of French alliances had been made. The jump on to the Nazi bandwagon had begun.

In the autumn, rumors began to circulate that Daladier and Hitler were planning a meeting in the Black Forest. These came from another of Daladier's emissaries to Berlin, Edouard Pfeiffer, General Secretary of the Radical-Socialist Party. He sang Hitler's praise in every register. The German Chancellor, he declared, wanted nothing better than an understanding with France. But these plans were abruptly wrecked when Hitler banged the door on the Disarmament Conference and the League of Nations.

It was a terrific shock for Daladier's histrionic Foreign Minister, Joseph Paul-Boncour. In October 1933 the delegates, reassembled at Geneva, were informed in a curt telegram by Hitler's Foreign Minister von Neurath that Germany felt constrained to withdraw from the Disarmament Conference, as well as from the League of Nations. Paul-Boncour had one of his periodic flare-ups and demanded that a forceful retort be sent to Germany. So a sub-committee to draft a reply was set up by the Conference. It consisted of Paul-Boncour, Sir John Simon (then British Foreign Minister) and Norman Davis, observer for the United States. The report these men submitted was watered down in meeting after meeting. When it finally saw the light of day, it was a clear indication to Hitler that he had little to fear.

For the first time Hitler had tested the will to resistance of the Western democracies—and had found it flabby, overblown, exaggerated. This lesson was to guide him in his subsequent political and military moves. A few days after this abrupt exit from Geneva, the Quai d'Orsay received a report from Berlin that most of Hitler's conservative Ministers and collaborators had opposed his action. He had forced their assent only after threatening to inflict a purely Nazi Government on the decrepit Marshal von Hindenburg. The reactions of the democratic powers to Hitler's bold step enhanced his prestige with German big business. These interests were delighted with his audacity in foreign, as well as in domestic affairs.

Another consequence of the Anglo-French fiasco at the Disarmament Conference was to make the small countries in Europe grow more alarmed. Foreseeing further French and British defections, they began to think seriously of making an agreement with Hitler. This was true of a section of the powerful Agrarian Party in Czechoslovakia, of the camarilla around King Carol in Rumania, and of the Stoyadinovitch group in Jugoslavia.

While the Disarmament Conference lay a-dying, the situation within France went from bad to worse. The depression raged. The Treasury was empty. Already in the early months of 1933, Finance Minister Georges Bonnet had secured a short-term loan amounting to $150,000,000 in London. But now he was again desperately searching for new monetary expedients. The attack of the political Right against the Government gained momentum. Alertly the opposition sniffed the approach of the moment when the Radical-Socialist Cabinet would "fall to the right"; that is, would be overthrown on an issue which would make it possible for the Radical-Socialists to form a coalition with the Right-wing parties.

Fascist and semi-fascist leagues and groups gathered strength. The most important of these, the "Croix de Feu," led by Colonel Casimir de la Rocque, grew in mushroom fashion. Originally a non-political ex-servicemen's group, the "Croix de Feu" was now organized along fascist lines. It held drills, conducted trial mobilizations and secret maneuvers, even using airplanes for these purposes later on. De la Rocque's connections with the Army rendered the "Croix de Feu" especially dangerous—it was already common gossip that its arms and weapons came from military arsenals.

By the middle of October a rumor flitted through the newspaper offices and through the lobbies of the Chamber of Deputies that a new financial scandal was due to explode in the next few days. I attempted to ferret out details of this mysterious affair, but without success.

After a dramatic night session, punctuated by heated altercations and fervid bursts of oratory, the Daladier Cabinet fell at dawn on October 24, 1933. Again a proposal to cut the salaries of the civil servants proved the Government's undoing. That night the Paris police were mobilized and out in force. Civil servants and taxi-drivers were reported planning a huge demonstration before the Chamber. The Prefect of the Paris Police was the Corsican, Jean Chiappe, whom Clemenceau had once called "the smartest cop in France." He was hated by the Leftists. He was personally supervising the work of the police from the main entrance of the Palais-Bourbon, which housed the Chamber of Deputies, when he was accosted by a passing Socialist Deputy.

"What are you doing here, Jean?" the Deputy asked.

"I'm protecting Daladier's life!" Chiappe replied with a meaning gesture.

In the next three months three more Cabinets were formed and as quickly forced out of office. The same faces, the same Radical-Socialist wheelhorses, the same old gang would always come back, holding slightly different posts in each successive Ministry. Daladier's successor was Albert Sarraut, a boss of the Radical-Socialist Party from the southwestern region near Toulouse, an epicure and an aging Casanova. Long active in French politics, he seemed to live a charmed life. Almost fatally wounded during his youth in a duel fought in the heat of the Dreyfus Case, he later went to Indo-China as French Governor of the colony. There he was the object of a number of attempts at assassination. He escaped them all. He became a solidly entrenched party boss and now, in the twilight of his life, women were more and more his destiny. Daladier retained the War Ministry in Sarraut's Cabinet and continued making political advances to Hitler.

But Daladier's plans for a *rapprochement* with the Führer were nearly nipped in the bud. The Nationalist Deputy, Georges Mandel, right-hand man of Clemen-

From Hitler's Rise to the Paris Riots 59

ceau during the World War, exposed the secret rearming of Nazi Germany in a speech delivered to his constituents. The largest morning paper in France, *Le Petit Parisien,* destined later to join the appeasement camp, followed Mandel's lead by publishing a series of articles disclosing the extent of Nazi rearmament. Daladier rushed the Count de Brinon to Berlin. And so in November 1933 the Count returned to France with a message from Chancellor Hitler, replete with "sweetness and light." At Daladier's request, the influential newspaper of the French Steel Trust, *Le Matin,* printed it. It had a stunning effect.

Count de Brinon prefaced the interview by declaring: "I suspect that Herr Hitler's ambition is to be the man who reaches an agreement with France in behalf of Germany. If his book *Mein Kampf* is filled with exclamations of hatred against France, it should be remembered that it was written while Herr Hitler was suffering martyrdom in prison. Since then the man has evolved greatly." And this is what Hitler confided to the Count: "I am convinced that once the question of the Saar, which is German territory, is settled, there will be absolutely nothing which can estrange France and Germany. . . . I have repeated many times that the fate of Alsace and Lorraine is settled and that we make no claims on them. . . . Those who say I want war insult me. I am not that sort of a man. War? It would settle nothing.

It would only make matters worse . . . it would mark the end of our races, which are the élite of the world, and make bolshevism triumphant."

De Brinon told Hitler of the uneasiness felt in France because of Germany's rapid rearming. The Führer replied by giving—as he has done so often before and since that occasion—his word of honor. He solemnly declared: "I alone decide the policy of Germany, and when I give my word I have the habit of keeping it."

This De Brinon-Hitler interview in November 1933 marked an important turn. Daladier had made himself the guarantor of Hitler's sincerity. So had *Le Matin*, whose ties with powerful industrial and banking trusts, and with the Right groups of the Chamber were notorious. From that time onward, whenever Hitler's sincerity was questioned his sympathizers in France could retort: "Haven't you read the interview in *Le Matin*? Don't you know that Daladier himself sponsored it?" From then on, Hitler's deceptive peace propaganda was under the protecting wing of the War Minister—that is to say, of the Army chieftains and the political reactionaries behind them. With the publication of this interview the Fifth Column in France made its initial bow.

Other bows followed. Jacques Chastenet, one of the editors of France's influential *Le Temps*, went to Berlin to see Hitler. He, too, returned an appeaser. The inner pincer movement against France's very existence was considerably reënforced.

From Hitler's Rise to the Paris Riots

The Left failed to grasp the significance of these moves. Deeply enmeshed in parliamentary combinations, petty intrigues and "backroom deals," the Radical-Socialists and the Socialists did not react forcefully against this first official contact between French reaction and Hitler.

Sarraut's Cabinet fell after three weeks. Another reshuffling brought Camille Chautemps to the Premiership. Daladier retained the War Ministry. It was at this point that the scandal, bruited about for weeks, broke into the open. The Stavisky Affair came to light and left traces in French history which were written in letters of blood.

Alexander Stavisky, "handsome Alexander," was well known for years in the *demi-monde* and underworld, as well as in fashionable Parisian society. Already under indictment for check forgeries to the extent of some $350,000, he had forged bonds of the municipal pawnshop of Bayonne, a small city in southwestern France, to the value of some twelve or thirteen million dollars. Tracked down by the police, he had, according to the official police report, committed suicide in Chamonix, Switzerland. But in the view of many Paris newspapers, especially those of the Right, he had been shot because he knew too much.

Now, the main feature of the Stavisky Affair was not the financial swindle itself. There had been others before involving much vaster sums of money. But this scandal implicated several Cabinet Ministers including Georges Bonnet, a number of deputies, leading judges, several newspaper editors, and Prefect of Police Chiappe. The Affair embraced politicians indiscriminately: Right-wingers and Leftist Radical-Socialists. But the French Right seized on it to pave the way for a controlled Government, an advance-guard of French fascism.

An attack of unprecedented vehemence against the Left began. The spearheads of this onslaught were *Action Française*, a paper of royalist-fascist tendencies, *Le Jour,* an extreme Right-wing sheet, and *Gringoire*, a rabid weekly edited by Chiappe's son-in-law. These publications increased their circulation by the tens of thousands during the Stavisky Affair.

Early in 1934, on the occasion of the reopening of Parliament, the first organized street riots took place in Paris. The most conspicuous of the rioters were the "Camelots du Roi," affiliated to the *Action Française* of Charles Maurras and Léon Daudet. They were soon joined by other fascist leagues. The demonstrations mounted *accelerando* until January 26 and January 27. Then, on the main boulevards of Paris and in the vicinity of the Chamber of Deputies, members of various ex-servicemen's organizations joined the crowds. Every day brought fresh evidence that these demonstrations were the result of a concerted effort by the fascist leagues and that they were directed by a common general staff.

The contagion spread. The whole of France was plastered with posters: "Kick the Deputies out! Chase the Deputies to hell!" The uproar was reaching its height.

As Georges Mandel later revealed, the startling material for the anti-democratic and anti-parliamentarian conspiracy was furnished to the fascists by Jean Chiappe, the Prefect of Police. His sympathies were blatantly Right wing. Through his position as boss of the Paris Police, he was able to collect a mass of incriminating data about many of the prominent Leftist politicians. He had no scruples about having these people shadowed. Their telephone wires were tapped. Many an unpublished financial scandal of the Third Republic lay buried in his archives. That was his source of strength.

Sarraut's intimate relations with women of doubtful character, Bonnet's financial jugglery and speculations, Chautemps' private secrets—these were among the treasures of Chiappe's confidential files. He gave only a portion of his collection to the newspapers. He kept another portion in reserve. And, in the opinion of several reliable Deputies, still another portion went to Berlin, to the archives of the Nazis. A former Minister confided to me that the willingness of Bonnet and Chautemps to come to an understanding with Hitler was partially explained by the fact that the German Chancellor knew too much about them. Nazi agents, my informant added, constantly held the threat of making public these revelations, like a Damocles sword, over the two politicians' heads. Was this true? We will know only after the Nazi archives are thrown open to the world. In them every foreign politician and statesman of note is card-indexed, with particular attention paid to his vices, financial and social connections, aptitudes, likes and dislikes.

The French Right considered the Stavisky Affair a godsend. It came at just the proper psychological moment! The country was tired of this fatuous cascade of Cabinets, of this reshuffling of the same greasy cards, of these monotonously repeated proposals to cut the civil servants' wages, of these eternal promises and this constant paralysis of action. Labor, the peasantry and the middle class were driven to despair by the crisis. The moment seemed ripe to shatter to bits the parliamentary system and the democratic forms of France, and to remold them nearer to the fascist model.

In the face of battle, Camille Chautemps deserted his post. Having received a substantial vote of confidence in the Chamber, he nevertheless resigned his office. This created a dangerous precedent. For the first time in the history of the Third Republic a legally constituted Cabinet, upheld by the Chamber, had resigned under pressure from the fascist and near-fascist groups which dominated the streets.

The remedy for this serious situation? A new reshuffle of the pack of cards. And now Daladier emerged face up. By the end of January 1934 he formed his second Cabinet. A few days previously, the aristocratic drawing-rooms of Paris had circulated a list; it was the "directorate" of five men who were to guide the destinies of France. The list contained the names of Marshal Pétain, former President of the Republic Gaston Doumergue, Pierre Laval, André Tardieu and Adrien Marquet.

The new Cabinet lasted less than ten days. It fell under the hammer blows of the first open revolt by Hitler's Fifth Column in France, the men who gathered on February 6, 1934 on the Place de la Concorde and near the Chamber of Deputies in order "to chase the Deputies to hell."

Here they were all lined up: the leagues and groups itching for weeks to smash the democratic institutions of France. "Croix de Feu" and "Jeunesses Patriotes" and "Camelots du Roi" were howling: "We want Pétain!" But it was like a tragic contrapuntal piece of music, a diabolical symphony. Another melody was also audible, a counterpoint over and above the howling mob on the Place de la Concorde. It rang out: "What we need is a Hitler." An ambassador of a foreign power stood in the midst of the wild-eyed yelling crowd. "It's a Hitler we need!" his neighbor told him. I spent several hours with the demonstrators and I heard these same phrases repeated time and again. One year after France's most implacable foe had taken power, French fascism was already demonstrating with his anti-democratic slogans.

The demonstration became a riot. The mob attacked the police. The officers resisted, then charged. When the smoke of battle had cleared away, twenty rioters and one police guard lay dead on the asphalt pavements. Over 2,000 were injured, half of them policemen and guards. It was a ghastly night of attacks and counter-attacks, of barricades in the streets, of fierce slashing and charging and shooting. The fascists burned buses; they set fire to the building of the Ministry of Merchant Marine; they attempted to storm the Elysée Palace, residence of the President of the French Republic.

While this first battle of Hitler's Fifth Column in France was raging, Daladier received a parliamentary vote of confidence by 343 to 237.

After the vote in the Chamber I went to the War Ministry where Daladier maintained his office. I caught up to him at the entrance of the building. He seemed undecided.

"What are you going to do?" I asked him.

"The riots will be suppressed," he replied. "The Government will not tolerate the disturbance of order. It has every means of enforcing the law!" With these words crisply flung over his shoulder, he disappeared into the War Office.

Then another momentous Daladier-Weygand conversation took place—this one during the night of February 6 to 7. Weygand faced Daladier, who was frantic and livid with fear. "It is said you intend to summon the Army," he told the Premier. "I cannot guarantee that it will march, but I can guarantee you that the Army will never forget you if you spare it this dilemma."

The President of the Republic, Albert Lebrun, joined forces with General Weygand. He threatened to resign if the Army were sent against the rioters.

In the early morning hours of February 7, Daladier, terrified, quit his post. He handed in his resignation without even consulting his colleagues. He made way for a Government which was counted on to introduce fascism. Behind it loomed the shadows of the fifteen regents of France.

3

THE REGENTS OF FRANCE

DURING THE almost seventy years the Third French Republic existed, many Governments came and went, over a hundred of them—but all the while the country was actually governed by the fifteen regents of the Bank of France. They were the real masters.

The Constitution of the Third Republic was brought into being by a precarious one-vote majority in a Parliament dominated by monarchists. This Constitution, which never in the ensuing years underwent any fundamental change, was carefully devised by its monarchist sponsors to foster the privileges of a small minority. Universal and direct suffrage—for male voters exclusively—was accorded only to the lower House, the Chamber of Deputies. The Senate was created as a check and a brake. This upper House was elected indirectly by municipal and county electors on whom private pressure could be brought to bear with telling effect. Such applications of pressure were the rule, not the exception. The President of the Republic was given almost no power at all. The President was more of a figurehead than a chief executive. However, he had one important prerogative: the right to choose the Premier. More than

The Regents of France

one President of the Third Republic deliberately chose a conservative Premier to tame or thwart a Chamber with a Left majority.

But over and above this structure, the framers of the Constitution left intact the Bank of France. This institution remained at the apex of the State pyramid, just as Napoleon Bonaparte had created it: autonomous, unassailable, with unrestrained power. At its creation more than a hundred years ago, the Bank of France was christened, in a widely circulated leaflet, "the new Bastille." This was what in reality it proved to be—a concrete fortress erected in the interests of the wealthiest men of France.

The "High Bank," as it was called, had its fingers on the pulse of every important corporation, credit establishment and commercial bank in France. It fixed arbitrarily the re-discount rate and the rate of advances against securities or gold. By discounting commercial notes it granted life to a business firm; by refusing to discount, it pronounced a death sentence. It held in its hands the fate of finance and industry. It determined the destiny of the Government in power. By granting the necessary credits, it allowed a Cabinet to continue. By its refusal to do so, it doomed the life of the Cabinet beyond recall.

In 1933 the capital of the Bank of France was divided among 31,000 share-holders. But of these only 200 had the right to vote at general meetings of the Bank. These 200 share-holders were called "the 200 Families of France"—they controlled the decisive levers of finance and industry in the nation.

The business of the Bank was directed by a board of 21 members: the governor, two vice-governors, 15 regents, and three financial auditors. The governor and vice-governors were appointed by the Government. But only an individual possessing at least 100 shares of the Bank's stock could be nominated governor. In 1933, 100 shares represented a sum of approximately two million francs. Only a man holding 50 shares could become vice-governor. It was customary for the 15 regents to provide the governor and vice-governors with the requisite shares. It was also customary for the governor and vice-governors to receive, upon their resignation from the Bank, lucrative positions in private business.

The fifteen regents came from the great banking houses, from commerce and industry. But to the most important among them, election to the board was a mere formality, because their seat was practically hereditary. Thus the Rothschild family was represented on the regency for over seventy years, the Mallets and Hottinguers for over a hundred.

The regency was as exclusive as the blue-blooded Jockey Club of the aristocrats. A handful of men, linked together by class ties, marriage alliances, business inter-

The Regents of France

ests, social bonds and snobbery, formed a solid forbidding phalanx against all newcomers. Frequenting the same drawing-rooms and the same ultra-fashionable clubs, they might quarrel and compete with one another. But whenever a serious threat to their common interests arose, they drew closely together and buried whatever differences may have arisen between them, in order to preserve intact the social order on which their strength was based. They controlled the money of the nation; hence they dominated most of its industrial mechanism. They enjoyed the closest connections with the leading members of the military caste, many of whom sprang from collateral branches of the same families. They were related to some of the highest prelates of the Church. Their sons, nephews and sons-in-law held key positions in the Foreign Office, in the Finance Ministry and in the State apparatus. They furnished the diplomats who represented France in foreign countries. They financed—and lavishly—their own political parties and groups. Through the newspapers they owned or controlled they molded public opinion.

Thus, by its stranglehold on the Cabinet, by its control over Right-wing political parties and some of the most influential newspapers in France, the High Bank in fact controlled French policy. Its history has been a long one; but always, in the words of the French publicist Francis Delaisi, "it has been on the other side of the barricades." In 1848 the Bank fought the Liberal Democrats and supported General Cavaignac, a militarist notorious for the brutality and ferocity with which he crushed a rebellion of the "have-nots," the common people of France. Later the Bank made common cause with Napoleon III and sustained his repressive dictatorship. After the Franco-Prussian War of 1870 the Bank of France was on the side of Marshal MacMahon and the monarchists against the people. During the Dreyfus Affair the Bank, in spite of the Rothschilds, subsidized the anti-Dreyfus camp. In the first decade after the War of 1914-18 it fought obstinately against the two Radical-Socialist Governments of Edouard Herriot and brought them crashing down. As Herriot then affirmed, it constituted a "money wall" which no Government was able to breach. Once, during the World War, Clemenceau complained that he did not possess enough power. A Deputy asked him: "But after all, who has more power than you?" The Tiger shot back: "The regents of the Bank of France!"

During the World War, Mussolini fought to induce Italy to enter on the side of the Allies. His efforts were generously financed by the French Government of that day. After the Duce's rise to power in Italy, he became a favorite of the regency of the Bank. Their newspapers supported him from the very outset of his régime, in spite of his numerous and violent attacks against France

The Regents of France

during the post-war period. Not even the fact that fascist Italy's territorial claims embraced French colonies or possessions could curb the regency's unilateral admiration. That was not the first time the Bank of France had placed its private interests above national interests. During the Franco-Prussian War, the Bank took its stand with Thiers, the "monstrous gnome" who sought an understanding with Prussian Chancellor Bismarck.

In 1933 when Hitler came to power the regents were enchanted with the Führer's enslavement of German labor, the smashing of the trade unions and the interdiction of all liberal and Leftist political parties. They were ready to forget that he had branded France Germany's Public Enemy Number One and that, in *Mein Kampf*, he had set the isolation and annihilation of France at the head of his program. From the first days of Hitler's régime the "200 Families" gazed with envy across the Rhine. They accepted Hitler, just as German big business before them had done, as the crusader and savior of Europe from bolshevism. During the early months of the Hitler Government they entertained some doubts as to its stability, permanence and eventual success. But by the beginning of 1934 the "200 Families" had definitely made up their minds to follow his example and to arrive at a political understanding with him. By then they judged France ripe for remodeling in the image of fascist Italy and Nazi Germany.

A report issued by the Finance Committee of the Chamber of Deputies in 1936 lifts a corner on the manipulations and ramifications of the Bank of France. It is charged with the following:

> (1) It is in the hands of an oligarchy which rules the country over the heads of its elected representatives;
> (2) It grants credit facilities more readily and bountifully to members of the oligarchy or their associates than to other firms;
> (3) It gives unlimited credit facilities to big corporations, while denying them to smaller business houses;
> (4) It drives to the wall and ruins many valuable small or secondary businesses, such as a number of private agricultural banks.

A statistical survey showed that the fifteen regents were chairmen or held seats on the boards of 250 companies. These included thirty-one private banks, two railway companies, seven steel and iron companies, six public utilities, eight mining, twelve chemical, and eight insurance companies. Like an octopus, the regents have spread their tentacles over the key industries and the monetary nerve-centers of France. But their grip extended over international boundaries, as well.

Eugene Schneider, the ironmaster, representing

The Regents of France

France's greatest armament trust—Schneider-Creusot—on the regency, was also the head of the Union Européenne Bank, which controlled the most important armament works in Czechoslovakia, the Skoda factories. The French Chamber was presented with convincing evidence that the French director of the Skoda works had made large contributions to the Nazi movement. After the rape of Czechoslovakia in 1939, Schneider sold his Skoda shares to German interests. The transaction was negotiated by the Paris bank of Lazard Frères, represented on the regency by Max David-Weil. Lazard Frères had intimate connections with the bank of Lazard-Speyer-Elison in Frankfurt, Germany, in turn connected with the Metal-Gesellschaft, an offspring of the giant German chemical trust I. G. Farben.

I. G. Farben collaborated in Spain, South America and China with the French chemical trust of Kuhlmann, represented on the regency by René Duchemin. Interestingly enough, 75% of the capital in one of the vital cellulose explosive factories of the I. G. Farben chain was owned by French sources.

The regent François de Wendel, Senator of France, is head of the De Wendel Trust, the greatest mining company in France. He is also the leader of the Comité des Forges, the all-powerful federation of France's heavy industry. The mines, steel mills and blast furnaces of the De Wendel group are situated on the Franco-German frontier: some of them are in France, others in the Saar region of Germany. In 1914, at the outbreak of the World War, one of Senator de Wendel's close relatives, Herr von Wendel, was a member of the German Reichstag.

President Albert Lebrun was always treated kindly by the Comité des Forges. Lebrun, a mining engineer and company director from Lorraine, was on the board of the Aciéries de Micheville, a member firm of the Comité. François Poncet, French Ambassador in Berlin from 1931-1939, had close ties with this gigantic outfit. Before leaving to assume his diplomatic post in Berlin François Poncet had edited the daily bulletin of the Comité in Paris. It was a tradition for the French Ambassador in Berlin to be the "man of confidence" of the French steel magnates.

The War of 1914-18 did not sever the contacts between German and French heavy industry. Early in the World War the ore mines in the basin of Briey fell into German hands and were exploited to capacity for the purpose of producing armaments. The French bombarded these mines on only one occasion. In 1916 the War Minister, General Lyautey, was asked why such an important source of German raw materials had not been destroyed. He declared that he had given the proper orders, but that the orders had not been carried out. After the war a letter in the Paris newspaper *Informa-*

tion, dated February 16, 1919, revealed the reasons for this failure to carry out instructions: a tacit agreement between the belligerents had been reached, sponsored on the French side by De Wendel and Schneider, and on the German side by the magnate Thyssen and the Saar ironmaster Roechling.

In 1933, at a convention of the Radical-Socialist Party, one of the delegates, Sennac, charged that he had proof that Schneider-Creusot had recently furnished Nazi Germany with a number of the latest model French army tanks, routing them through Holland to avoid suspicion. In March 1940, at one of the secret sessions of the French Chamber, it was disclosed that from September 1939 France had delivered huge quantities of iron ore to Germany and had received German coal in return. The route of transit was by way of Belgium.

Such is the partial record of the men who, as regents of the Bank of France, really ruled the French. In peacetime as well as in wartime they have shown that national interests mattered to them only so long as their own private interests were thereby furthered. They were the financial backers of extremist fascist groups and leagues. François de Wendel's membership card in the "Croix de Feu" bore the number 13. The electricity magnate, Ernest Mercier, closely linked with the German electricity trust A.E.G., was reputedly member number 7 of the same group. In 1934 it was reported that his donations to this, the strongest of the fascist leagues, as well as to other organizations of a similar character, exceeded the sum of ten million francs. With the contributions of men of wealth, such as these, Colonel de la Rocque purchased rifles, ammunition, machine guns and airplanes for the militarized formations of his "Croix de Feu." With this money the riots were organized in February 1934 on the Place de la Concorde in Paris. And the Third French Republic was brought to the brink of catastrophe.

When the February riots had achieved their purpose, and Daladier had resigned his office, a "favorite son" of the "200 Families" became his successor. He was Gaston Doumergue.

4

PAPA DOUMERGUE

The Savior Who Failed

THE APPOINTMENT in 1934 of seventy-two-year-old Gaston Doumergue was hailed by the "Croix de Feu" as an important success. Colonel de la Rocque flashed a bulletin of victory by telegraph to his cohorts all over the country: "FIRST OBJECTIVE ATTAINED."

Addressing a conference of the leading functionaries of his movement, De la Rocque expressed the conviction that fascism would be in the saddle in France by the end of 1934 at the latest. He miscalculated by approximately six years.

The Doumergue Government was the first of a series of "national" Governments extending over a period of two years. These combinations were made up of a coalition of the Radical-Socialist and Right-wing parties, and dominated by the latter. These years were marked by attempts to change the democratic Constitution of the French Third Republic, to invest the President of the Republic with semi-dictatorial powers, and to curtail the jealously guarded right of Parliament to control State finances. It was in this epoch that the Popular Front, an alliance between labor and the middle class, was formed.

A week before the sanguinary clash on the Place de la Concorde, Doumergue, in a radio broadcast, had declared, "Parliament is to blame for the present situation. It has done nothing to fulfill its duty. A revision of our Constitution seems to me an urgent necessity." Thus was sketched the program for his newly formed government.

During his entire political career Gaston Doumergue had been the typical "dark horse." Whenever there was a stalemate between Right and Left, or when it was essential to achieve the political objectives of the Right in the guise of a so-called government above parties, Doumergue was among the candidates. Nothing distinguished him especially from the typical, mediocre French politician save his broad genial smile. For forty years the Doumergue smile was arched like a fixed rainbow across the sky of French politics.

In 1913 he became Premier for the first time. He was a member of practically every Cabinet during the World War. He won particular fame when, returning from an official mission to Russia in 1917, he predicted that the Czar had never been as firmly entrenched as at that moment. One month later the Czar and czarism were swept aside by the Russian Revolution.

In 1924 he was elected to the Presidency of the Republic. Shortly after his election, Edouard Herriot complained: "We have chased Reaction out through the

Papa Doumergue

front door; but in the person of Gaston Doumergue it has sneaked in again through the back door."

A week before the expiration of his term, Gaston Doumergue married an elderly lady friend of many years' standing. Asked why he had chosen almost the day of his departure to quit the ranks of bachelorhood, he confided to an intimate friend: "I wanted to give her the satisfaction of being Madame Président for at least one week."

When his tenure of office came to an end Doumergue received the reward for services rendered. He was made one of the directors of the Suez Canal Company—with a neat little nest-egg of 200,000 francs a year. He retired to a country village in the South of France, Tournefeuille, where, on a comfortable estate, he passed his time cultivating wine grapes and playing cards with his neighbors. "He always wins," his rural card companions complained. "He's almost as good at playing cards as he is at selling wine."

Doumergue's picture was again spread across the papers in 1933. The Right was searching for a likely candidate for the Premiership. But now the man with the benign smile was no longer dubbed "Gastounet." He was graced with the epithet "the wise man of Tournefeuille." He prepared his candidature by broadcasting regularly and frequently to the French people. At the same time Colonel de la Rocque of the Croix de

Feu extolled Doumergue in one of his speeches, calling him "the future savior of France." So it was as a savior from liberalism and democracy that Doumergue was inducted into office. This time the "200 Families" meant to settle accounts with liberal ideas once and for all.

Doumergue's plans for revision of the Constitution were outlined in a book by Senator Maurice Ordinaire, for which Doumergue wrote the preface. It advocated: first, the right of the President of the Republic to dissolve the Chamber and call for new elections; second, that the Chamber was to be elected by indirect (not direct) suffrage, the number of deputies to be reduced, and the terms of those elected to be lengthened; third, that the State budget was to be drawn up and put into effect by governmental decree, without parliamentary procedure or approbation.

But before the new Doumergue Cabinet met Parliament, two events occurred which induced the Premier to go slow with his projects. Two hours after the official formation of the Ministry, during the evening of February 9, 1934, street fighting broke out in Paris. The Communists had issued a call for a demonstration against the Doumergue Cabinet in the poorer section of Paris, the Place de la République. The police banned it. Very few people penetrated as far as this section, which was guarded by a heavy cordon of police and troops. The Government had called out the soldiers and police to prevent the gathering. However, demonstrations spread like wildfire over the entire East End of Paris—to historic Belleville and Ménilmontant, to the railway stations Gare du Nord and Gare de l'Est. Behind high barricades, an unarmed mass faced the police. Guns and machine guns chattered until the early hours of the morning. A hail of stones replied in kind. When the smoke of battle had lifted, the beginning of the Doumergue Cabinet was marked with blood. Official reports estimated the losses on both sides at over 200 dead and wounded. There were more than a thousand arrests in Paris. For the first time it was officially asserted that the fighting was due to the influence and machinations of foreign agitators. From that time forth the specter of "foreign agitators" was an oft-repeated refrain in sections of the Paris press.

Three days later Paris and the great provincial cities of France witnessed a general strike. According to impartial estimates, it was almost 100% complete in such vital administrative services as the post offices, telegraph and telephone exchanges, street-car, bus and subway lines. Laborers in the most important key industries joined the strike. Railway service, water, gas and electricity were exempted by order of the strike leaders.

The Doumergue Government was frightened at the scope and proportions of the strike. Not only that— that very day the Socialists and Communists, although ostensibly in two separate gatherings, came together on the vast expanse of the Vincennes Park in Paris. At the close of the two meetings over 100,000 people of Paris merged into one impressive demonstration. Government circles were profoundly shocked and alarmed. It was the first united demonstration of the Socialists and Communists since the two parties had sharply split in 1922. And it came on the heels of a bitter, internecine struggle which had raged between the two organizations for the past twelve years.

On the morning after the strike Doumergue consulted for hours with his two closest collaborators, the former Premiers André Tardieu and Pierre Laval. Although it was later publicly denied, Laval admitted in private that he and Tardieu had outlined the main points of Doumergue's initial declaration before the Chamber of Deputies. The strategists decided to proceed cautiously with the projected constitutional changes. The temper of the people of Paris was riding high. Doumergue and his advisers had expected them to be downhearted and momentarily stunned by Premier Daladier's hasty exit and by the powerful show of force displayed by the "Croix de Feu." Instead, they found the population stubbornly resolved to fight back. Even if Parliament should commit suicide by swallowing Doumergue's so-called "reforms," the people would not let democracy perish without sharp resistance. So, at its very first appearance before Parliament, the Doumergue Cabinet, which had intended to expound its program of drastic constitutional changes, postponed these plans. The new Government went before the Deputies and Senators suavely and modestly as "a government of party truce." Savior Doumergue again wrapped himself in the mantle of Papa Doumergue with the amiable, cherubic smile. The first attempt to introduce "cold" fascism had been checked.

The Doumergue Ministry, twenty-four strong, included only six Radical-Socialists, with Herriot as Minister of State. Its reactionary members were united in their desire to end the system of parliamentary democracy in France; but they were divided as to ways and means of accomplishing it. Tardieu, Minister of State representing the Right, wanted a corporate State. But he also desired to continue the traditional French diehard policy, that of Clemenceau and Poincaré, toward Germany. Pierre Laval, Minister of Colonies, sought to combine fascism in France with an understanding with fascist Italy and Nazi Germany. His point of view was destined to become that of the so-called "national" parties of the Right.

But to put through his foreign policy, Laval had to wait until the death of Louis Barthou, whom Doumergue had made Foreign Minister. It was not out of love or esteem that Doumergue had included Barthou in his Cabinet. He appointed him only because "Barthou in the Cabinet would be difficult, but Barthou out of the Cabinet would be disastrous."

Louis Barthou was seventy-two years old when he installed himself at the Quai d'Orsay. His career had been a brilliant one. Born in the Basses-Pyrenees region in southwestern France, Barthou was the son of a tinsmith. His alert mobile face, with the lively eyes and the Napoleon III beard, had appeared in more than a dozen Cabinets.

A few weeks after he took over the Foreign Affairs portfolio, I interviewed him. He asserted then that he was the only Cabinet Minister in France who had read Hitler's *Mein Kampf* in the original, unexpurgated edition. Barthou spoke German flawlessly. He could recite long passages of Heinrich Heine by heart, Heine having been one of his favorite authors.

I had gone to see him because Paris was buzzing with rumors that Hitler had demanded a standing army of 300,000 men and that the Doumergue Cabinet, under pressure from Great Britain, was ready to concede. Now, six years after the event, it sounds like a fantastic fairy tale that serious minds calmly discussed the possibility of buying Hitler off by granting him the right to have an army of 300,000. But Laval's agents were all over the place, affirming that this was a way to ensure peace. Count Fernand de Brinon was busy paying calls on newspaper editors. So was Stanislas de La Rochefoucauld, of the nobility who worked for Laval. Leaders of Nazi ex-servicemen's organizations bustled into Paris giving assurances on every hand that Hitler was going to omit the passages insulting to France in his *Mein Kampf*, and that a new bowdlerized edition was in preparation. They convinced the head of an influential French ex-servicemen's group, Deputy Jean Goy, who buttonholed colleagues in the lobbies of Parliament to assure them of Hitler's good faith. One of Hitler's cleverest agents, Otto Abetz, made his first visit to Paris. He made the rounds of the fashionable drawing-rooms, accompanied by the correspondent of the *Frankfurter Zeitung*, Friedrich Sieburg, a notorious turncoat from liberal democracy to Nazism.

Louis Barthou expressed himself to me in the strongest terms possible. He denied categorically that he was on the point of making concessions to Hitler. "If we take that fateful step," he cried, "we will be faced with new and higher demands in a short time. One day we will have to make a stand. It is better that we make it now while the trump cards are still in our hands."

Louis Barthou, small, robust, urbane, civilized and versatile, seemed to have a love for politics in his blood. He wrote once: "The political tribune is the altar of the word. One has to fear the tribune in order to be equal to it." He loved music almost fanatically. He was an ardent bibliophile and art collector. When his library was auctioned after his death, it was revealed that he possessed the most extensive collection of erotic literature in France.

This statesman, a kind of twilight figure of grandeur in the epoch of France's decline, was a curious mixture of Poincaré's matter-of-factness and Briand's tremulous warmth. In his spare hours he wrote a number of books, mainly on French literature. One of his volumes was a personal tribute to Richard Wagner, for by a strange quirk of history the voluble little man from the Pyrenees adored the harmonies of Nazism's precursor in music.

Barthou was the last representative of traditional French policy at the Quai d'Orsay. This policy was dictated by the fear of Germany's industrial and military potentialities, as well as by a distrust of Great Britain's continental policy of the balance of power. Although he sought to preserve Franco-British collaboration, Barthou was haunted by the idea that in that partnership France, as Clemenceau had once put it, would be the horse and England the rider. His doctrine was that France must be the first continental power in Europe. For him the network of French alliances—with Poland, Czechoslovakia, Rumania and Jugoslavia—was indispensable to maintain the European balance. With Barthou as Foreign Minister, the initiative in European foreign policy rebounded to France, which in the previous year had lost it to Tory Britain and to Nazi Germany.

Papa Doumergue

Barthou had been an implacable foe of Soviet Russia in the first period after the World War. He was a dyed-in-the-wool conservative in his internal policies. But now, in the face of the heightened danger of Hitlerism, he strove tirelessly to come to an understanding with the Soviets. In May 1934 he coöperated with Litvinov in Geneva in laying the groundwork for the entry of the U.S.S.R. into the League of Nations. At that same session of the League he fought the attempts of Sir John Simon to make concessions to Hitler. In an impassioned speech, a rejoinder to one of Sir John's tortuous, legalistic declarations, Barthou attacked the Nazi spirit of militarism and war, to which he applied, with a deft substitution, the words of the eighteenth-century Mirabeau: "the national industry of Germany."

"I am too old to spout rubbish," he told us waiting newspapermen as he stalked from the conference room in high dudgeon. Sir John Simon, the cold-blooded apostle of appeasement, was not seen again at Geneva during that session.

Barthou as Foreign Minister immediately set to work to reorganize and reënforce the system of French alliances. With that in mind, he made a "grand tour" of Europe, which led him to Poland, Rumania, Jugoslavia and Czechoslovakia. His basic idea was to complement the Locarno pacts (which guaranteed France, Great Britain, Germany, Italy and Belgium in the West the help of all the other signatory powers in the event that one of these powers was attacked by a co-signatory) with an "Eastern Locarno." This was to embrace Germany, the Soviet Union, Poland, Czechoslovakia, and the Baltic countries.

In the course of this trip Barthou narrowly escaped death when his train was bombed by the Nazis on its passage across Austria. The French press thereupon received explicit instructions from the Premier's office to minimize the incident.

He met Poland's aging dictator, Marshal Pilsudski, in the Belvedere Palace in Warsaw. The Polish leader seemed resolved to adhere to the pact of non-aggression he had recently signed with Hitler. On leaving the palace, Barthou appeared worried and distraught. "I could not make him change his mind," he confessed.

He entered Rumania like a triumphal conqueror. The jubilant Rumanians made him an honorary citizen of their country. He was received in audience by King Alexander of Jugoslavia, who renewed his attestations of loyalty to France. He talked with the aged President of the Czechoslovak Republic, Thomas Masaryk, and with his pupil, Foreign Minister Eduard Beneš. Both gave him pledges of collaboration against any eventual Nazi expansion.

His voyage was a resounding personal triumph for him and a political triumph for France. But he clearly saw the danger signals. On his return to Paris, he avowed: "I have underestimated this Hitler. He is working feverishly in the East and Northeast of Europe. I think I have checked him. But it will require hard work to keep him permanently in check."

The Führer did not underestimate Barthou's achievements. In October 1934, while King Alexander of Jugoslavia was paying a state visit to France, both he and Barthou were assassinated in Marseilles by Croatian terrorists. The murderers were members of the notorious "Ustachi" gang, and their connections with the Nazi Party were confirmed by incontrovertible evidence. The newspaper of the "Ustachi" organization was published in Berlin with financial support from the Foreign Section of the Nazi Party. The assassins at Marseilles had received their false passports at Munich. The machine gun which they fired bore the trademark of the Mauser Arms Factory at Oberndorf-am-Neckar, an important German munitions concern.

It was the third political assassination committed by the Nazis or their agents in that year: they had murdered Chancellor Dollfuss in Vienna; the Rumanian Prime Minister Duca in Sinaia near Bucharest; and now King Alexander and Louis Barthou at Marseilles. Indeed, it was while endeavoring to shield the King with his body that the French statesman lost his own life. Even the reactionary *Journal des Débats*, a paper which bears a heavy responsibility for the events of the ensuing years, admitted grudgingly: "Murder has become an integral part of foreign policy."

Barthou was laid to rest. Pierre Laval moved into the Quai d'Orsay to succeed him. After the man who had exclaimed at Geneva that "a promise from Nazi Germany is not enough!" came the man who declared: "I shall not hesitate to conclude an agreement with Berlin, if it is possible." Less than two months after the *attentat* in Marseilles, Joachim von Ribbentrop, then Hitler's special roving envoy, was received by Foreign Minister Laval at the French Foreign Office.

It was not only in Berlin that the end of Louis Barthou was greeted with a sigh of relief. Premier Doumergue seized the occasion to reshuffle his Ministers. One fall from grace was significant. Out went the Minister who had in his possession too many secrets of the Stavisky Affair, especially choice bits concerning the instigators of the riots. His name was Henri Chéron, a shrewd and chubby Norman. Chéron insisted on making a thorough, far-reaching investigation of the Marseilles murders.

Up spoke Marshal Pétain, Minister of War. "We have a dead weight in this Government!" It was a rare occasion when the marshal opened his mouth.

"Whom do you mean?" Chéron asked.

"You!" retorted Pétain.

So the dead weight was unceremoniously flung over-

Papa Doumergue

board. Chéron was replaced at the Ministry of Justice by Senator Henry Leméry, a big landlord from the French colonial possession of Martinique. Leméry, who was supposed to take charge of the investigation of the Marseilles outrage, was himself a member-at-large of the "Croix de Feu." Later he became an ardent champion of the appeasement policy and an admiring visitor to General Franco in Burgos. No wonder the investigation marked time! As a matter of historical record, the accomplices of the assassin, who had himself been lynched on the spot by the crowd in Marseilles, were brought to trial two years later—under a Popular Front Government.

The Doumergue Government survived the murderous attack in Marseilles by little more than a month. It had failed, in spite of its slashes in the wages of State employees, to cover the budgetary deficit. It could not stem the tide of increasing unemployment, and it was helpless before the cancerous spread of the depression. In spite of the fact that a Marshal of France was its War Minister and General Denain, its Air Minister, the Doumergue Cabinet neglected the defense exigencies of the nation. It had before its eyes a mass of precise and detailed reports about Hitler's furious rearmament, yet it did almost nothing to modernize France's timeworn military equipment. In the early weeks of the Cabinet's life a scheme to reorganize the Air Force was glibly introduced by General Denain. He suggested that the air arm be strengthened by an addition of 1,000 planes. This was at a time when Nazi Germany was already driving full speed ahead to gain air parity, and then soon after air superiority, over France and Great Britain. More than two years elapsed before these 1,000 planes were delivered to the Army. By that time the models were outdated!

Two people advocated intense mechanization for the French Army. One of them, General Charles de Gaulle, in his book *Towards a Professional Army*, expressed the view that a mechanized army of 100,000 men could defeat any under-mechanized foe of far superior numbers. The other champion of mechanization was Paul Reynaud, the little Paris Deputy with big ambitions, who was known to enjoy excellent connections with high finance and the General Staff. He, too, had published a book in which he demanded the creation of at least six armored divisions.

Meanwhile the two parties of the extreme Left—the Socialists and the Communists—were conferring with each other. The first impulse had been given by the united demonstration on February 12, 1934. This was followed by repeated offers from the Communists to the Socialists for joint action. After five months of negotiations, the two parties concluded a pact of united action which pledged them "to mobilize the entire working population against fascism, to defend democratic liberties, to fight both against the new war danger and for the liberation of the victims of fascist terror in Germany and Austria." On that same February 12, when the anti-fascists of Paris massed on the grounds of Vincennes, barricades were erected in Vienna. For several days civil war raged in Austria between the forces of labor and the army of Chancellor Dollfuss. The famous workers' housing developments of Vienna were shattered by cannon and machine-gun fire. Clerical fascism was enthroned in Austria; the once powerful Austrian trade unions were smashed, and Socialists and Communists outlawed.

These events made a deep impression on the French people. The Nazi terror in Germany also drove home important truths. It is unquestionable that these considerations hastened the signing of the pact of united action.

The French Socialist leaders accepted this new alliance with the Communists only reluctantly and with many misgivings. One month before the pact was officially signed, the administrative committee of the Socialist Party—the leading national body—rejected by a vote of 22 to 8 a motion in favor of unity. Included in the 22 was Léon Blum, the leader of the Socialist Party.

The committee adopted a resolution that it deemed the moment an inopportune and inexpedient one to continue conversations with the Communists. But this motion obviously ran counter to the desires of many Socialist members. One Socialist-Communist demonstration after another followed. Blum voiced his own apprehensions in his party's newspaper *Le Populaire*: "One feels as if on a steep slope and carried down, more by force of gravity than by one's own volition. . . . The feeling of not knowing exactly where we are going is quite natural. . . ."

On July 27, 1934 the pact was signed. The next day some 50,000 people gathered at the Pantheon in Paris to commemorate the twentieth anniversary of the assassination of the great French Socialist, Jean Jaurès, at the outbreak of the first World War.

The underlying sentiment of the common people of France was hatred of fascism. Life itself was the cement of fusion. The rôles were now reversed in French politics. From the signing of the Treaty of Versailles, the policy of the French Right had been to defend the treaty as immutable and inviolable. The French Left, on the other hand, had assailed the iniquities and injustices of the treaty. Now it was French Labor which fiercely demanded resistance to Hitlerism; while the parties representing French big business were espousing the idea of making concessions to the Nazis.

Papa Doumergue

The Socialist-Communist pact could not fail to have repercussions in the ranks of the Radical-Socialists. The Left wing of the Radical-Socialist Party swung into action. More than half of the prescribed legislative period of four years had run its course. Elections were looming ahead. The Radical-Socialist deputies began to hearken more wholeheartedly to the prospects of an electoral alliance with the Socialists and Communists. Only thus could they guarantee their return to the Chamber. They received batches of letters and reports from their constituents back home. Public opinion showed no swing in Doumergue's favor—quite the contrary.

By the end of October 1934 the atmosphere in Paris was again electric with tension. Rumors were rife that the "Croix de Feu" was planning a new *putsch*. Colonel de la Rocque made vainglorious, menacing speeches against "those who conspired to overthrow this great patriot Doumergue." He ordered renewed large-scale military drills and trial mobilizations in which many airplanes participated. He was received by Marshal Pétain. This encounter was to have remained a closely guarded secret, but somehow the news leaked out and served to heighten the tension. The stock market reacted in jittery fashion. Paris was again living in an atmosphere bordering on civil war.

The Doumergue clique manned its guns. *Le Temps*

thundered: "Doumergue is on the right road; we must aid and follow him. The card he asks us to play is at once the last and the best one. If the State is not reformed as Doumergue proposes, then in a few years, perhaps in a few months, it will be all over with our liberal régime."

Coming from such a semi-official source, the seriousness of the threat was apparent to everybody. A specific date for the showdown was whispered in informed circles: the "Croix de Feu" had chosen November 11, Armistice Day, as their M-day. Every Armistice Day saw a big parade of the "Croix de Feu" and other ex-servicemen's organizations, with a traditional march past the tomb of the Unknown Soldier and the eternal flame at the Arc de Triomphe in Paris. This time, it was reported, the paraders would not disperse. While their air pilots would darken the skies over Paris, the "Croix de Feu" would seize the key points in the metropolis and in several provincial centers. Then they would close up "the talk shop" of Parliament and install the notorious Directorate of Five. This time the names were Doumergue, Pétain, Laval, Marquet and General Weygand. Tardieu was not on the list. He never forgave De la Rocque for having eliminated him from the list of prospective dictators. He took his revenge on the Colonel a few years later.

The Left made its preparations too. Paris was excited. Parades followed one another in quick succession. The most impressive demonstration of the Left forces came on the eve of the Radical-Socialist convention. Nearly 100,000 men and women marched through the streets of Paris demanding the resignation of Doumergue and the revocation of his drastic financial decrees.

Help came from a totally unexpected quarter. Georges Mandel spoke up. He sat in the Chamber as an independent Republican. As Clemenceau's intimate and closest collaborator, he enjoyed unusual prestige with the Rightist parties in the Chamber. He persuaded a majority of the most influential members of the Rightwing group that an attempt to introduce fascism by means of a *putsch* would lead to a prolonged and bloody civil war. And it was by no means certain that fascism would prevail. The masses were in a belligerent anti-fascist mood.

Curiously enough, the man who in the last analysis decided the issue and dissuaded Doumergue from seeking an open fight was his Minister of Public Works, Pierre-Étienne Flandin. A few days after the Radical-Socialist Party meeting, Flandin made a thinly veiled offer to the radicals to join forces in the formation of a new Ministry which would not include Doumergue. Herriot got the idea. He avoided a head-on conflict with Doumergue on the vital question of constitutional changes. He chose to fight on a relatively insignificant budgetary issue. Doumergue, adamant, insisted on his point of view. The Radical-Socialist Ministers promptly walked out behind Herriot's huge bulk. The Doumergue Cabinet was a thing of the past.

Now the moment for the long-dreaded *putsch* of the Right was at hand. On Armistice Day the "Croix de Feu" paraded along the broad Champs Élysées in Paris, grimly shouting: "We want Doumergue! Pétain in power! We want Weygand!" But it was all sound and fury signifying nothing. The tired old mediocrity—again he was "Gastounet" to his supporters—had to take the train back home to Tournefeuille.

Doumergue's successor was Flandin. Six feet six inches tall, called "the skyscraper of the French Parliament" and "the unfinished one," Flandin was the youngest Frenchman ever to become Premier. He assumed that office at the age of forty-five.

Flandin offered the War Ministry to Pétain who, on the advice of Weygand, refused. "Save your strength," cautioned Weygand. "Perhaps you are fated to play the same rôle in France as Hindenburg in Germany." Edouard Herriot stayed on in the Flandin Cabinet as Minister of State, Pierre Laval as Minister of Foreign Affairs.

Papa Doumergue

Flandin comes from a wealthy upper-class family. His father had been a French Resident-General of Tunisia in northern Africa who had left a considerable fortune to his children. Pierre-Étienne was destined to follow the legal profession, but at twenty-five he entered the Chamber from the rural district of the Yonne. He was "the baby deputy" in Parliament. He was one of the first French military aviators in 1914. In 1917 he became director of the Inter-Allied Aeronautical Service.

Flandin's education was what the French call, with an ill-concealed grimace, an English one. So are his habits and tastes. He is inveterately fond of hunting, shooting and fishing. A fast-driving motorist, he has collected more police tickets for speeding than any other politician in France. He prefers tame English dishes to the rich sauces and delicacies of the French *cuisine.* His long head, partly bald, towers over extremely broad shoulders. He likes to stand very erect; and thus he gives the impression of being even taller than he really is.

He had held seven Cabinet posts before he became Premier. He was the party leader of a group in Parliament known as the "Democratic Alliance." Poincaré had once been chairman of this group. But here we run up against another of the baffling intricacies and complexities of the French political system. The Left wing of this fairly loose coalition was not very far politically from its neighbor immediately to the left of it; while its Right wing was hardly distinguishable from its neighbor to the right. Be that as it may, Flandin's views were outspokenly on the Right. He had served solely in Cabinets dominated by the Right. Hence the maneuver by which he contributed decisively to the fall of Doumergue was all the more startling.

It is one of the classic examples of the contradictions in the political life of the Third French Republic. Bound closely by social and economic ties to those circles which stood behind Doumergue and used him as a convenient screen, Flandin ought normally to have followed his chief through thick and thin. But in the complex situation arising in the autumn of 1934 he spied a chance for himself to become *the* leader of public life in France. So rather than let the opportunity go by, he seized time by the forelock and made a brusque turn to the Left. His calculations proved correct.

The great surprise of the Flandin Cabinet was the new Minister of P.T.T. (Post Office, Telegraph and Telephone): Georges Mandel. At last Mandel had reached ministerial rank. It was a minor post, no doubt, but one which gave him a golden opportunity. Now he could have the wires of all his political friends and enemies tapped indiscriminately. Flandin, fearing that the Police would listen in to his telephone conversations, had a special private wire installed. He outwitted the Police, but not Mandel's diligent listeners. Unbeknown to Flandin, they remained at their post.

The Socialists and Communists adopted a hostile attitude toward the new Government. For them, Pierre-Étienne Flandin was the man of the Aero-Postal scandal. This firm, which was involved in fraudulent speculations, had been exposed in 1931. Its corrupt practices created a minor sensation and dragged three Parisian banks into bankruptcy. Flandin had been the legal adviser of the Aero-Postal Company. Evidence indicated that he had been on the company's pay roll even while he had been Minister of Finance in a previous Cabinet. When Flandin presented his Government to the Chamber of Deputies, cries of "Aero-Postal! Aero-Postal!" savagely greeted him from the benches on the Left. But he won a comfortable majority in the Chamber just the same.

His Cabinet lasted seven months. Then he was made to pay the penalty for what the "200 Families" considered a betrayal: his part in the overthrow of the Doumergue Government. In May 1935 the Flandin Cabinet badly needed credits from the Bank of France. A few weeks before, Flandin had asked for the Bank's support and had been given a modest advance. But the Bank issued a communiqué stating: "The Flandin Government will have to ask for more credits. The reply will depend on whether the Bank is satisfied with the actions of the Government during the first breathing spell given it as a reward for its expressed determination to defend the franc." That was, as everybody understood, the death warrant for the Flandin Cabinet. When the Premier again turned to the Bank of France for additional credits, the regency refused flatly and with cold finality. The Government of Pierre-Étienne Flandin staggered, floundered helplessly, and then fell in May 1935.

5

FIFTEEN MONTHS OF LAVAL

SOLIDLY entrenched, since the murder of Louis Barthou, in the historic edifice at the Quai d'Orsay, with its multitude of narrow corridors and its old-fashioned offices, Pierre Laval for fifteen months guided the foreign relations of the Third Republic. He was Foreign Minister in the Flandin Ministry which lasted seven months. After it toppled, and after a half-serious, half-comic interlude of a one-day Government under his friend, Fernand Bouisson, Laval headed a Cabinet of his own. This, too, lasted seven months.

He was already intimate with the Quai d'Orsay, having occupied it three years previously, after the resignation of Aristide Briand. With Briand, Laval, then Premier, had traveled in 1931 to Berlin to visit German Chancellor Bruening. "We need more men like you in France," Laval is reported to have declared to the stern, ascetic-faced Catholic Bruening. The German Government was then ruling by means of emergency decrees. After his conferences with Laval, Bruening told colleagues that the Frenchman had been alertly interested in the functioning of these semi-dictatorial methods of government.

Laval brought to the Quai d'Orsay the astuteness and stubbornness attributed to the people of Auvergne, where he was born. This volcanic, mountainous country in the south central part of France, with its weird beauty and harsh contrasts, produces rugged, thrifty individuals. Thrifty is an understatement—stingy and avaricious would be more to the point. The Auvergnats are the Scotchmen of France—and they play an analogous part in countless Gallic jokes and anecdotes.

Some biographers of Laval maintain that he is the son of a butcher; others claim that his father was a café proprietor. Judging from his face, he himself might pass as a butcher. He is of medium height, with a tendency to squatness and dumpiness. He has the olive-green complexion of his countrymen, dark and heavy-lidded eyes, prominent thick lips and cigarette-stained teeth. In fact, for years the Nazi newspapers delighted sadistically in running a picture of Laval in their columns as an outstanding example of "the Negroid, bastardized French people." But memories are short; a nod from Dr. Goebbel's propaganda bureau and Laval's features took on Nazi grace.

There is, as a matter of fact, a brutality in Laval that makes an indelible impression. Not even the man's suavity and cunning, his keen sense of what pleases his interlocutor, and his subtle exploitation of every weakness he finds in others, can efface that faint sticky feeling of discomfort.

Fifteen Months of Laval

Laval comes originally from the French Socialist Party. For a short while as a young man he taught school in his home town. Then he studied law in Paris. His first important assignment was in the legal department of the trade unions in the Paris region. He achieved prominence just prior to the war as a "poor man's lawyer." In the Socialist Party he met Aristide Briand shortly before the latter left its ranks. The Laval legend has it that the young man made such an impression on Briand that the latter mentioned him in glowing terms to the Socialist leader, Jean Jaurès. Some of Laval's acolytes even quote Briand as follows: "Today I met a remarkable young fellow. I recommend him to your attention."

However that may be, Laval rose swiftly in the Socialist Party. In 1914, at the age of thirty-one, he was elected to the Chamber of Deputies from the Paris suburb of Aubervilliers.

His negative, defeatist attitude toward the first World War was common knowledge. The French Secret Service put his name on the celebrated "Carnet B," a list of people to be arrested on the spot or to be closely watched in the event of war. Laval was in the second category. "My movements were shadowed, my mail opened, my telephone tapped. That's how I learned governmental technique. The quintessence is to know what your foes are preparing; then you can never be taken by surprise." But there is even a better story. One day Laval bribed the Police inspector who was shadowing him, and then proceeded to win all his money back again by rolling dice with him.

He never saw the front during the war, although there is some evidence that he may have served in the Army for a brief period. But he did have a good opportunity to study the home front. In the hinterland he met a number of politicians from various parties who shared his defeatist viewpoint. These were mainly in the circle of Joseph Caillaux, a former Premier. Himself a patrician, Caillaux had excellent relations with the men of high finance. He introduced Laval into these charmed circles, and as the war drew to a close, the influence of this exclusive set began to tell on Laval. He switched from the Left wing to the Right wing of the Socialist Party. Since then he has continued to switch like a prestidigitator. Léon Blum once said of him: "You never can tell where Laval will be tomorrow, except that he's always moving to the Right."

Laval's clientele changed too. He became a very prosperous corporation lawyer. He picked and chose his clients carefully, favoring only those in high places. His main source of income came as a result of his connections with François de Wendel, the potentate of the Comité des Forges. He became de Wendel's intimate law counsel.

He had entered politics in 1914 penniless. In 1935,

Fifteen Months of Laval

when his daughter José married Count René de Chambrun, nephew of the American Nicholas Longworth and an American citizen by virtue of his descent from the Marquis de Lafayette, Laval's fortune was estimated at higher than three and a half million dollars. He was made a Papal Count. He was said to own three vast country estates, an ancient chateau, a racing stable and a priceless collection of antiques. He is the owner of a chain of provincial newspapers and a mineral-water concern. The Chamber of Deputies knew him as an uncannily successful speculator on the Stock Exchange. Anatole de Monzie, who had sat by his side in several Cabinets and who was himself no slouch at feathering his nest, used to assert: "I don't always agree with Laval's political ideas, but on the stock market I follow him blindly." There was only one fly in Laval's ointment. With all his amassed wealth, he was forbidden to partake of rich food and drink. By doctor's orders he was kept on a strict, meager diet.

Laval is a man without illusions, without scruples and without ideals. His cynicism goes hand in hand with his Auvergnat toughness and predilection for a hard bargain. His shrewd instincts, his thorough unscrupulousness and his quick grasp of an adversary's vulnerable points, have formed his character. He received his first Cabinet post in a Leftist combination, as a reward for acting as a go-between for Painlevé and Briand. He first became Premier in 1931. Since that time he has been prominently mentioned as a candidate in practically every ministerial crisis.

Year in year out he wears the same washable white necktie. Some attribute it to his stinginess. Others to its publicity value. And still others say he needs at least something clean about him. A Socialist Deputy once interrupted a speech by Laval in the Chamber with the shout: "I wish your hands were as clean as your necktie!"

He is the last person in the world to give something away for nothing. One of his intimates of the press was the foreign editor of an influential morning paper. Once in a thoughtless moment, this man wrote an article which ran contrary to Laval's wishes.

That same day Laval phoned the editor-in-chief of the paper: "Here's what I want your foreign editor to write in tomorrow's issue!" He proceeded, in an extremely harsh and domineering tone, to explain his desires.

The editor was offended by this peremptory note of command. He retorted: "You've no right to dictate what we should write!"

"Oh, yes I have," Laval shot back. "Ask your foreign editor." The latter was then fired from the paper —not because he had accepted subsidies from Laval, but because he had failed to give his own editor-in-chief a cut. That was Laval's revenge. Later he placed the same man on the afternoon paper *Paris-Soir*. That was after he had made sure that the foreign editor would never again swerve out of line.

The Ministry of Foreign Affairs controls most of the secret funds at the disposal of a French Cabinet. Laval made the most lavish use of this money. He dealt it out right and left. His manipulations were so flagrantly shameless that Léon Blum once proposed in the Chamber that the secret funds be taken away from him.

Describing the state of the French nation on the eve of 1935, Julien Benda, a noted moralist and historian of ideas, wrote: "A taint of Caesarism affects one whole section of the French people—a certain organic hostility to democracy which will yield to no proofs however convincing. . . . France may be said to live in a state of perpetual civil war."

Laval was the leader of this trend to Caesarism. It also signified an understanding with the other Caesars of Europe, Mussolini and Hitler. Laval's deep-seated contempt for democracy, his admiration for demagogy and his flouting of the League of Nations, combined to make him think of himself as the man who could reach an agreement with the two dictators. He was wary and suspicious of British policy. But he felt confident that between his outlook and that of Hitler and Mussolini a common denominator could be found. Thus a community of interests between France, Germany and Italy might result, if necessary at the expense of other nations, even those allied with France. He made no secret of his conviction that the days of democracy in France were numbered. The "new order" he sought would be easier to impose by a pre-arranged accord with fascist Italy and Nazi Germany.

During his stay at the Quai d'Orsay Laval not only demolished Barthou's work, but also laid the foundations for the future defeat of France. He helped Hitler win a smashing success in the Saar plebiscite; he allowed the Führer to commit the first open breach of the Versailles Treaty by introducing military conscription in Germany; he signed the Franco-Soviet Treaty of mutual assistance only to do everything to render it valueless. He backed Mussolini in his war against Abyssinia. He ruined the system of collective security of the League.

Outwardly he did not break sharply and abruptly with the traditional foreign policy of France. He used almost the identical phrases and catchwords of his predecessors at the Quai d'Orsay. But an air of mystery and intrigue hovered about his actions. His colleagues were puzzled; so was the London Foreign Office. He appealed to the inchoate sentiments, the vague unformulated ideas, the fuzzy unexpressed desires of the middle-class French-

Fifteen Months of Laval

man. The man in the street listened. He wanted no war. Laval declared: "I will guarantee peace for you. Just let me come to terms with our two great neighbors, Italy and Germany. Then you'll enjoy a long and lasting peace." Jean Frenchman lent a more willing ear. After all, he was not particularly concerned about the League of Nations or France's alliances in the East and Southeast of Europe. Those factors were so remote, so lacking in immediacy and appeal. Nor was he overfond of Great Britain. His affection for Italy, "the Latin sister," overrode his contempt for Italy's failure at Caporetto and elsewhere in the first World War. The fear of Hitler, riding from victory to victory, coupled with respect for his achievements, made it seem all the more desirable to the middle-class Frenchman to come to terms with him and thus avoid or divert Nazi attack.

Immediately upon entering the Quai d'Orsay, Laval sent emissaries to Berlin and Rome to sound out the possibilities for an agreement. Mussolini, then putting the finishing touches to his plans for the conquest of Abyssinia, was only too eager to get the support of France. Hitler in Germany had not yet dissipated the uneasiness caused by his "blood purge" of June 30, 1934. There was still considerable unrest in the Nazi Party and among the Storm Troopers. The German Army had not yet forgotten the stain of dishonor left by the murder of General von Schleicher. Hitler was desperately in need of a success. Hence Laval's envoys were received with open arms. When the Right-wing deputy Jean Goy, together with Paris Municipal Councillor Mounier, visited Berlin, he had an audience with the Führer. He was lavishly entertained by Joachim von Ribbentrop, then Hitler's roving envoy and head of the so-called "Ribbentrop Bureau," in reality the Special Foreign Office of the Nazi Party. During Goy's sojourn in Berlin the idea of a visit by von Ribbentrop to Paris was hatched. Ribbentrop painted in vivid colors the picture of a Franco-German understanding which, he affirmed, nobody desired more than the Führer. So at the end of November 1934, Herr von Ribbentrop, accompanied by Hitler's specialist in the matter of a Franco-German *rapprochement*, Otto Abetz, came to Paris as the guests of Deputy Jean Goy. Von Ribbentrop was introduced to the smart set of Parisian society by Count Fernand de Brinon. The Count also scurried about to arrange a number of interviews between von Ribbentrop and various Right-wing politicians.

During his stay, von Ribbentrop was received at the Quai d'Orsay on December 2, 1934, by Foreign Minister Laval. Their conversation was cloaked in deep secrecy. But when Laval bade his visitor good-bye, an arrangement had been reached guaranteeing Hitler a success in the forthcoming plebiscite in the Saar.

The Saar region had been separated from Germany

by the Treaty of Versailles in 1919 and placed under the control of the League of Nations. France was to receive the output of coal from its rich mine deposits for fifteen years. After that interval a plebiscite was to be held: the inhabitants of the Saar would then decide whether they wanted to return to Germany, remain under the supervision of the League or join France.

There could be no doubt that the overwhelming majority wished to return to Germany. But to a Nazi Germany?—that was another question. Thoroughgoing investigations by neutrals demonstrated that the bulk of the population in that predominantly Catholic region preferred not to join Nazi Germany. They wanted to be given the possibility of voting again, after the downfall of the Nazi régime. The League of Nations Commission administering the region, as well as some leading political figures in France and Great Britain, worked hard to win the approval of the French and British Governments to such a solution. A member of the League Commission in Saarbruecken told me at the end of November 1934 that an agreement had been reached in principle. A declaration would be made at the beginning of January 1935 that the Saar plebiscite would be held after an additional ten years.

This statement never saw the light of day. In the course of von Ribbentrop's visit, Laval made a solemn promise that no such declaration would be forthcoming from the League of Nations. In exchange he received a renewed affirmation from Hitler that, after the settlement of the Saar question, Germany would have no territorial claims on France. Laval obtained the support of Marshal Pétain for his Saar policy. The Marshal expressed himself as strongly against any repetition of the Saar plebiscite. Pétain asserted that he would not permit the Saar to become another Alsace-Lorraine. When Laval informed the Cabinet about his conversation with von Ribbentrop, he was opposed by only two Ministers, Georges Mandel and Edouard Herriot.

At this Cabinet meeting Laval went into an exhaustive analysis of foreign affairs. It was an optimistic Laval addressing his colleagues. He presented them with the report of the French Ambassador in Rome, who said that Mussolini was looking forward to meeting him. The Duce was anxious to discuss all outstanding differences "man to man" and was hopeful of a settlement. The report was replete with details concerning the biting remarks Mussolini was making about Hitler. From Berlin Ambassador François Poncet reported that at his last meeting with Hitler, the Führer had again stressed his desire to reach an understanding with France. M. Poncet added: "It is true, of course, that I am not without my doubts as to Hitler's sincerity; still there is reason to believe that the Führer, loaded down with the tremendous burden of rearmaments, is looking for a breathing space. It seems reasonable to believe that Germany is in no position to continue for another twelve months under the present economic strain induced by rearmament."

Laval laid before the Cabinet Council a plan for an agreement with Mussolini: France would cede to Italy a portion of her territory in French Somaliland and south of Lybia; it would transfer to Italy some of its Djibouti-Addis Ababa railway shares; it would extend the present status of nationality of Italian settlers in Tunisia until 1960. In return France asked Mussolini to agree to mutual consultations in the event of any threat to Austrian independence or to the *status quo* in the Danubian and Balkan nations. Furthermore, Italy was asked to consult with France and to associate itself with steps necessary to prevent any further extension in Germany's rearmaments.

At that point one of the Ministers asked Laval whether he possessed any new information concerning Mussolini's rumored designs on Abyssinia and about the conversations again under way between Germany and Italy. Laval replied that the Berlin-Rome conversations were, according to his reports, being highly exaggerated as to their scope and importance. (In reality he knew that the web, badly damaged in the course of Hitler's visit to Italy in June 1934 and by the assassination of Chancellor Dollfuss of Austria, was being rewoven.) As far as Mussolini's plans in Abyssinia were concerned, the Foreign Minister added, his information led him to believe that Mussolini contemplated gaining some minor territorial concessions from Haile Selassie. And in his opinion France ought not to be concerned if Il Duce collected a few more square kilometers of desert.

After the Cabinet meeting I talked to one of the Ministers present. He was discouraged: "Here we are," he complained, "facing two dictators, each of whom is straining every nerve to build up a vast empire for himself. And Laval thinks he can tame them by offering to one of them a patch of desert and a few shares in a railway, and to the other the Saar territory. He handles foreign affairs as if they were a matter of a by-election in his home district. I fear we are in for trouble."

Although Mussolini had expressed acceptance of only a part of the French proposals, Laval started for Rome early in January 1935. Taking leave of the diplomats who had come to see him off, he exulted: "I have high hopes that a new era in Franco-Italian relations is about to begin." As the train slowly moved out of the station, Spalaikovich, the Jugoslav Minister to Paris, burst out in tears.

Laval insisted peremptorily that the "Croix de Feu" stage an enthusiastic reception for him in Paris on his

Fifteen Months of Laval

return from Rome. As was later revealed he paid from the secret funds, on a *pro rata* basis, for every demonstrator the leader of the "Croix de Feu" had sent to greet him at the Paris railway station.

The Chamber and the Senate both gave him a rousing ovation. The Rome agreement was overwhelmingly passed, with only a handful of Communist deputies voting against it. Laval went out of his way to draw up personally the communiqué describing the meeting of the Chamber and the Senate.

The initial reception awaiting Laval in Rome did not correspond to his great expectations. No crowds, no banners, no popular demonstration greeted him. For two days Rome showed the visiting statesman a polite but coldly reserved face. Hinting broadly that he had expected more from France than Laval actually proposed, the Duce declared in his toast at the state banquet: "This significant visit is the first meeting point in the policies of the two great Latin States."

Laval's answering toast was warmer by far. "Mussolini has written the most beautiful page in the history of modern Italy," he said. "We have given rise to great hopes. All who are animated by the ideal of peace, today have their eyes turned towards Rome." But even this declaration of love failed to warm up the frosty Italian atmosphere.

The change did come—abruptly. But only after a

conversation without witnesses between Laval and Il Duce at a brilliant reception given by the French Embassy. There in the spacious Palazzo Farnese, with Caraccio paintings looking down from the richly decorated ceilings, the two men were left strictly alone. The tête-à-tête lasted half an hour. These brief thirty minutes sufficed to settle the fate of Abyssinia, an independent nation and member State of the League of Nations. Mussolini and Laval were beaming with satisfaction as they rejoined the other guests. The atmosphere immediately changed—from stiff politeness to melting cordiality. A phrase launched by Mussolini to the French Ambassador made the rounds: "Laval is the only statesman who understands fascism."

No sooner had Laval departed from Rome, than the Fascist Grand Council met and declared that all the necessary military measures had been taken for whatever eventualities might arise.

Nine months later, in October 1935, Mussolini invaded Abyssinia.

Several days after Laval's return to Paris in January 1935, the plebiscite was held in the Saar territory. It resulted in a resounding international victory for Hitler. Laval had smoothed the way for that triumph of the Führer.

Fifteen Months of Laval

Over 90% of the Saarlanders were officially recorded as voting for a return to Germany. True, the outside world knew that, in spite of international supervision, the population had been terrorized and browbeaten. Hitler's Storm Troopers threatened those voting against Germany with the direst punishments after election day. Nevertheless, the plebiscite did foster the belief the world over that the German people were behind the Nazi leader. Hitler's success helped him to surmount serious difficulties from inside the Nazi Party. The Nazi dictatorship now established itself firmly in the saddle. The result of the plebiscite also considerably strengthened the Nazi movements in Austria, Czechoslovakia and other countries with large German minorities. But most important of all, it again proved to Hitler—and this time in a most convincing fashion—the weakness and shortsightedness of the statesmen representing the democracies. He saw how eager the masters of France were to reach an agreement with him. He noted the contents of a multitude of reports by his undercover agents: voices in France were growing bolder, demanding that the French Republic turn its back on Great Britain and join forces with the authoritarian nations. While making the rounds of the drawing-rooms of Parisian high society, Von Ribbentrop had been told time and again that France would not oppose the re-introduction of general military conscription in Germany. Ribbentrop reported this to Hitler. After the Saar plebiscite the Führer held long discussions with his associates. He insisted that the moment had come to risk the first open breach of the Versailles Treaty. Again he was right—against the opinion and advice of many of his more cautious advisers.

Two months after the Saar plebiscite Hitler tore up Part Five of the Treaty of Versailles. In March 1935 he decreed universal military conscription in Germany.

During that eventful January 1935 General Weygand, Army chief and Vice-President of the Supreme Council of Defense, reached the age limit and was retired. His successor was General Maurice Gustave Gamelin. This appointment was fraught with the gravest consequences for France.

To keen unbiased observers, the Rome Pact and the Saar plebiscite seemed milestones on France's path to the abyss. For Laval, however, they were proofs that he was engaged on the right road. During the next few months he kept a shower of agreements, pacts, accords, declarations, promises and projects—"a rain of papers," as it was called—falling down upon France. His hirelings called him the "traveling salesman of peace," because of

Fifteen Months of Laval

the many trains and airplanes he boarded to visit different countries. But almost every one of these trips further weakened France's diplomatic position.

He journeyed to Geneva and sought, by a "speech of faith in the League," to dispel the misgivings his trip to Rome had evoked in the States of the Little Entente. He had a hard time with Rumanian Foreign Minister Titulescu. In a heated discussion the Rumanian statesman accused him of having betrayed the friends of France. A Jugoslav diplomat who was present said that had he been in Laval's place, he would never have stood for Titulescu's insults. But Laval swallowed them all—and grinned.

In February 1935 he traveled to London with Prime Minister Flandin. The meeting in London was described to me by one of Laval's colleagues as the encounter in the jungle of two strangers who have each lost their way. They stare at each other with ill-concealed suspicion, ready at any moment to face a hostile attack. But they cannot attack each other, for it is better to seek a way out of the dangerous jungle together than to face the perils alone. That was the London conference: suspicious of each other, each seeking a separate understanding with the dictators, the British and French Ministers dared not quarrel openly for fear of the "beasts in the jungle."

Laval's opinion of the London meeting was best expressed by Senator Henri de Jouvenel, one-time French Ambassador to Rome, who said: "I don't know where we stand with Great Britain, but I have profound confidence in Mussolini."

The next month the London soap bubbles burst abruptly when Hitler introduced military conscription. Pale and motionless, Laval and Flandin sat on the front bench of the Chamber of Deputies while the nationalist Deputy Franklin-Bouillon lashed at them for their "abdication in the face of German rearmament." As Franklin-Bouillon ended his speech, he looked expectantly at the Right of the Chamber, apparently anticipating a storm of applause from those benches. Only a few of his colleagues clapped their hands. Franklin-Bouillon's face reddened, and he hurried in discomfiture to the lobbies of the Chamber. Bumping into a veteran journalist, one of his old friends, he cried intensely: "France is lost!" Inside the Chamber, on the Government bench, Laval was sitting with a broad grin covering his face.

Still, something had to be done. So the French Government applied to the League of Nations for an immediate summoning of the council. Relying fondly on Mussolini, it proposed a tri-partite discussion between representatives of France, Great Britain and Italy.

But before this meeting was held, Sir John Simon, England's Foreign Secretary, and Anthony Eden were packed

Fifteen Months of Laval

off to Berlin for conversations with the Führer. These had already been postponed once—and in a hurry—because of a sudden "cold." (In reality the postponement was due to the startling revelations in a British White Paper of the extent of Nazi Germany's rearming.) In Berlin Sir John Simon was bluntly informed that already Germany's air force had outdistanced Britain's. Imperturbable as ever, Sir John declared in an interview with the newspaper men that he regarded Germany's rearmament as a factor for peace.

The meeting of the French and British Ministers with Il Duce took place in Stresa in northern Italy. On the story-book island of Isola Bella, behind a solid wall of Black Shirt guards, Mussolini protected himself from outbursts of affection on the part of his people and from the inordinate curiosity of foreign journalists. It was a strange play the five actors—Mussolini, Ramsay MacDonald, Sir John Simon, Flandin and Laval—staged in the lovely setting of the Palazzo Boromeo, where the Duce was housed. They did not say what they meant; they did not mean what they said. Mussolini's thoughts were in sun-baked Africa, where Marshal de Bono was preparing troops and military equipment for an attack on Ethiopia. Laval thought of the forthcoming meeting of the League of Nations, where a formula had to be produced which would pacify those who wanted to take a strong attitude against Hitler and still be acceptable to those who, like himself, desired to come to terms with him. Sir John Simon's thoughts were in Berlin. He expected a sensational move from Hitler—something like a declaration that Germany was returning to Geneva. The move of course did not come.

The Stresa conference ended with several paper-declarations. One regretted Germany's violation of the Versailles Treaty, but expressed the pious hope that an agreement could be reached with Hitler on the limitation of armaments. Italy and Great Britain renewed their solemn pledges as guarantors under the Treaty of Locarno. And the three powers—Britain, France and Italy—asserted that they would oppose any unilateral repudiation of treaties which might endanger the peace of Europe. This document received the proud name of the "Stresa Front." But one discerning commentator called it "a wall of paper incapable of withstanding the first gust of wind."

After signing the Stresa agreement, Mussolini let it be known to Hitler that it was by no means as serious as it sounded. In one of his invaluable indiscretions, Nazi Propaganda Minister Goebbels has since revealed that, while the so-called Stresa Front was being erected, an understanding between the Führer and the Duce had already been reached.

From Stresa, Laval traveled to near-by Geneva. There he collected another scrap of paper: a unanimous declaration from the League condemning Germany's uni-

Fifteen Months of Laval

lateral action in introducing universal conscription. Only Denmark abstained from voting. Five years later, almost to the exact day, Denmark was invaded by Nazi troops.

Pierre Laval's next journey sped him across Europe to Moscow. Herriot and Barthou had cleared the ground for a mutual assistance pact between France and the U.S.S.R. To Laval it seemed of the utmost expedience to continue Barthou's negotiations. This pact was by no means a contradiction, in his own mind, with his plans to buy off Hitler and Mussolini. It was, like every other step he took in foreign affairs, an offspring of his domestic political policy. The understanding between the Left forces in France was gaining momentum. Communists, Socialists and Radical-Socialists were calling for an agreement with Soviet Russia as a counterweight to Hitler's and Mussolini's plans of expansion. The French General Staff at that time also favored the Franco-Soviet pact, as did one section of the reactionary politicians. By signing the pact Laval thought he would take the wind out of the sails of the Left, particularly the Communists whose influence as the initiators of the Popular Front was rapidly growing. Laval had a trick up his sleeve. He was confident this would be a knockout blow for the Communists. He planned to ask Stalin for a declaration of approval for increased French armaments. With this public statement Laval hoped to crush the

Communists at the forthcoming municipal elections, especially in his own constituency of Aubervilliers, where he was Mayor and where he felt his position was menaced by the mounting Communist tide. Laval's idea was over-clever; it proved later to be a boomerang.

Before quitting Paris, Laval went to great lengths to assure Hitler that the agreement with Soviet Russia would by no means preclude a Franco-German get-together. He informed the German Ambassador in Paris in no uncertain terms that he would be ready at any moment to drop the Franco-Soviet pact in favor of a far-reaching, definitive Franco-German agreement. After drafting the text of the pact in Paris with Potemkin, Soviet Ambassador to France, Laval went to Moscow to sign it, accompanied by a legion of newspaper men. As he passed through Warsaw, capital of Poland, the Polish dictator, Marshal Pilsudski, lay dying of cancer.

While Laval was expressing his admiration for Stalin to the journalists in his retinue and affirming that France was genuinely anxious to maintain good relations with the Soviets in the spirit of the pact, François Poncet, French Ambassador in Berlin, was having another of his frequent talks with Hitler. He had particularly sought this interview at the time of the Moscow negotiations, in order to repeat to the Führer what Laval had confided to the German Ambassador in Paris before departing for the Soviet capital.

Fifteen Months of Laval

On his way back from Moscow, Laval officially represented France at the funeral of Marshal Pilsudski. Here he met German Air Chief Goering. For two hours Laval and Goering remained together in secret conversation at the Hotel Europe in Warsaw. When the meeting terminated, the Franco-Soviet pact was a dead letter. Back in Berlin, Goering informed foreign diplomats that he had made it perfectly clear to Laval that the latter's desire for a Franco-German agreement would remain a fanciful dream as long as there was a pact in existence between France and Soviet Russia. "I think," he added with a laugh, "that Laval understood what I meant."

Goering met another personality during his stay in Poland. He walked by the side of Marshal Pétain in the funeral procession. The two men had met once before at the funeral of King Alexander of Jugoslavia. On that occasion, the press had noted the cordiality with which the two soldiers of the first World War treated each other. This time they met after the funeral for a confidential talk. Marshal Pétain returned to France convinced that the Franco-Soviet treaty must be rendered meaningless. He had previously shown no signs of opposition to it.

As soon as he was back in France, Laval saw that his calculations about the internal repercussions of the

Franco-Soviet pact had gone astray. The municipal elections in Paris brought a spectacular victory of the Left parties. The Communists, especially, made gains, winning a majority of the communities surrounding the metropolis, the industrialized "red girdle" of Paris. In Aubervilliers some of Laval's associates were defeated by the Communists, in spite of an energetic election campaign directed and led by the Foreign Minister himself.

Immediately, Laval began to sow obstacles along the path of ratification of the pact with the Soviet Union. Although the French Constitution did not require a ratification of such documents by Parliament, Laval asked for that procedure. Thus, final ratification was deferred until after his downfall. He dug up devious ways and means of postponing indefinitely the conversations between the French and Soviet General Staffs which, according to the agreement signed in Moscow, were to have begun in June 1935. It was clear to every political observer that the Foreign Minister had no desire whatsoever to breathe life into the pact. He was determined to make it another in his collection of scraps of paper. Neither could Hitler help noticing his behavior. As the Paris edition of the *New York Herald Tribune* stated a few months later: "Laval is a strong partisan of an agreement between the French Third Republic and the Nazi Third Reich and is reported to be willing to scrap the Franco-Soviet alliance, which has been signed but not ratified by the French Parliament, for an agreement whereby the Hitler régime would guarantee France's Eastern frontier in exchange for complete freedom of action in the Memel region and in the Ukraine."

In June 1936, after the fall of the Flandin Cabinet, Laval headed the new Government. He took over the Foreign Office as well. At about this time Colonel de la Rocque had declared in the name of the "Croix de Feu": "The moment when we shall take power is near, very near. Our airplanes will not be seen again until the instant we actually strike. That instant is drawing near." A few days after Laval was installed in the Premier's office, the "Croix de Feu" resumed large-scale demonstrations in Paris and the provinces. At Algiers, in French North Africa, thousands of supporters gathered, while thirty "Croix de Feu" airplanes roared and wheeled overhead. This caused considerable excitement. Did the Right, shocked by the Left victory in the municipal elections and by the spread of the People's Front throughout the country, intend to strike while the iron was hot?

The Left, too, was mobilizing its forces to parry the blow. The first official Popular Front meeting was called in Paris. The main speakers were the Socialist leader Léon Blum, the Communist leader Maurice Thorez and, emerging from his political eclipse, the Radical-Socialist leader Edouard Daladier. This was an event of more than usual significance. It officially consecrated the political coalition between the middle class and labor. Addressing the crowded hall, Daladier expressed his gratitude in speaking before Socialist and Communist workers. He was in a militant Jacobin mood. "As a representative of the *petite bourgeoisie*," he orated, "I affirm that the middle classes and the working class are natural allies." This Paris meeting met with a tremendous response in the country. All over France, Popular Front committees were set up to arrange united Left demonstrations on the occasion of the approaching national holiday of July 14.

This Bastille Day saw in Paris the greatest, gayest, liveliest and most colorful demonstration in modern French history. Half a million people marched in the procession, with Daladier, Blum and Thorez at the head of the seemingly endless columns. At the historic Place de la Bastille the leaders took the solemn oath to fight against fascism and war, to fight for liberty, equality, fraternity.

On the Champs Élysées 30,000 "Croix de Feu" demonstrated, guarded and blocked off from the Popular Front columns by a serried wall of police. One thing was obvious. In Paris, at least, Colonel de la Rocque's legions would find it difficult to carry out his threats.

Shortly after Laval had taken power, Mussolini sent

Fifteen Months of Laval

word that he favored a revival of the Four Power Pact. Laval agreed immediately and proceeded to enter into conversations with the German Ambassador in France. These were suddenly interrupted by a startling political surprise. In July 1935 an Anglo-German naval agreement was announced. By it Germany was given the right to construct a navy up to 35% of the total British tonnage. In the race between Britain and France for Hitler's favor, the British had stealthily crept up and won a lap.

To lessen the shock produced in Paris by the agreement, Captain Anthony Eden was dispatched to the French capital. Laval handled him roughly. With no tangible results to show from his policy of making friends with the dictators, he had now suffered a very severe frontal blow from the British.

England's solo waltz with Germany undermined Laval's prestige. He sought to strengthen it again by a series of emergency decrees. Railwaymen, dock workers, and civil servants were forced to bear the brunt of the new wage cuts. Strikes flared up in the seacoast towns of Toulon and Brest, and were suppressed by colonial troops. The result was six dead and a score of injured. The atmosphere, charged with electricity by the constant provocations of the fascist leagues, grew more tense almost every day. General Weygand was reinstated in active service.

As summer approached the air was thick with rumors of a clash. The slightest incident would entail the gravest consequences. Although there could be no doubt that the sentiments of the majority of the people were on the anti-fascist side, Laval did not lift a finger to stop the demonstrations, marches and trial mobilizations of the "Croix de Feu." In this atmosphere of heightened nervousness and anxiety, portending riots and street-fighting, Laval left Paris for Geneva.

The League of Nations was about to convene. Ominous storm clouds loomed on the horizon. The Duce had completed, or all but completed, his preparations for the conquest of Abyssinia. For the first time since the inception of the League, a great European power was on the verge of committing aggression against a member State. Would the League survive this, its most serious test? Would collective security, preached by its members for years, win the day?

Laval was accompanied to Geneva by his Minister of State Herriot and by Paul-Boncour, both ardent defenders of the League and of collective security. They stood on guard like watchdogs to prevent Laval from aiding Italian aggression. But when the test came they failed.

England was represented by its new Minister of Foreign Affairs, Sir Samuel Hoare. He shared Laval's viewpoint. Later he was destined to become a notorious champion of the appeasement policy, but now he had come to Geneva to make a strong stand—in words only—for collective resistance to any act of unprovoked aggression. Sir Samuel's attitude, like Laval's, was dictated by inner political considerations. General elections in Britain were approaching. As Prime Minister Baldwin later explained, any British Government which at that precise moment had condoned Italian aggression and done visible damage to the League of Nations would have been swept out of office by the outraged vote of the people. Hence the British Government had to take a stand against the potential aggressor Mussolini, while it had only yesterday come to terms with the potential aggressor Hitler.

For reasons of home policy Laval prepared to assume a contrary position. The impending invasion of Abyssinia had split France irremediably into two camps. On the one side the Popular Front was strongly advocating resistance; on the other French Reaction was advocating an agreement with the dictators. The French Right fought its fight with the cry that the Left was leading an ideological crusade which would inevitably end in war. With this platform Laval hoped to pilot his Cabinet safely until the 1936 elections.

In the course of this struggle the French Right also disclosed a pronounced anti-British attitude. Almost every day newspapers whose close ties with Laval were well known, continued a barrage of attacks against England. Their violence recalled the days of the Fashoda incident of 1898, when Britain and France were on the point of war. The fascist weekly *Gringoire* featured a sensational article by Henri Béraud: "England must be reduced to slavery. . . . The day will come when the world will have the strength and wisdom to enslave the tyrant with his reputation for invincibility. Concord between the continental nations alone can save Europe and the world. Who knows? Perhaps the day is near."

That was in 1935! In the light of later events Béraud's article has a special significance. Every word in it was paid for in gold. For a long time *Gringoire* had been receiving regular subsidies from Mussolini. A high official at the Quai d'Orsay told me once that during the Abyssinian affair Mussolini's agents had distributed more than a hundred and thirty-five million francs to the French press and to various fascist organizations.

The British Foreign Office retaliated against this anti-British campaign with a campaign against Laval. As one American correspondent phrased it in a cabled dispatch to his paper: "Premier Laval is now considered by Whitehall as just around the corner from fascism himself."

At the beginning of October, Italy invaded Abyssinia. The League then decided on a series of sanctions against Mussolini. For three months Laval intrigued and

Fifteen Months of Laval

maneuvered to prevent the sanctions against Italy from becoming really effective. "Sanctions mean war," the leading journals of the Right screamed at the French public. They singled out for special fury the one act which could have changed the course of the Italian-Abyssinian war—oil sanctions. Whenever the talk of oil sanctions was renewed, Italian Ambassador Cerruti would pay a visit to Premier Laval. Each time he left, the news would get around as if spontaneously that Cerruti had declared that Italy would answer the application of oil sanctions with a declaration of war. This blackmailing threat of war was successfully kept alive by Laval and his press disciples until Italy's victory was assured.

The Left accused Laval of selling out Abyssinia during the famous half-hour talk with Mussolini in Rome. He strenuously denied the charge. "There was nothing either in the agreements or in the conversations which preceded or followed them that could encourage Italy to resort to war," he said in a speech before the Chamber of Deputies.

He sent a special envoy to Rome to demand that Mussolini give him documentary proof that in those conversations he had made no commitment on behalf of France in the Abyssinian question. In due course he received a letter from the Duce. But it was so unsatisfactory that Laval did not dare to publish it.

The truth about the Rome conversations was revealed by two of Mussolini's closest collaborators, Marshal de Bono and Roberto Farinacci. The marshal, who led Mussolini's Abyssinian venture in its first phase, wrote in his book about the campaign, *The Year 16*: "About this time [January, 1935] the conversations with Laval took place in Rome which gave us reason to hope that if we did have to take action in East Africa, France would put no obstacle in our way."

Roberto Farinacci, former Secretary General of the fascist party, declared in the *Lavoro Fascista* that both during the Rome conversations and at Stresa, Laval had given Mussolini a free hand in Abyssinia.

So, after all, Laval's denials were just another scrap of paper. He had sold out Abyssinia.

The senatorial elections in October exhibited a distinct trend to the Left. For the first time in the Third Republic two Communist Senators entered the upper house. That same month the Socialist-influenced and Communist-influenced trade unions decided to unite in one organization with a combined membership of one and a half million workers. Popular feeling was unmistakably moving toward the Left. If this swing was to be checked by the Right, no time could be lost.

On October 31 our paper received information that Colonel de la Rocque had told Laval that his organization had completed preparations for the *putsch*. At a conference with his associates, De la Rocque assured them that this time nothing would stop him. With tough hard-boiled Laval instead of that weakling Doumergue, as the Colonel put it, the *coup* would succeed.

For the third time in two years Paris was only a hair's breadth away from a violent and bloody insurrection. Documents found later have proved that Colonel de la Rocque's preparations were really completed down to the last detail. Backed by the Army and supported by Laval, he had strong odds in his favor. The masses opposing him were unarmed. He expected to crush their resistance in Paris in four or five days.

He never got a chance to fight. At the last moment Laval called it off. Early in November, Laval spent one whole night in his office with his intimate advisers, discussing whether to take the plunge or not. He had reports from all over the country lying in front of him on his desk. They showed that the Popular Front idea had gripped French labor and a large section of the middle classes. The trade unions of the C.G.T. and the two labor parties had issued warnings to their followers to be ready for the onslaught. Any attack would be immediately answered by a general strike. With the temper of labor as it was, the strike would probably be almost one hundred per cent effective. There were also stirrings of restlessness in the Army. The majority of the officers were in sympathy with the "Croix de Feu" and other fascist leagues, but the common soldiers felt otherwise. Their sentiments were guided by the feeling prevailing back home in their native towns and villages. They were mainly sons of peasants. Their parents had told them that Laval's economic and agricultural policies had hurt, not helped, their situation.

So, in spite of the heavy odds which Colonel de la Rocque believed to be on *their* side, Laval backed down. Armistice Day passed with jitters and high tension, but without serious incidents. The fascist movement had lost another round.

Responding to the sentiment of its voters, the Radical-Socialist convention had definitely sided with the "powerful gathering of forces in the country resolved to bar the road to the enemies of the Republic." The Laval Cabinet looked lost.

It was saved by a surprise move which Laval made in the Chamber of Deputies. In the midst of a heated debate, the Basque Deputy Jean Ybarnégaray, representative in Parliament of the "Croix de Feu," had arisen to affirm the readiness of his organization to disarm, if the militarized groups on the Left would do the same. The gesture was well-timed. Ybarnégaray had been expected to upbraid the Left with savage, unbridled fury. That was his usual procedure. Instead he came out with

Fifteen Months of Laval

this totally unexpected proposal for a truce. Immediately after his speech, Léon Blum for the Socialists and Maurice Thorez for the Communists affirmed their agreement with the offer. They acted thus without mental reservations or afterthoughts. The Left had no armaments and no militarized formations. The arms of the "Croix de Feu" were of course never surrendered to the authorities. But the theatrical maneuver pumped life into the Laval Cabinet.

The tussle between England and France over the Abyssinian affair now entered a new stage. Each attempted to make the other responsible for the failure of the League of Nations. In order to corner Laval, London asked bluntly whether the British Fleet, if attacked in the Mediterranean, could count on the French Fleet. Laval replied in "too many words to be taken for a 'yes.'" But it was impossible to interpret them as a "no" either. Laval coupled his answer with the query: Would the British help France, if Hitler seized the opportunity to launch an attack on Austria and Czechoslovakia? This in turn gave the British pause.

The diplomatic game came to an end after the British general elections. London approached Laval with the proposal that the two Western democracies draw up a plan of mediation to end the Italo-Abyssinian war.

"They are beginning to show some sense," muttered Laval. So after the League of Nations officially charged France and Great Britain with the task of drafting a plan for mediation, the two leading appeasers, Hoare and Laval, set to work.

The result was the Hoare-Laval plan. This virtually handed Abyssinia over to Mussolini, lock, stock and barrel. Italy was to receive the greater part of Abyssinia. Economic preferences would be granted in the remaining portions. This would have put the Duce in a position to swallow up what was left whenever he wanted.

This plan was elaborated in secret. Nothing was to be divulged until Mussolini had signified his acceptance, for then Haile Selassie, under terrific pressure, would be left no other alternative than to accept. The plan would be published only after both sides had agreed to it. Then, no matter how violently public opinion reacted against the sell-out, it still would go into effect.

Hoare was so confident of success that he left London for a holiday in Switzerland. Laval waited anxiously in Paris for Rome's answer.

Two French journalists upset these well-laid plans. Pertinax and Madame Geneviève Tabouis published the Hoare-Laval plan before Mussolini answered. Laval maintained that they had obtained the information from a high official of the Paris Foreign Office. In journalistic circles it was believed that one of Laval's own Ministers

Fifteen Months of Laval

had purposely committed the indiscretion. There were even rumors that Mussolini had himself allowed the information to leak out. Thus he would wreak revenge on Hoare and Laval for the sanctions which he bitterly resented, notwithstanding their ineffectiveness and lax enforcement.

However that may be, the publication of the plan provoked a storm of indignation. In England the Baldwin Government tossed Sir Samuel overboard as harmful ballast. He could scarcely finish his speech of self-justification in the House of Commons. When he left the House he was weeping.

Laval left the Chamber smiling. He had eked out a pitiful majority of twenty in the Chamber. "Enough for me to carry on until the elections," he told me in the lobby of the Chamber.

But the Laval Cabinet fell before a month was out, in January, 1936. Yielding to the temper of the country, Herriot withdrew. That sealed the fate of the Laval Ministry.

6

THE TWO EDOUARDS

THE LAVAL CABINET was the fourth which Edouard Herriot had overthrown in the course of his political career. He represented the Radical-Socialist Party in these Cabinets. This cautious middle-of-the-road Party was, I must again repeat, neither radical nor socialist. Like Herriot himself, radicalism was now old, creaky and comfort-loving.

In December, 1935, when Sir Samuel Hoare resigned under fire in England, Herriot withdrew from the Presidency of the Radical-Socialist Party, a post he had occupied for a good many years. He was not overzealous about the People's Front. On the last Bastille Day the Radical-Socialists of Lyons had not marched side by side with the Socialists and Communists. Herriot, their Mayor, had kept them aloof. Now he felt that the time had come for Edouard Daladier, the leader of that wing of the Radical-Socialists which favored the Popular Front, to take over the chairmanship of the party.

Daladier had been a pupil of Herriot, first in school and then in politics. But around 1928 their ways parted. Daladier, fired with ambition, cut loose and strove to become the leader of the party himself. When he first

The Two Edouards

became Premier, Herriot viewed it with an extremely critical eye.

The rivalry between these two men has powerfully influenced the fate of the Radical-Socialist Party. After 1933 they did not see eye to eye, either in foreign policy or domestic affairs. The February riots had pushed Daladier, after a temporary eclipse, more to the Left. He became an outspoken advocate of the Popular Front. "In case of trouble, go to the Left!" was his watchword. But later, when he made his sharp about-face in the opposite direction, events moved Herriot further to the Left. Then for almost a year it seemed as though these two individuals had exchanged their political dress.

The Battle of France showed the terrible inadequacy of both of them in the moment of crisis. These two men, so different in character, make-up and ways of thinking, had one fatal common denominator: weakness. They were both Radical-Socialists. That in the final analysis tells more about them than long biographies or psychological studies.

In outward appearance the two friendly enemies had scarcely anything in common.

Herriot comes from an army officer's family. But there is nothing whatsoever of a soldier's appearance about him. His head and belly are massively proportioned; his eyes are small but keen and penetrating. The Herriot pipe, stuck between thick fleshy lips, is famous throughout France. Herriot's voice knows every stop and register and gamut. His oratorical talents were second to none in the recent parliamentary history of France. When Herriot took the floor at a Radical-Socialist party convention, he could make men weep. He could make them roar with laughter; he could set them wild with enthusiasm. For fifteen years he towered, figuratively and literally, over party conclaves. He could swing them in the direction he chose, either to the Right or to the Left. When his eloquence failed, he bristled and threatened to resign. A party convention without a resignation by Herriot to enliven the proceedings was dull. His fellow deputies used to call him, with a mixture of admiration and contempt, "the Tenor of Democracy."

Herriot had won the highest scholastic honors at the École Normale Supérieure, a school which turned out the best products of French culture and politics. He became a successful professor. But politics fascinated him early and he was soon at home in the public arena. Long before 1914 he was already Mayor of Lyons, the third city of France and the center of the silk industry. He was still a young man when he entered the French Senate. Aristide Briand made him Minister of Public Works in his World War Cabinet. After the war Herriot switched from the Senate to the Chamber of Deputies. The victory of the Left coalition in the general elections of 1924 swept him into power as Premier. It was then that he was forced to cross swords with the finan-

The Two Edouards

cial magnates of France. They checkmated his Government. He took a seat in the Poincaré Cabinet which succeeded his own and which adopted a strongly Rightist program. Again in 1932, after an even more sweeping victory at the polls by the Left coalition of his own party and the Socialists, he assumed the Premiership. After seven months of wrangling, his Cabinet fell. Entering the Doumergue combination, he again lent the weight of his authority to a Government with manifest anti-liberal and anti-democratic tendencies.

Herriot's vision was of a liberal Europe grouped in the League of Nations around the French and British democracies. He hoped to achieve his goal by means of a disarmament campaign and by concessions to the German Weimar Republic. But he was keenly aware of the danger to France in the rise of reactionary and ultra-nationalist forces in Germany. While France was still the first military power on the European continent, while French economic strength was bulwarked and unchallenged, he was haunted by the fear of France's declining birth rate and Germany's tremendous industrial and military potentialities. He sought to conjure up these perils by an understanding with Soviet Russia and closer ties with the United States. He envisaged France as the guardian of liberalism in Europe, bound by an alliance with Great Britain and flanked by the U.S.S.R. and the United States of America as potential allies.

For this conception—liberalism, disarmament and

French security—he labored strenuously. But his will power was not equal to his piercing intelligence. Whenever he faced energetic resistance, he gave in. He could have smashed through the "money wall"; he could have unloosed the stranglehold of big business on French politics. His adversaries never hesitated to mobilize public opinion against him. But Herriot had compunctions; he yielded. He did not dare to summon up the extra-parliamentary forces of French labor and the democratic-minded middle classes arrayed behind him. He contented himself with verbal denunciations of the monetary powers, passionately declaiming that they were responsible for riding roughshod over every honest French Government. Yet rather than fight them with every weapon at his disposal, he compromised with them. He despised graft; yet he felt incapable of dealing with it. His name was never mixed up in a scandal or questionable deal. Nevertheless, he shielded many of his party colleagues who, he knew perfectly well, used politics for personal aggrandizement.

He was a firm believer in collective security. Yet he kept silent when Daladier and Bonnet, leading members of his own party, ruthlessly torpedoed it. He confided to me that he considered a victory of the Loyalist Government in Spain vital to the national interests of France. In private conversations he vehemently condemned the policy of non-intervention; yet he gave his

The Two Edouards

tacit blessing to the Cabinets that pursued it. He laid the foundations for the Franco-Soviet Pact of mutual assistance. But when Daladier and Bonnet wrecked the pact, Herriot surrendered abjectly to "realism." There were times when a gesture by Herriot, a word from his lips, a single public outcry from him against the sinister intrigues of the men of Munich, might have changed the entire course of French policy. The gesture was not forthcoming; the word was left unspoken.

He has been fond, too fond, of the spacious easy-going life of the French Republic. A man of letters, a connoisseur of the arts, he has written excellent works on Beethoven, on Madame Récamier, on the beautiful city of Lyons—and on the beautiful democracy of France!

He likes food as other people are fond of drinking. I often felt that Herriot could get drunk on food. It was after an exquisite yet hearty meal in the best traditions of French cooking that his wit and verve were at their best. His conversation sparkled. He outlined his projects with an air of authority and passionate conviction. His companions, fascinated, listened to the cadences of his voice.

What was the central hard core of Herriot's life? He was a deep-rooted pessimist. He told me once that he really did not have faith in the possibility of a decisive change in French politics. He took his own weaknesses for national attributes. His charm and magnetism and cultural sheen covered over a void of pessimism and disbelief. He was not in the camp of the appeasers. He was opposed to fascism. Yet it cannot be denied that his vacillations, his love of comfort, his fondness for the easy life and the easy way out, his corroding pessimism and his lack of courage at crucial historic moments have contributed in no small measure to the downfall of the French Republic. Herriot's fine words have buttered no parsnips!

Short, stocky, bull-necked Edouard Daladier does not belong to the circle of France's outstanding speakers. It is not given to him to arouse people to great heights of enthusiasm, to inspire conventions and dazzle Parliament with scintillating displays of brilliant oratory. He is the machine politician *par excellence.* While Herriot generally renewed his grip on the party at conventions, Daladier preferred to work in the intervals to prepare for them. He had a predilection for men who had enough ambition to want influence but were too subservient to compete with the boss. While Herriot fostered individuals like Daladier and Chautemps who later seized leadership away from him and betrayed him, Daladier encouraged people of the secretarial, subaltern sort.

The Two Edouards 151

Daladier liked to play the son of the people who had made his way to the top because of his own innate ability. He enjoyed telling stories about his difficult younger days; how he had made good without any outside protection. He often depicted himself as a product of French democracy, where everybody "carried a marshal's baton in his knapsack."

His taciturnity and suspiciousness were forbidding. He was surrounded by only a few persons, official collaborators rather than friends.

He had served in the World War with distinction, reaching the rank of a captain. He was as proud of his war veteran's record as Hitler was of his.

When he entered the Chamber in 1919 he began to specialize in military matters. Soon he became the spokesman of the Radical-Socialist Party on the Army Committee. When he assumed the Premiership he also kept the War Ministry for himself. This doubling of functions was a special feature of the French parliamentary system.

Daladier is a man of average tastes and habits. He rolls his own cigarettes and, on rare occasions, smokes a pipe. He is very fond of a kind of absinthe drink known as *pastis*. Daladier's *pastis* has been for years the delight of wags and cartoonists. Although some of the stories about his excessive drinking have certainly been exaggerated, there can be no doubt that he indulged in *pastis* more than was good for him. I recall how once, at the request of my editor, I came to the War Ministry to ask Daladier for some vitally urgent information. One of his secretaries advised me not to insist on being received: "It's better to come before the *apéritif* hour. After that, Monsieur le Président is usually in a very bad mood."

Very often he had violent fits of temper, almost like Hitler's. On such occasions he treated his associates with extraordinary harshness but, unlike Hitler, he made no efforts to give them any credit in public. He was subject to peaks of exhilaration and troughs of depression. At times he fancied himself a strutting strong man, a little Napoleon; at other times he was abject and cowering. Of peasant stock, he is stingy to the point of miserliness, and very small-minded.

I was always struck by the air of mediocrity which clung to Daladier. I have seen him often, but I never remember having heard him utter one striking phrase, one formula which really pierced to the heart of a question.

Even his henchmen called him a mediocre man. I recall an occasion when I was at a luncheon with Albert Chichéry, a Radical-Socialist Deputy, who during Daladier's last Premiership was his party whip in the Chamber. Chichéry spoke in a slighting tone of Daladier. "I wouldn't trust him with the management of my fac-

The Two Edouards

tory," he declared in the presence of a dozen people. But he trusted him with the Premiership of France.

On another occasion I saw Daladier besieged by several deputies who were impressing on him the effects of Nazi propaganda in France. They demanded energetic counter-measures. "All right," he said, "I'll think about it. But you people exaggerate. The French cannot be fooled by propaganda. That's an invention of a few literary *salons*." This was the judgment of a provincial mind who deeply resented Paris and who never felt at home there.

Clemenceau once said he had a horror of Philistines —they were the most insincere of human beings. This description fits Daladier. Although he gave the impression of frankness and genuineness, he was without a doubt one of the slyest foxes in French politics, and slyness carried him a long way forward.

His favorite trick was to place the blame on somebody else's shoulders. During the civil war in Spain, Daladier expressed himself several times in my presence in support of the Loyalists. He asserted that he would like to furnish them with arms but that Léon Blum was restraining him from doing so. But once he became Premier, one of his first acts was to seal the Franco-Spanish border hermetically, so that not even the most trifling amount of Russian armaments could be transshipped to the Loyalists.

I have heard him thunder and rage against Georges Bonnet, who in 1938 became his Foreign Minister. He liked to say dramatically that he would fire him within the next twenty-four hours. But Bonnet remained his Foreign Minister for a year and a half.

He called himself "the last Jacobin." But he had neither the fire nor the sincere convictions of the Jacobins. He waxed eloquent about "France, the last trench of liberty." But it was he who surrendered it to the enemy. One of France's outstanding political commentators once called him "a sinister comedian." That, I think, is a just and correct appreciation of Edouard Daladier.

7

HITLER MARCHES—FLANDIN WEEPS

THE POLITICAL defeat of Laval was a clear-cut verdict on foreign policy, a rupture between the head of a Government and public opinion. The heritage he left was far from enviable.

A year previously Laval had asserted: "In this world there are five or six men on whom peace depends. Destiny has placed me among them." Now as he departed temporarily from the political stage, he left a tell-tale balance-sheet: his policy had emboldened and strengthened the dictators and had seriously weakened the prospects for peace. He left behind him a heap of ruins. The League of Nations had received a mortal wound from which it was never to recover. Collective security had been wrecked. Laval had hoped for a *rapprochement* with Italy and Germany. Instead, the two powers had drawn fundamentally closer to each other, so that less than a year after Laval's retirement the Rome-Berlin Axis was an historic fact. Franco-British relations were cooler than ever before. Franco-Russian relations, so promising a year previously, had lost much of their glow and warmth.

When Laval slunk from the limelight, his political

opponents thought that his removal was permanent. But he was destined to come back again. It takes a long time before history hands down its final verdict.

The damage Laval had wrought could be repaired only by a strong Cabinet. He was a man without doctrine, without moral scruples, and with no sense of the given historic situation. His successor should have been a man with deep democratic convictions, strong morals, and with an intimate knowledge of France's possibilities, an understanding of its necessities and the energy to translate his judgments into action. But the man picked by President Lebrun was the proverbial old warhorse of Radical-Socialism, Albert Sarraut. He formed a Centrist Cabinet, composed for the most part of nonentities.

Everybody knew—including Sarraut—that this Cabinet was a stop-gap affair. Just the type of government France could least afford! The incoming Foreign Minister was Pierre-Étienne Flandin who proceeded to announce that he was in complete agreement with Laval's policy on the Abyssinian question. Sarraut and Flandin in a time of crisis!

As the new Cabinet set to work, it became more and more evident that Hitler was determined to reoccupy the Rhineland. This section of Germany bordering on France had, according to the Versailles Treaty and the Locarno Pact, been declared a demilitarized zone.

Hitler Marches—Flandin Weeps

A few days after the inception of the Sarraut-Flandin combination, King George V of Great Britain died. Flandin represented France at the funeral in London. His conversations with Baldwin and Eden convinced him that the British Government would offer no energetic resistance to Hitler's Rhineland plans. He reported this impression at a Cabinet council. This meeting showed how many "Lavalists" were included in Sarraut's Cabinet. Their leader was saturnine Marcel Déat, a "Neo-Socialist" who had bolted the Socialist Party together with Adrien Marquet and thirty other deputies in order to strive for "order, authority and the nation." Déat declared bluntly that it was not worth the bones of a single French soldier to fight against the remilitarization of the Rhineland, which was, after all, German territory. Furthermore he opposed Sarraut's proposal to hasten the long-delayed ratification by Parliament of the Franco-Soviet Pact.

Hitler's agents, who were circulating freely in Paris— the notorious Otto Abetz paid a long visit to the French capital in the winter of 1936—received frequent assurances from drawing-room denizens and nationalist politicians that France would not fight against the remilitarization of the Rhineland. French visitors to Berlin spoke the same language. One of the French correspondents in Berlin told me that a French Deputy had declared at the luncheon table of the French

Ambassador in Berlin, in the presence of high officials of the Wilhelmstrasse, that the feeling in France was against war, and that no Government could arouse French public opinion against remilitarization.

The French Ambassador, François Poncet, had himself long favored a "negotiated remilitarization." He had told the Führer so on several occasions. In view of these facts, Hitler had no reason to fear grave consequences should he take that step.

The Right-wing press, getting wind of Sarraut's intention to ratify the Franco-Soviet Pact, instituted a brisk campaign against the plan. General Loiseau, attending the Russian military maneuvers in the autumn of 1935 for the French General Staff, had stated: "In regard to tanks I consider the Red Army the first in the world." In spite of that, the Rightist press asserted that the technical equipment of the Red Army was faulty, that it lacked leadership, and that it was at best a defensive army of no value to the French in the event of a German attack. The Right papers stressed the idea that the Franco-Soviet Pact was the only barrier to an understanding between the Third Republic and the Third Reich. Once this was cast aside, France and Germany would quickly come to terms. This was the identical tune played by the coördinated Nazi press of Germany.

In the Chamber one orator after another of the Right argued against the Pact. The spearhead of the opposition was Jacques Doriot, ex-Communist turned fascist.

Hitler Marches—Flandin Weeps 159

Pierre Laval worked strenuously behind the scenes. Georges Mandel, Minister of Posts, best explained the attitude of the Right: "As the elections drew nearer, the political parties began to show fight. Quite a number of political problems assumed a different aspect. The question of relations with Moscow was scrutinized from the viewpoint of internal politics, and the tragic misunderstanding which had handicapped the Franco-Russian alliance even before the World War was now repeated. Just as, forty years ago, the extreme Left had denounced the close friendship between Paris and St. Petersburg as a danger to the Republic, so now many nationalists showed their alarm that the pact might encourage the French Communist Party. Their hostility, which was shrewdly stimulated by foreign propaganda, grew more intense when the French Communists took steps to weld the Popular Front."

While France was wrangling about the Pact, Hitler summoned his leading generals to Berchtesgaden. He explained his intention to reoccupy the Rhineland. He was sharply opposed by the aristocratic Chief of the Army, General von Fritsch, who considered that Germany would be in no position to resist if France took retaliatory military action. Hitler insisted that no military resistance would be forthcoming. But in case there was, he would permit the generals to withdraw their troops.

A week after this meeting at Berchtesgaden, the

official French news service, *Agence Havas,* carried a report originating in London diplomatic circles that England was considering no military action in the event of the re-militarization of the Rhineland. Such a Havas dispatch could not have been published in France without the consent of the Foreign Minister. The fact that it appeared served as a clear go-ahead signal to Hitler.

A few days later Marcel Déat, the Air Minister, lunched with the German Ambassador in Paris. Later the German diplomat informed his associates that Déat had assured him that "the French would shoulder arms only in defense of their own frontiers."

The Franco-Soviet treaty was ratified by 353 to 164 votes in the Chamber. Two days after the bill was passed *Le Journal* published an interview with Hitler by Bertrand de Jouvenel. He was a young writer who had joined Jacques Doriot's fascist group. In the interview Hitler not only indulged in his usual ranting about bolshevism as the world menace, but also warned that France was in danger of falling into the hands of the bolsheviks. "Don't you realize what you are doing?" he cried. "You are allowing yourself to be dragged into the diplomatic game of a power whose only aim is to work havoc among the great European nations." And then he concluded with a reiterated offer to France: "Today if she wishes, France can put an end for all

Hitler Marches—Flandin Weeps

time to the 'German menace.'" He added the solemn pledge that he had no territorial demands in Europe.

The parties of the Right and their press hailed this interview as the avowal of a statesman who put peace above everything else.

A week after De Jouvenel's article appeared in print, on March 7, 1936, Nazi troops marched into the Rhineland. The second breach of the Treaty of Versailles was a fact. Just a few weeks previously Hitler had assured the French Ambassador that he would remain faithful to the Locarno treaty. Now it was torn to shreds.

When Hitler's long-awaited move came, it found France split as it was during the Abyssinian crisis. "Down with Sarraut! No sanctions—sanctions mean war!" was the attitude of the nationalist press to Hitler's action. At the Cabinet meeting Georges Mandel demanded mobilization. Déat, Flandin and a majority of the Ministers opposed it. The ultimate decision was to demand a session of the League of Nations Council and a meeting of the Locarno guarantor powers.

That same evening Sarraut made a strong speech: "I do not propose to negotiate while Strasbourg is under the fire of German guns!" Then he met with his three defense Ministers and the Chiefs of Staff of the Army, Navy and Air. All of them, except War Minister Paul-Boncour, declared themselves opposed to mobilization. The only decision made was to reënforce the garrisons of the Maginot Line with a few colonial regiments. Sarraut's thunderous speech was just another declamation which was never backed up.

The meeting of the Locarno powers in Paris—France, England, Italy and Belgium—was attended by British Foreign Minister Anthony Eden and Lord Halifax. The latter had been instructed to supervise the activities of the dapper young Foreign Secretary. The conference ended without results.

A similar fate befell the League of Nations meeting, held in London. Lanky Foreign Minister Flandin looked like a beaten, helpless man. At one of the conferences he flew into a fearful rage; at another he burst hysterically into tears. Finally all that emerged to condemn Hitler's breach of Locarno was a new "paper declaration."

The retreat of France and Great Britain was covered by a British statement that Britain still felt herself bound to the Locarno pact, and hence would come to France's assistance in the event of an unprovoked aggression.

When Flandin returned home, he found on his table an article in *Candide*, a weekly with fascist sympathies. It read: "As recently as January 23, we pointed out that the ratification of the Franco-Russian alliance

Hitler Marches—Flandin Weeps

would automatically be followed by the remilitarization of the left bank of the Rhine. But you had the Franco-Russian pact on the brain. For the last three months you have been trying to starve Italy. You are treating Mussolini like an outcast. You are advocating revolution against him. You are a scoundrel. Clear out!"

It soon became apparent that Hitler intended to follow up his Rhineland victory. On March 21 the famous Brown House on Paris' Rue Roquépine was opened, and almost immediately it became the headquarters of the Nazis' intelligence system in France. . . . The inner prong of the pincers was beginning to close.

In April, General Gamelin was dispatched to London to consult with the British General Staff. Not much came of the meeting, save the General's emphatic declaration that France, securely entrenched behind the Maginot Line, could resist any German attack. However, Gamelin's confidence was not shared by a large group of European statesmen and military experts. One of the best informed of the foreign correspondents wired his paper: "Never since the end of the Franco-Prussian War has Europe had less confidence in France's ability to maintain her position."

Those were the conditions under which the country went to the polls that year. A nation which had been longing for a change from the vacillating Cabinets which had been moving in and out of office now turned toward the Popular Front, presenting it with an impressive victory over its opponents. The Popular Front received 5,500,000 votes (1,900,000 for the Socialists; 1,500,000 for the Communists; slightly over 1,400,000 for the Radical-Socialists; and the remainder for splinter groups) as against 4,300,000 for the combined Right and Center. In the incoming Chamber it had 375 out of the 618 Deputies.

There is little question that the Popular Front was elected because of the people's desire for a change—any change—which would throw out of office the Doumergue-Laval-Flandin type of reactionary politicians whose policies had accomplished nothing to stem the tide of fascism or to relieve the depression. At the time the Popular Front first came into power, France was on the brink of civil war, agricultural prices were at their lowest ebb, and unemployment had risen to 3,000,000. The Popular Front, in spite of the extreme radical faction which it included, was the most democratic coalition which could have swung sufficient votes to gain office.

It advocated freedom of the press, defense of peace, the reorganization of State finances, a general amnesty, disarming of the fascist leagues, and close coöperation

Hitler Marches—Flandin Weeps

of the member States of the League of Nations to enforce sanctions against aggressor nations. Léon Blum described its defense policy to me as a "disarmed peace." He also told me that he intended to introduce legislation which would abolish private trade in armaments. "With regard to the Bank of France," he said, "I intend to make it the bank of the State. It will become not the private monopoly of the fifteen regents, but the servant of the people of the nation. . . . The regency will be abolished by placing the Governor of the Bank under the permanent control of a new council composed of representatives of Parliament, State administration, labor, the farm groups, industry and commerce."

This, in brief, was the nature of the program the Popular Front had pledged itself to put into effect. As was to have been expected, the victory of the Popular Front was hailed with misgiving by the reactionaries. They could not forget that a large number of Communists were included in the party, nor that many of their traditional privileges would be curtailed. Signs of panic became visible. Pantries were stored with food, children were sent to the country with their nurses, jewelry and gold were shipped to England and America. I personally knew one well-to-do family which kept its trunks and bags packed, in instant readiness for flight. Like an army after a terrible rout, capital fled pell-mell from France.

While Léon Blum was in many ways a capable—and even a brilliant—man, he lacked one quality which the crisis demanded. He did not have that ruthless courage which would have ensured the success of his program; his innate timidity betrayed him at the very moment when the least sign of weakness must result in panic. Although he sensed as well as anyone else that the reactionary groups were desperate, he permitted an entire month to elapse before taking office. It was traditional for the Cabinet presiding over the elections to resign only after the induction of the new Chamber of Deputies. Blum, as Premier-designate, adhered to this needless procedure.

Suspicion immediately took root among the people who had hailed the victory of the Popular Front. Rumors began to circulate that in May the fascist leagues, with the support of the Army and the tacit consent of the President of the Republic, planned to stage a *coup*. The fall of Addis Ababa, capital of Abyssinia, to the Italian invaders contributed to the new tension. It was at this point that Blum, had he been as resourceful as the occasion demanded, could have taken office promptly and begun to put his reforms into operation. This would have satisfied the Popular Front voters.

Hitler Marches—Flandin Weeps

Instead he made speeches. He spoke at the American Club in Paris and at a special convention of the Socialist Party. And the tenor of his speeches always was—patience. He asked the panicky "200 Families" to be patient; he asked the same of the Popular Front voters who wanted some positive proof that he intended to initiate significant reforms; and, worst of all, he ignored the Abyssinian question which at that moment was dividing France into two camps. Regarding the dictators he said: "We want to collaborate with all the nations of the world, whatever their internal policy, in eliminating the causes of conflict which might some day lead to war. We reject war absolutely." How Hitler and Mussolini and Stalin must have smiled with satisfaction! Blum had "rejected war": here, indeed, was the type of French Premier with whom they knew how to deal.

The Paris Stock Exchange seemed slightly reassured, but the people were not. Their suspicion grew that the reactionaries were sabotaging the formation of the Blum Government because they hoped to stimulate a fascist uprising. To show their displeasure, the Popular Frontists organized sit-down strikes throughout the country.

The first wave embraced about 70,000 workers, mainly in the large Renault automobile factory, an aircraft plant and a few other industrial establishments in the Paris area. The Whitsuntide week-end holiday brought a slackening of the strikes, the number of strikers declining to somewhere above 10,000.

The beginning of June saw the start of a second wave. Factories, warehouses, department stores, printing plants and private shipping firms were closed down by strikes. However, even at the peak of the stoppage, public utilities functioned normally.

By June 4 approximately 800,000 people were on strike. Finally, during the evening hours of that day, the first Popular Front Government, headed by Léon Blum, was formed.

8

THE POPULAR FRONT IN ACTION

THE PRESIDENT of the Chamber, Edouard Herriot, rapped his gavel. "I now give the floor to the President of the Council!" he said.

Léon Blum mounted the tribune to read the Government's statement of policy. It was June 6, 1936.

As he stood facing the Deputies in this crucial moment, Blum awakened many memories and stimulated endless speculation. He was no newcomer to them. His grey hair, his long face with the spectacles and the wispy walrus mustache, his bent lean figure, and the flailing motions with which his stringy arms accompanied and emphasized his words, were a familiar sight to many of the parliamentarians. They had listened to his high-pitched voice—a girl's voice, somebody called it—time and again. They knew his indefinably sinuous, involved method of thinking, his flair for the *mot juste*, his weaknesses and his virtues.

Léon Blum was sixty-four years old when he became Premier of France. It was his first Cabinet post. He had entered the arena of practical politics comparatively late in life. One of his boyhood friends told me that his family had expected him to become a brilliant writer or an illustrious lawyer, or both. But nobody predicted a political career for him.

Son of a wealthy Jewish silk and ribbon merchant, young Léon had exhibited no acute interest in his father's business. He was given an excellent secondary-school education, after which he went through the École Normale Supérieure. He was a contemporary of Edouard Herriot at that training-ground for so many of France's future dignitaries.

Léon Blum early developed a passion for the theater. For many years he wrote dramatic criticism for one of France's most snobbish publications, *La Revue Blanche*. He was also a contributor to *Le Matin*, and later to *Comoedia*, one of the leading periodicals of the theater. Blum was as much at home at the exciting first night of a play as he was at the elegant gatherings of horse-racing enthusiasts at Longchamps.

He was a prominent figure in that "mauve decade" in France's literary and aesthetic world. He wrote a daring book on marriage, a penetrating analysis of the novelist Stendhal, and countless articles on the wits and dandies of the 'nineties.

Being a lawyer, he entered the civil service. There he attained the highest rank. He became a Councillor of State in the Supreme Court of France on constitutional issues.

The erudite librarian of the École Normale, Professor

The Popular Front in Action

Lucien Herr, imparted the first ideas of Socialism to him. Herr brought him in touch with Jean Jaurès. Léon Blum spent more than a decade in the shadow of that great tribune of labor.

When Jaurès founded *L'Humanité* as a Socialist daily, Blum was one of its contributors. But he did not forswear the field of the arts. He still clung to the habits of his youth. He retained his feeling for the exclusive, his fondness for the preciosity of the élite. He was a good fencer and fought his last duel in 1912.

Jean Jaurès paid with his life for his struggle against war. He was assassinated by a fanatic youth of the royalist *Action Française* on the first day of the World War in August 1914.

It was during that war that Blum made his first real advances in practical politics. He became Chef de Cabinet of Marcel Sembat, Socialist Minister of Public Works in the "National Union" Cabinet. Since then Blum has been in politics every minute of his life.

He entered Parliament in 1919. Two years later he was among the leaders of a Socialist group which split away from the party at the national convention at Tours, where the majority declared in favor of the Communist platform. Blum bolted the gathering with a minority. Shortly thereafter he became the leader of the re-constituted Socialist Party and the editor of the official organ *Le Populaire*.

The secret of Blum's strength lay in the "strategy of synthesis." When various groups inside the Socialist Party met in convention and sharply crossed swords with different at times seemingly irreconcilable motions, Léon Blum found the synthetic formula acceptable to the divergent camps. That was his weakness too. For right after the convention ended, each group continued to sponsor its own viewpoint. The synthesis saved the convention, but it did not bridge the fundamental differences which very often split the Socialist Party from top to bottom and made it incapable of action.

The Left wing of his Party was in sympathy with the Communists, while the Right wing was led by Paul Faure, who in foreign policy essentially shared the views of Laval, Flandin and Bonnet.

This tendency to compromise is the most striking feature of Blum's character. Perhaps it arises from the synthesis he had to make between the predilections of his youth and his adult political activity. There always remained a gulf between his private tastes and his public responsibilities.

The Popular Front movement was born not out of a will to compromise, but out of a dynamic desire for change. Léon Blum, called upon to represent this feeling, was at once shocked and—as some of his speeches show—even frightened by it. He preferred debates on a lofty plane in the intimacy of a conference room to

The Popular Front in Action

the storm and stress of huge mass meetings. Very rarely did he achieve a sense of organic, personal contact with the people whom he led. There was something remote, even unconsciously supercilious, in his attitude to the common people.

The success of the Popular Front Government depended on its maintaining close contact not only with its parliamentary supporters, but also—and especially—with its electorate. The People's Front was not a mere parliamentary coalition, such as those of the past. It could broaden its achievements and defend them against the inevitable attacks only if the Government had the firm backing of its parliamentary representatives *and* the voters outside Parliament. This was the "Ministry of the Masses." As soon as the Government cut adrift from its voters, it became vulnerable. Then, like its predecessors, it was at the mercy of parliamentary combinations and liable to succumb. Blum's duty was to keep this contact, this reciprocal interplay which alone could secure the success of his Government and the Popular Front. In this he largely failed. He separated himself from a large section of his electorate, as we shall see, at the very outset of the Spanish War. From that time on he was incapable of synchronizing the will of the people with that of the Government. A year after his fall, practically all that the Popular Front had given to the country disappeared. This was fundamentally due to the gap between Léon Blum's Government and his electorate.

The Cabinet he formed was composed of Socialists and Radical-Socialists. Edouard Daladier became Vice-Premier and War Minister. The big surprise was the new incumbent at the Quai d'Orsay. A new man, Yvon Delbos, became Foreign Minister. Delbos had taken a leading part in the fight against the disastrous foreign policy of Laval. A journalist by profession, he had enjoyed a successful career on several Radical-Socialist publications and later on in Parliament. Here he had specialized in foreign relations and had held minor posts in several Cabinets. During the Laval era he had earned the reputation of being an ardent defender of collective security.

Unimpressive, shy, halting, Yvon Delbos lacked the energy necessary to build a new edifice of foreign affairs on the ruins left by Laval and Flandin. Instead of courageously taking the bit between his teeth and becoming the leader of a new foreign policy for France, Delbos weakly followed the trend in his own party which led back to the path of Laval.

Under the pressure of the sit-down strikes, Parliament rushed through a series of social reforms which the Blum Government had laid before it. The forty-

The Popular Front in Action

hour week and vacations with pay were introduced; collective bargaining was made obligatory. All in all, 65 bills were passed in two and a half months of the legislative session. The age at which children could leave school was raised to fourteen. Nationalization of the armament industry was decreed. The regency of the Bank of France was abolished. The representatives of the "200 Families" were superseded by a general council consisting of a governor, two vice-governors and twenty councillors—nine of them named by the Government, six chosen from a list of persons proposed by the trade unions, farm groups, chambers of commerce, coöperative societies, artisans' associations, and business organizations. One member was appointed by the National Economic Council, two were elected by the staff of the Bank, and two by the share-holders. The Senate made a few inconsequential changes in the bill. When it became a law, it was hailed by the Popular Front press as a victory of great magnitude. The head of the C.G.T. trade union federation, Léon Jouhaux, with substantial paunch and trim goatee, was appointed to the General Council of the Bank. One of the Council members, a hold-over from the old personnel, later confessed: "It gave me the creeps, the first time I saw Jouhaux enter the conference hall of the Bank of France. But we really got along fine," he added with a twinkle.

Another bill ordered the dissolution of the armed leagues. On the basis of this law, Minister of the Interior Roger Salengro, a veteran Socialist and Mayor of the important city of Lille, disbanded the "Croix de Feu" and several other armed groups. But this measure did not put an end to fascist activities. Colonel de la Rocque transformed his league into the "French Social Party" which, under this innocent-sounding name, carried on along the same lines as the banned "Croix de Feu." The law simply produced a change of name—that was all. In spite of demands from some members of his party, the Premier refused to check the activities of De la Rocque's new creation. The Colonel's followers continued to parade through the streets, shouting vengeance against the Popular Front.

The first blanket agreement between the trade unions and the employers' organization was signed in Premier Blum's office, at the Hôtel Matignon. It gave to the industrial and white-collar workers an average wage increase of about 12%, and granted recognition of their duly elected shop committees. Jouhaux greeted the Matignon agreement, as it was called, "as the beginning of a new era."

Indeed, the social legislation of the Popular Front Government had converted France from one of the most backward to one of the most advanced countries in this direction. A special innovation, an Under-Secre-

The Popular Front in Action

tary for Sports and Leisure, established recreation grounds and provided cheaper railway tickets for about 500,000 workers. The beautiful summer resorts of France—on the Riviera, on the Channel, in the Pyrenees, in Brittany—were thronged with men and women from the factories and offices. Most of them were leaving their home towns for the first time in their lives to enjoy vacations with pay and visit some of the show-places of France.

These vigorous social reforms inspired tremendous enthusiasm. The Cabinet's initial declaration on foreign policy, however, stunned many of its supporters. Foreign Minister Delbos somehow gave the impression of uneasiness. In the fight against Laval, Delbos had contributed a brilliant speech on the Government's Ethiopian policy. Now he seemed to begin on the assumption that, with the end of sanctions, Italy would be brought back into a new kind of Stresa Front. Delbos in his maiden speech as Foreign Minister asserted: "France would be glad if the efforts of Italy could gradually be harmonized with our own." Turning to Germany he said that France "had no intention of doubting the words of a man who for four years had lived through the horrors of the war." The man whose word he did not doubt was Adolf Hitler.

From a Foreign Minister of the Popular Front, which had achieved power in the fight against national and international fascism, these were strange words indeed. One of Blum's staff attempted to interpret the situation to a group of journalists. He explained that Blum, as a Socialist and a Jew, had to be doubly careful in foreign policy, and that that was why he had agreed with Delbos on a prudent, friendly wording of the statement. It would please the British, he concluded, and would not fail to impress the Italians who had no love for Germany.

The keystone of Blum's foreign policy was Franco-British amity. This was the axis of his diplomacy. He felt that only the closest coöperation of the two Western democracies could restore at least a part of the League of Nations' lost prestige. For the sake of this collaboration he was ready to handle his totalitarian neighbors with kid gloves and to cold-shoulder Soviet Russia. This much is certain: under Blum relations between France and the U.S.S.R. did not undergo any startling improvement. No conversations between the General Staffs of the two nations occurred, although the Russians made several requests for them. Thus the Franco-Soviet Pact was emasculated and stripped of most of its value.

The 1936 anniversary of Bastille Day was celebrated all over France with impressive displays of

The Popular Front in Action

enthusiasm. A year before the three chiefs of the coalition—Edouard Daladier, Léon Blum, and Maurice Thorez—had marched at the head of the demonstrators as leaders of the opposition to the Laval Government. Now two of them were at the head of the first Popular Front Cabinet, and the third led a party with seventy-two Deputies pledged to support the Government. The 14th of July celebration promised to be the great popular festival of the people's victory. Estimates of the demonstration varied between 500,000 and 700,000 persons. Blum and Thorez again walked in the front ranks of the procession. Daladier, sullen and stubborn, was not present. It was the last harmonious major demonstration at which Léon Blum appeared.

I did not see it. Word came to my editor through diplomatic channels that a military uprising was expected in Spain. I was sent there. On the day of the giant Paris demonstration I was received by the Spanish Prime Minister, Casares Quiroga. I questioned him about the rumors buzzing through Madrid that in a day or two the generals would take up arms against the Republican Government. He did not take the affair seriously. "I assure you," he said, looking me straight in the eye, "that the Army is loyal. As long as the Constitution is respected, there is nothing to fear from the Army. I cordially invite you to make a tour throughout Spain. See for yourself."

Four days later General Francisco Franco, supported by Nazi Germany and fascist Italy, launched his uprising. It shook not only Spain but all Europe to the foundations. There is an old Spanish proverb: "The world trembles when Spain moves." It was prophetic.

A week previously an agreement had been concluded between Austria and Germany by which the Nazis guaranteed Austria's independence. If that guarantee augured no good for the future of Austria, it did demonstrate how far the understanding between Italy and Germany had progressed. This accord alone ought to have sufficed to shatter the illusions which even sincere anti-fascists in Paris nourished, that Italy would return to Stresa. They overlooked the fact that whatever Mussolini's personal feelings might be, he was still linked to Hitler by a common fate. If the strongest fascist dictator, Hitler, were overthrown or even suffered a serious reverse, Mussolini's structure would come tumbling after. And inasmuch as the dictators put their own above national interests, it was clear that sooner or later Mussolini would have to make common cause with Hitler.

A day before the Spanish War began, there was a "cold" Nazi *putsch* in Danzig. On July 17 the Nazi Party became the totalitarian master of the Free City. "Whoever has Danzig," Frederick the Great once remarked, "has more to say in Poland than the King of Poland himself." But Colonel Beck, the enigmatic Polish Foreign Minister, seemed unperturbed.

General Franco's rebellion placed the French Government in a difficult and complicated situation. Its foreign policy was undergoing its first major test. For many decades the French-Spanish frontier had been regarded as safe. The Spanish Balearic Islands dominated the lines of communication between the homeland and its North African possessions. France's national interests unequivocally demanded that no foreign power be allowed to gain influence with, let alone dominate, the Madrid Government. The Spanish Cabinet, at grips with General Franco's uprising, was supported by the Spanish Popular Front, which had won a crucial victory in the elections of February 1936. The relations of the rebellious Spanish generals with the Nazis and the Italian fascists had long been an open secret. The Quai d'Orsay was in possession of reports that General Sanjurjo, prevented by sudden death in an airplane crash from assuming command of the rebellion, had been in Berlin in the winter and spring of 1936. There he had purchased arms and received advice. Strategic considerations and democratic faith combined to demand that France support a friendly democratic Government, constitutionally elected and victim of a fascist conspiracy.

The first shots in Spain reverberated with a rumbling

echo in France. Public opinion was galvanized. The supporters of the Popular Front immediately took sides with the Loyalists, the Right with General Franco's Insurgents. The reactionary newspapers, with *Le Jour* and *Gringoire* leading the pack, painted the ghastliest horror-pictures of alleged atrocities committed by the Loyalists. General Franco was depicted as a knight in shining armor, a resplendent savior of civilization from a godless, blood-crazed mob. It mattered little to the French Right that during the World War the Spanish generals, the lofty prelates and the big businessmen had supported Germany and Austria-Hungary, while the Spanish Left had upheld and even fought for France. At that time King Alfonso, the scion of a decaying Bourbon dynasty, had said: "Only I and the *canaille* are for France." But for *Le Jour*, *Gringoire* and their ilk, the *canaille* was still the *canaille*, even if it was pro-French.

Blum's first move was to make a trip to London. The conversations lasted two days. Then both Blum and Delbos decided to follow the British lead. Information leaked out about the meeting. It was said that the British had warned the French that any attitude other than neutrality in the Spanish affair would displease them highly. General Franco was regarded in London Tory circles as "the gentleman whose victory was eminently desirable." Talking to several French deputies,

The Popular Front in Action

Anthony Eden, then Foreign Minister, expressed his pleasure at the reasonable attitude shown by the French Cabinet Ministers. The communiqué published at the termination of the discussions was, as one French Deputy put it, "as if issued from another planet." It spoke vaguely about plans for a new Locarno conference, saying that "if progress could be made at this meeting of the Locarno powers, other matters concerning the peace of Europe would then come under discussion."

Was the era of unrealistic declarations and "scraps of paper" beginning all over again? Would the Popular Front Government lend the weight of its prestige to another game *à la* Laval?

It seemed so. The steps taken after the return of the French Ministers from London pointed clearly in that direction.

While Foreign Minister Delbos was collecting assurances from the Italian and German Governments that they would refrain from interfering in the Spanish struggle, five Italian warplanes on their way to General Franco made a forced landing on French soil in Northern Africa. A German plane, mistaking the Madrid airdrome for an Insurgent base, landed there on its way to the rebel general. It was seized by the Loyalists.

The Right press now began to accuse the Government of surreptitiously sending arms and airplanes to the legal Spanish Government. The youthful Air Minister Pierre Cot was the main target of the attacks. "Cot the murderer! Cot the war-monger! *Cot-la-Guerre!*" the headlines shrieked. The only reply made by the Blum Cabinet was the bald assertion that no arms had been delivered to the Madrid authorities. And, in fact, after the dispatch of a few airplanes which Pierre Cot arranged, the deliveries did stop.

Many times stronger in manpower than Franco, the militiamen of the Spanish Republic had to retreat before the fascist columns because of their lack of arms, munitions and expert well-schooled military commanders. The first reports from Spain described what had taken place in the villages and cities taken by the Franco forces. The massacre at Badajoz, where 2,000 civilians were murdered by the rebels, became known. A roar of anger went up. It seemed as though loudspeakers everywhere in Paris were shouting: "Arms for Spain! Airplanes for Spain!"

The tumult and the shouting were in vain. Planes and arms were pouring into the Franco camp from Germany and Italy. The Spanish Republic was deserted, left by the democracies to its fate. In the opinion of experts, fifty airplanes at that juncture could have ruined Franco's plans. He had counted on a surprise victory and was frankly worried.

In vain the Spanish Government demanded that or-

The Popular Front in Action

ders for planes and armaments placed before the outbreak of the civil war be filled. The Blum Government refused.

On August 8 it officially banned the export of all planes and armaments to Spain. In a communiqué it disclosed that it had approached several other governments for the conclusion of an agreement to the same effect; and it added that the answers thus far received gave grounds for the hope that an agreement would soon be reached with Germany and Italy prohibiting the shipment of arms to both of the warring sides in Spain. The policy of "non-intervention" had been born.

On August 8, shortly after the Cabinet meeting, I ran into a Socialist Minister. The momentous decision of the Government was a fact. He was terror-stricken. "This is the end," he moaned. "Mark the date well! It means in reality the resignation of the Blum Cabinet. Oh, I know outwardly it is continuing in office. But the Blum Government you have known is gone. From now on it is different. When we came into office, a new era had begun for France. Today it is ended. We're going back to the old days."

This outburst impressed me at the time as highly exaggerated. But subsequent events proved that the man was right. Here is a summary of the story he gave me concerning the Cabinet meeting, an account later confirmed from several other sources:

Yvon Delbos had laid before the Council of Ministers a plan of non-intervention. By its provisions, Germany, Italy, France and Great Britain pledged themselves to ignore the Spanish civil war and to ban the export of arms of any kind to either side. He declared that the Italian and German Governments had exhibited their readiness to accept the plan.

A storm broke loose. At the outset, a majority of the Cabinet was against the plan. Premier Blum was forced to hurl the full weight of his authority into the controversy. He declared that the British Ambassador, Sir George Clerk, had informed him that "the British Government was in no position to support France if, because of her attitude toward the Spanish conflict, she should be drawn into war." The Radical-Socialist Minister of State, stealthy Camille Chautemps, joined hands with Blum. Delbos threatened to resign if his proposal were not accepted. He was supported to the hilt by two Socialist Ministers—dry, sardonic Paul Faure and Charles Spinasse, who was in charge of national economy. They argued that any other attitude would drag France into war.

Pierre Cot, blunt Radical-Socialist Air Minister, was the spokesman for the group in the Cabinet which demanded support of the Spanish Republican Government. He outlined the strategic dangers to France of a conquest of Spain by the puppet of Hitler and Mussolini.

Three times the session was interrupted. President Lebrun, who backed Delbos' plan, acted as intermediary and finally persuaded Pierre Cot and his supporters to yield to "reality." During the entire fight, Daladier hardly uttered a sound.

The Cabinet's decision was taken in the full knowledge of extensive Nazi and Italian intervention. There could be no doubt about the plans of Hitler and Mussolini. Their blue-prints were common knowledge. These had appeared in numerous articles and books in Germany and Italy, where all publications were under strictest censorship, and had dealt with the strategic importance of the Balearic Islands, the Spanish Mediterranean, and Spain's ports on the Atlantic. Above all, the German Army journals had exhaustively analyzed the Spanish problem for the past six months. As for Léon Blum, had he not previously professed in numerous speeches that no reliance could be placed on the words of the dictators? Had not he and his Government pledged themselves to halt direct and indirect aggression? When they took the fatal road of non-intervention, they could not pretend to a lack of knowledge of the plans of the dictators.

Later on, in a discussion with a Spanish Cabinet Minister, Léon Blum explained why he could not advance any other policy. He offered two reasons: first of all, sharp pressure from the British; second, the Spanish civil war had created a profound dividing-line in France.

The Left—men of the People's Front—was vigorously pro-Loyalist; the Right—the "200 Families," the fascist groups, the snobbish Parisian drawing-room society and part of the Army—were just as ardently for Franco.

It is true that the war in Spain cut an unbridgeable chasm through France. But so had Mussolini's invasion of Abyssinia. So had the Hitler terror in Germany. So had the re-occupation of the Rhineland by the Nazi troops. The line cleaving the Right from the Left could not be whisked away with the legerdemain of compromises. Experience was there to prove that. Never had the Left been so united and the Right so discouraged as in the first weeks of the Popular Front Government. At the start of the Spanish civil war Blum was backed by a solid compact mass. The people had just greeted the social reforms with joy; they showed a fierce resolve to defend a foreign policy of "standing up" to the aggressors. It was impossible for Blum to invent a foreign policy which would satisfy both the Right and the Left. There was no such policy. But he could pursue a line corresponding to the sentiments of the French Popular Front and the national interests of France. And he would thereby be helping a friendly government and a potential ally. There was not a chance in the world of uniting Right and Left. But there was the ominous risk that the non-intervention policy might sap and disintegrate the Popular Front; that it might bring

The Popular Front in Action

confusion into its ranks and split them wide open. As a cemented bloc the Popular Front might carry on for many years. Disunited, it would fall victim to the maneuvers of the Right. The reactionaries were lying in ambush, lynx-eyed, waiting to spot the first signs of weakness.

Moreover, Blum, striving for national unity on the Spanish issue, was chasing a phantom. Meanwhile, he forgot the solid reality of the Popular Front. He leaped for the shadow and ignored the substance. His coalition was knitted together by common hopes and common ideals. Whoever sought to attack France had first to disrupt this bloc. Every attempt of Hitler's agents and propagandists to undermine the morale of France, every effort of the pincer-men to "soften up" the country first, successful as it had been and would be with the parties of the Right, had made no headway among the people of France. Just the opposite: the Hitler danger was one of the elements which had cemented the Popular Front. If the morale of this coalition was to be weakened, it could only be done by actions which its leaders took—or failed to take. The non-intervention policy was contrary to the basic strategic interests of the French Republic. But more than that it was devastating in its effects, for it shattered a solid phalanx of the masses which alone was capable of stopping the aggressive designs of fascism.

The non-intervention agreement incorporated none of the spectacular features of the Munich pact which was to follow two years later. But its dramatic significance and its tragic consequences for the fate of France were no less terrible than of Munich. It had the same characteristics: the iniquitous abandonment of a democracy to the dictatorships. The surrender was explained and justified—as later was the case at Munich—on the grounds of the necessity of preserving peace. Peaceful desires and compliance with treaties were attributed to the Rome-Berlin totalitarians at the signing of the non-intervention accord, just as they were after Munich. Without this non-intervention pact—which in reality sanctioned intervention in Spain—Hitler's triumph in Czechoslovakia would have been inconceivable. The road from Spain led straight to Munich.

The decision of the Blum Cabinet was hailed with delight by the reactionary papers and politicians. They enjoyed even more the reports they received concerning the behind-the-scenes proceedings at the Cabinet meeting. The leaders of the Right saw that the Socialist Party, the largest in France, was splitting wide open, just as the Radical-Socialists had done whenever they had assumed the reins of government. The Right realized that the "realism" of governmental practice was already taking effect on the Blum Government. From that day on, they could become bolder in their fight

The Popular Front in Action

against it. They had succeeded in driving a wedge into the leadership of the Popular Front.

It took some time before the lower ranks were also split. In August 1936 the overwhelming majority of the Socialists and a large section of the Radicals joined the Communist-led campaign for aid to the Spanish Republic. The Government's decision came as a great shock to the people. They recognized instinctively that the struggle beyond the Pyrenees was a struggle against an enemy similar to their own. They could not understand why France, still the first military power on the Continent, should be intimidated by the threats of the dictators. For the past two years they had been reading in their papers that resistance to Hitler and Mussolini was the only way to keep France free of fascism. Neutrality toward the Spanish Loyalists seemed to them utterly unfair, unbelievably wrong. Many, especially the Socialists, felt for quite some time that the non-intervention proposal was a clever ruse on Blum's part. He would keep the Germans and the Italians from sending arms to Franco; and meanwhile he would quickly and generously equip the Republicans with all the weapons necessary to crush the rebellion.

The Government clung for a long while to the belief—or, at least, professed to cling to it—that the Italians and the Germans were faithfully observing the agreement. If it was an illusion, it was a tragic one.

To a delegation of Spanish Republicans appearing before him to ask for aid, Blum replied that "all the information available proved that the Nazis and the fascists had ceased to deliver arms to Franco." Then he burst into tears. Mme. Blum interrupted the conversation indignantly: "You have no right to excite my husband so!"

A committee from the French Metal Workers Union was told by the Premier: "What do you take me for? My efforts to obtain neutrality and non-intervention in Spain have just borne fruit. Do you expect me to reverse my policy?"

In September, at a party meeting in Paris' Luna Park, Blum gave public utterance to what he had previously expressed to various delegations in private. The Socialists had become restless under the influence of events in Spain. Before a large crowd Blum asserted: "As far as I know, there is not a single proof, not a single piece of circumstantial evidence to show that the agreement [i.e. of non-intervention] has been violated since it was subscribed to."

Those words were uttered on September 16, 1936. At that same time a group of British parliamentarians who had traveled to Spain, brought home the material evidence—unexploded German and Italian shells and armament parts—that the Rome-Berlin intervention was continuing. The French Secret Service was in possession

The Popular Front in Action

of a list of the sailings of German and Italian ships bearing arms to Franco between September 1 and September 12, when Blum made his declaration. But the words of the Premier could not fail to make a deep impression on a portion of his followers. If Léon Blum guaranteed that no injustice was being wrought to the Republican cause, then they were ready to believe it. Many of them, too, had been powerfully moved by another part of Blum's speech, in which he had dealt with the danger of war. This, he implied, would be heightened by French help to the Loyalist Government. With consummate art and dexterity he painted the horrors of war, thus appealing to the deeply rooted pacifist sentiments of the French masses.

He was not altogether original. Laval had acted thus before him. The Lavalist press had screamed: "Sanctions mean war!" At that time Blum had insisted that resistance to the aggressors and collective security meant peace. Now he was using Laval's arguments. True, with this thesis he swung a portion of his followers into the non-intervention camp. In that sense he was successful. But now the dividing-line which cut through the Popular Front robbed it of its original striking power. While the Right was, with a few honorable exceptions, united on this issue, the Left was split. The Communists, the trade unions, and a part of the Socialists and Radicals cried for aid to Loyalist Spain; other Socialists and

Radicals opposed it. And as time went on, this fissure widened, until finally the pressure of the reactionaries succeeded in transforming the disunion into a complete rupture. The non-intervention policy was the beginning of the end of the Popular Front.

It also had decided repercussions in the sphere of foreign affairs. Rumanian Foreign Minister Nicolas Titulescu, a brilliant statesman with the face of a gargoyle, was an advocate of collective security and of close collaboration of Rumania with France and Soviet Russia. In June he had made an offer to Blum in Geneva to enlarge the alliance of the Little Entente into a military alliance between that group, France and Soviet Russia. In August, Pierre Cot was dispatched to the South of France to discuss the proposition with Titulescu. At length Titulescu's proposals were rejected by the French Government. On August 31 he was unceremoniously sacked by King Carol of Rumania, who then began his policy of *rapprochement* with Berlin and Rome.

Also rejected were the advances of the Turkish Government, unnerved by the Italian conquest of Abyssinia. The Turks wished to coöperate on the Franco-Soviet Pact in one form or another. Likewise rejected were the proposals of the Soviet Government prior to the conclusion of the non-intervention agreement. The Russians were willing to discuss ways and means of aiding Republican Spain; and were ready to agree upon the req-

The Popular Front in Action

uisite measures should help for Spain lead to a general conflict.

In Belgium, the non-intervention policy led the Government to serve notice that it intended to repudiate the Franco-Belgian Alliance. In the autumn of 1936 Leopold, the uneasy King of the Belgians, withdrew from the Locarno agreement, which pledged Belgian aid to France in the event of attack. He announced that his country would revert to the status of "absolute neutrality." Already for many months there had been reports that the Nazis were gaining influence at the Royal Court, as well as among important Belgian politicians. Belgium's neutrality was unilaterally guaranteed by France and Great Britain. Chancellor Hitler gave the Belgian monarch another guarantee which, as a French Deputy told the Foreign Affairs Committee, was "similar to a death warrant."

In the midst of the turmoil in France brought on by the Spanish war, Paris received the first visit of a German Cabinet Minister since the Second Empire. Hitler's economic wizard, Dr. Hjalmar Schacht, was received by Léon Blum on the very day the Führer doubled the length of military service in Germany. This, of course, the rigid stiff-necked German Minister hastened to explain, was not aimed against France but against the peril of bolshevism. Blum later revealed that his first remark to Schacht was: "You know that I am a Jew and that I do not agree with the anti-Semitic measures in Germany. And now we can talk things over." This revelation is interesting, for its light on Blum's estimation of fascism. He probably thought that such a confession from man to man would clear the air for frank mutual explanations. As if Dr. Schacht had come for frank explanations!

Following on the heels of Dr. Schacht, the successor of Pilsudski, Marshal Smigly-Rydz, the artist turned warrior, arrived in Paris. He was returning the visit of General Gamelin, who had gone to Poland to investigate the state of Polish military preparedness. On his return Gamelin had confided to his associates his genuine disappointment and shock at the condition of the Polish Army and, as he termed it, "at the foolish strategic conceptions of the Polish General Staff." Marshal Smigly-Rydz was rewarded with a French loan for armaments to the tune of $100,000,000.

The autumn of 1936 saw the Right in France begin the counter-attack along the entire front. The Senate had voted the initial legislation of the Blum Government with ill-concealed bad grace. Now its temper grew uglier and testier. The fissure in the ranks of the Popular Front led to another attack on the national currency by big business. Capital began to flee France again in

The Popular Front in Action

huge quantities. The Government's financial situation grew precarious. In an abrupt about-face it decided to devaluate the franc.

After a dramatic night during which Finance Minister Auriol was glued to the telephone, conversing long-distance with London and Washington, the devaluation was announced. It was coupled with the so-called Tripartite Monetary Agreement between France, Great Britain and the United States for the defense of their currencies and prices on the world market.

The Government had attached to the devaluation measure a bill introducing a sliding scale for wages. This had to be sacrificed to get a majority in the Senate. It was the first major legislative defeat of the Government at the hands of the reactionaries in Parliament and revealed that in four months the Government's position had weakened considerably. It further contributed to the friction in the Popular Front because the Communists and a majority of the trade unions opposed devaluation. The annual Radical-Socialist convention had already demonstrated that there were powerful forces inside this party arrayed against the People's Front. The most vocal group was led by two friends of Georges Bonnet, Émile Roche and Pierre Dominique, editors of the paper *La République*. In the lovely resort town of Biarritz, a few miles from the Spanish border, a considerable section of the delegates called for an open break with the Communists because of their attitude in the Spanish affair. The rupture was prevented only with great difficulty. The press of the Right was jubilant.

There is a street car that runs from Biarritz to the French-Spanish frontier. A bridge separates the border town of Hendaye from Irun on the Spanish side. When the Radicals convened at Biarritz the Franco flag was already flying over Irun. The Insurgents had entered the city in September. The Loyalists retreated across the International Bridge into France, after having fired their last rounds of ammunition. When they rushed into Hendaye they saw six freight cars standing in the station, loaded with Spanish munitions. These had been sent from Catalonia through French territory for the defenders of Irun. The French Government had halted the ammunition almost a stone's throw from the beleaguered, martyred city.

The press war over Spain was interrupted for a few days by the suicide of the French Minister of the Interior, Roger Salengro.

The name of Salengro had been affixed to the decree dissolving the fascist leagues. This was an unforgiveable crime; it had to be avenged. The fascist weekly *Gringoire* started a campaign of vilification against the Socialist Interior Minister. It charged Salengro with

The Popular Front in Action

having deserted to the enemy in the World War. The paper claimed it had evidence of this desertion, evidence given by six soldiers who had served with him. It accused him of a still more heinous crime—that of divulging military secrets to the German Command. It stated that proof of this was in the possession of the Nazi Government.

This campaign of slander was waged with incredible venom not only by *Gringoire* but also by several other reactionary sheets.

The case was taken to the floor of the Chamber of Deputies. Salengro was acquitted by an overwhelming majority. General Gamelin joined the defenders of Salengro, swearing that the Interior Minister had not deserted.

I met Salengro shortly after this parliamentary session. I congratulated him, but he refused to accept my felicitations.

"I'm finished," he murmured. "You cannot stop those filthy scoundrels. An example must be made."

"What kind of an example?" I asked.

"That's just what I'm thinking about."

Two days later he brought his life to an end.

Roger Salengro's death had a depressing effect on the people. Here they saw a Minister, member of a Cabinet which a few months before had been swept into office by a remarkable victory, unable to defend himself against the reactionaries whom they had believed defeated. They saw him finally driven to suicide because there seemed to him no other way of silencing the slanderous campaign of a fascist weekly subsidized by the Italians. This rag then must be more powerful than an important Minister of the Left. The public was profoundly stirred.

A bill prohibiting libel was passed; it did not prevent libel in the least. *Gringoire* continued its campaigns. There was not a single prominent anti-fascist in France who, on one occasion or another, did not suffer incredible insults and attacks from *Gringoire*. Fed with material from the archives of the former Police Prefect Chiappe, father-in-law of the proprietor of the defamatory sheet, financed by Italian fascism, the imagination of its editors was inexhaustibly evil. There was no more sordid sheet in France, none that has done more harm to French democracy.

Blum's most trusted lieutenant, bearded Max Dormoy, succeeded Salengro at the Ministry of Interior.

While the League of Nations was busy tabling the Spanish Republican Government's appeal for help, the Rome-Berlin axis was born.

On October 19 Count Ciano, Foreign Minister of Italy and son-in-law of the Duce, came to Berlin. He

The Popular Front in Action

was accompanied by his wife Edda, Mussolini's favorite daughter. As far as could be gathered, the agreement reached there embraced a common policy in Spain, a concerted attitude toward the League of Nations, and a common drive in the Balkans to definitively undermine the position of France and Great Britain in that part of Europe. Further proposals were made for the coördination of Nazi and fascist foreign propaganda and the exchange of diplomatic and military information involving Russia and the Western democracies. The goal Ciano and Hitler sought was the isolation of France, which was already encircled by Germany and Italy and would, Berlin and Rome hoped, soon be further encircled by Franco Spain. Should such an encirclement become a fact, France would either have to align herself with fascism or be crushed.

A secret report received at the Quai d'Orsay shortly thereafter contained not only news of these agreements but also choice details concerning a monetary deal supposedly arranged between Count Ciano and Marshal Goering. It stated with assurance that Count Ciano, badly in debt, had received a present of several million marks. The news was not at that time confirmed from any other source. Two years later it was repeated by a Catholic journalist after a visit to the Vatican. Again no further confirmation was obtainable. At any rate, it popped up in the French press only after Italy's entry into the war. If really confirmed, this information would cast a peculiar light on the activities of Mussolini's son-in-law.

Soon after Ciano's return to Rome, Mussolini delivered a speech at Milan in the course of which he coined the phrase: "Rome-Berlin Axis." This event had been rehearsed by the Italian propaganda bureau with minute care. Its importance was underlined by the presence of many uniformed Nazi officials on the platform reserved for distinguished guests. Mussolini referred to Nazi Germany as "a great nation which has recently attracted to herself the powerful sympathies of the Italian people." He maintained that the Berlin agreement covered "specific problems, some of which are especially crucial." Did he mean only Spain? Or was Austria included? It appears that while concluding the accord, Mussolini had already changed his mind about Austria. He had turned his eyes exclusively toward the Mediterranean, dreaming of gains in Africa and in the Balkans, and of a reënforcement of his position in Spain. It seems now in retrospect that the two Axis powers had by then roughly staked out their respective spheres of interest, if not in a pact, at least in a gentleman's agreement—if such an expression may be used in reference to them.

Some days later Hitler tossed out a bait which the French Right eagerly swallowed. In Berlin he signed the Anti-Comintern Pact with Japan. This measure, he said, was directed against the Communist activities of the

The Popular Front in Action

Third International. At the Nazi Party convention in Nuremberg in 1936, Hitler had avowed that he never would sit down at the same table as the Communists. The French Right was gleeful—this was a new sign for them that a settlement of accounts between Soviet Russia and Nazi Germany was drawing near. The reactionary French papers, from the cautious *Le Temps* to the poisonous *Gringoire*, greeted the Anti-Comintern Pact as "a powerful element of French security." As soon as bolshevism—this was their designation for the Spanish People's Front—was crushed in Spain, the Führer would turn on Soviet Russia. The Soviets, weakened by the purges, morally at a low ebb, would fall an easy prey to the efficient Nazi military machine. "The Anti-Comintern Pact," one of the papers stated, "should be an example for France in dealing with the Red menace."

The first meeting of the recently created "Non-Intervention Committee" was held in London under the chairmanship of Lord Plymouth. It manifested no desire to prevent German and Italian shipments of arms and soldiers from reaching Franco. In fact, while the Committee could find no evidence of German or Italian intervention, it appeared eager to discover proofs of Russian help to the Loyalists. In October the Soviet delegate, Ambassador Maisky, declared that his Government felt no more bound by the Non-Intervention Pact than did the other powers.

The whole political life of the Blum Government

was dominated by the Spanish issue. Franco was driving on Madrid; the ill-equipped Loyalist militiamen were forced to retreat. The French Right confidently expected the war in Spain to come to a quick close after the anticipated fall of Madrid. A Franco victory! What a blow it would deal to the French People's Front. On November 7, 1936, most of the reactionary Paris papers printed glowing descriptions of General Franco's entry into Madrid. A flood of pro-Franco literature poured into France, most of it issued from the so-called "Anti-Comintern Office" in Geneva, which had been set up by the Nazis some years before. Hitler and Mussolini recognized the Burgos Government as the only representative of Spain, hoping thereby to hasten a victory they deemed already within their grasp. But the wish was father to the thought. The fervid accounts of the conquest of Madrid stumbled on grim reality. The march of the Franco forces was stopped dead at the gates of Madrid by a few thousand Spanish militiamen and international volunteers, supported by Russian planes and tanks. One of the enterprising French journalists had already envisioned General Franco on a white horse in the heart of Madrid; it was almost two and a half years more before the fascist Caudillo penetrated the city.

The Blum Cabinet nearly resigned before the year 1936 was out. During a debate on the Spanish question

The Popular Front in Action

the Communists refused to endorse the Government's policy and abstained from voting confidence. On that occasion Blum divulged his decision to let the Axis powers have their way. He quoted Metternich: "I have never sent an ultimatum without being ready to back it up with guns." Even as he spoke, a massive contingent of German troops was on its way to Spain.

The new year began with a sudden burst of French energy which vanished as swiftly as it had gathered. While Yvon Delbos was away on vacation, the Under-Secretary for Foreign Affairs, Pierre Viénot, received reports that 6,000 German troops had disembarked at Cadiz, Spain. They were to be transported within a few days to Spanish Morocco, bordering on French Morocco. After due consultations with the Premier and the General Staff (whose undercover agents confirmed the information), the Under-Secretary summoned the French diplomatic press. He divulged the news and suggested that it be published together with sharp editorial comments. At the same time, the French Ambassador in Berlin was ordered to make a strong *démarche* with the Nazi Government, informing it that France would not tolerate the presence of German troops in Spanish Morocco.

In the face of this French display of firmness Hitler

withdrew. The German troops were re-routed to the interior of Spain. A joint communiqué, signed by Hitler and the French Ambassador, stated that no dispatch of German troops to Spanish Morocco had been intended. Thus, Hitler saved his face—and at the same time caused Under-Secretary Viénot to be disavowed. Immediately the whole reactionary press accused Viénot of seeking to drag France into a war with Germany, in order to save the bloody bolshevik régime in Spain. That was the first large-scale campaign of the Right against *"fausses nouvelles."* Henceforth, whenever an item did not suit their plans they labelled it "false news." Ambassador François Poncet, confidant of the Comité des Forges, had undoubtedly not overlooked that aspect of the communiqué when he drew it up. For him the mere existence of a Foreign Minister of the People's Front, even though as weak as Delbos, was an intolerable thought.

Apart from the Moroccan episode, 1937 passed without any sensations in French foreign policy. The war of nerves, with sharp little daily stabs, continued on its course. Hitler was waiting for the termination of the Spanish war; or at least for a decisive victory by Franco, prelude to a final triumph. But with the unexpectedly heroic defense of Madrid, the struggle in Spain began to drag on longer than the Axis had foreseen. Its end,

The Popular Front in Action

thought so near at hand two months before, was not now in sight. Hitler held a conference with his chief advisers in January 1937. According to advice reaching the Quai d'Orsay, the Führer declared that as long as the Spanish adventure was not finished, no sensational moves were to be expected. Before definitely planting "the Spanish fly in the neck of France," the Führer did not feel it was safe to embark on the series of aggressions he was planning. While the slaughter in Spain continued, the Nazis concentrated on gaining key political and economic bases in the Franco-ruled regions.

The central targets of the attack were the French Popular Front Government and the Franco-Soviet mutual assistance pact. It was claimed that the pact—and it alone—stood in the way of a French-German *rapprochement.* Those who defended the treaty as essential to France's national security were dubbed either bolsheviks or "Franco-Russes." In other words, they were in the pay of Moscow. The Nationalists Georges Mandel and Paul Reynaud were counted among the more notorious "Franco-Russes." Daladier and Chautemps were depicted as true patriots because they were cool to the pact. Rightist Deputies, some influential ex-servicemen, and aristocrats like the Count de Brinon had been frequent visitors to Nazi Germany. But now pro-Nazi opinions dropped more and more often from the lips of Radicals and Socialists as well.

The strategy of the French reactionaries was evidently

to break up the Socialist-Radical-Socialist coalition; to separate the Radicals from the Socialists, and the Socialists from the Communists. The Right did not yet seek a "national government" in the image of Doumergue and Laval. The time was still unripe for men like Laval to be trotted out before the French people. Discredited, dishonored and despised, their public appearance would have aided the cause of the steadily disintegrating People's Front. Instead of a national government, the French Right was scheming for a purely Radical-Socialist combination. This, once it had broken with the Socialists, would depend on the support of the Right and would become its prisoner, while still offering a Left face to the country. These plans help explain the change of attitude toward Daladier and Chautemps, men who, barely a year before, had been reviled as murderers and assassins.

Early in 1937 another exodus of capital from the country began. This time it assumed the shocking proportions of a billion francs a day.

Faced with this onslaught, the Government had to choose between counter-attack and appeasement. The counter-attack would have taken the form of water-tight legislation against "the desertion of capital." Such a measure could have electrified the country; it could have roused the Popular Front forces from their lethargy and rallied them anew behind the Government.

The Popular Front in Action

Exchange control—in other words, forbidding the purchase and sale of foreign currency without governmental permission—would have been the key point of such legislation. In previous years Blum had urged such measures. But under the pressure of French high finance and the City of London, Blum decided for appeasement. In February 1937 he proclaimed the necessity of a "pause," a breathing spell. No new social or financial laws were to be laid before Parliament; no budgetary increases were to be demanded. The execution of that part of the People's Front program, still unrealized, was to be postponed.

Instead, Professor Charles Rist, theoretician of orthodox "financial behavior," and Paul Baudouin, Director of the Bank of Indo-China, were placed in charge of the currency-exchange fund.

The hopes of the Government were concentrated on the Paris World Exhibition, scheduled to open in May. Early in March a Cabinet Minister explained to me that now, with financial stability secure for the next few months, the Paris Exhibition would help the Government survive the year 1937 without undue difficulties. The vast crowds of visitors expected would not only mean a large influx of gold, but their visit to Paris would have an inestimable propaganda value, and one which could not fail to have repercussions on foreign policy. Nazi propaganda in Europe and America was portraying the France of the Popular Front as rapidly succumbing to labor troubles, disorders, internal dissensions and chaos. The Exhibition would give foreigners the picture of a calm, orderly, charming France. Paris, he concluded, would regain its dominant cultural position in Europe.

Nazi Germany was forging a new army. Nazi agents had just won an important victory in the Balkans. Mussolini was on the eve of signing a treaty with fascist-minded Stoyadinovitch, binding Jugoslavia more tightly to the Axis. Spanish Malaga on the Mediterranean was in Italian hands. Hitler obtained control of the Spanish ports on the Atlantic Ocean.

And France's answer to all that was—a delightful and stimulating World Exhibition.

But before the Exhibition was opened, the Blum Government had to wrestle with the "Clichy incident." In Clichy, an industrial suburb of Paris administered by a Socialist mayor, a throng of people had staged a counter-demonstration to a "Croix de Feu" meeting which the Interior Minister had permitted to assemble. Police protecting the "Croix de Feu" had opened fire, killing six civilians and wounding several hundred others. Among the casualties was André Blumel, secretary-general to the Premier, who rushed to Clichy when he heard of

The Popular Front in Action

the rioting. Later, on his return from a gala concert, Blum and Dormoy visited the scene of the incident.

An investigation disclosed that there was no justification for opening fire against the civilians. They were completely under the control of their organizers. It, therefore, may be assumed that the shooting was deliberate, ordered to create new and serious difficulties for the Blum Government. The Paris Left demanded severe penalties for the guilty parties. In a speech before Parliament, Blum promised a thorough and merciless investigation. The results of the inquiry never were revealed.

Unfinished, with many of the pavilions still under construction, the Paris Exhibition officially opened in May. It soon made a tremendous and unforgettable impression. It was as though French democracy, before its abdication, sought to give the world a last and indelible twilight-picture of its genius and grandeur. In a narrow corridor along the Seine River, the Exhibition buildings were so skilfully placed and the limited space so tastefully utilized, that the scene offered the panorama of a vast, seemingly endless flow of striking, multi-colored monuments of the modern world. In the evenings a sea of lights flooded the entire area, attracting millions of visitors. A special area was devoted to the French provinces, where the products of these regions were presented with taste and pride. To a foreign visitor wandering through the many French pavilions it must have been a splendid picture of the culture and strength of France.

But, alas, politics were not brought to a standstill by the success of this display. In June a few bankers met in a rear private-room at Larue's, the famous restaurant close to the Madeleine church. Their guest of honor was Joseph Caillaux, the monocled President of the Senate Finance Committee. Several days later a new flight of capital began. The currency of France was again in peril. As if by coincidence, Rist and Baudoin resigned from the exchange-control committee. The rediscount rate of the Bank of France jumped from four to six per cent. It was obvious that the final assault was under way.

Blum endeavored to stem the tide by asking Parliament for decree powers. He had always fought against similar demands by his predecessors. Once in the course of a debate on this subject he had cried: "I would rather have a king than grant full powers!"

Of the 375 Deputies constituting the governmental coalition, 346 voted for the decree powers. The Opposition garnered only 247 votes. The crushing blow had to come from the Senate.

Caillaux had waited for this moment. Ambitious, domineering, revengeful, he did not forget that a year before, the Senate was forced to bow to the will of the people. He knew that he would never again fill one of

The Popular Front in Action

the highest posts of government, but if he could not command a Government, he wanted at least to be its executioner. With his monocle stuck in his eye, with his sharp voice and arrogant manner, Caillaux snapped one insult after another at the Premier. He could not, he sneered, give the Government his vote of confidence. It was unworthy of it. He did not know who the real master of France was: the Cabinet or the "Ministry of the Masses." He was not even sure that this Government wanted to adhere to its parliamentary platform.

Laval, listening, thought the time was ripe for him to break his long silence and joined in Caillaux's attack. The Blum Cabinet was defeated 188 votes to 72 in the Senate.

That did not necessarily mean the resignation of the Cabinet. According to the French Constitution, a bill upheld three times in the Chamber against the Senate became a law nothwithstanding. Blum could have returned to the Chamber and forced the Senate to bow. He still retained a decisive majority in the lower house. If Blum had taken this step, the overweening influence of the Senate on French policy, the grip of that body created as a brake on universal suffrage and elected only indirectly, could have been broken once and for all.

The decision before Blum was fully as momentous as that which had faced Daladier after the riots on the Place de la Concorde. The stiff-necked resistance of the

Senate was another boom of the same rebellious drive. But Léon Blum followed the example of Edouard Daladier. He resigned.

The explanation offered for Blum's resignation was his desire to ease his party for a while of the burden of supreme governmental responsibility. He wished, he said, to play second fiddle to the Radicals for a time, in order, strengthened by this respite, to stage a new and more powerful comeback. But two years later Blum made a precious admission when he said: "It was not the financial difficulties which conquered us; it was not even the adverse votes of the Senate—nothing would have overthrown us if we had not had the feeling that the working class was no longer responding to our advice."

9

CHAUTEMPS: ANTI-CLIMAX

IN THE ten months after the resignation of Léon Blum, four Cabinets came and went. Two of them were headed by the master of maneuvers, Camille Chautemps, the man with the poker face. He was Blum's immediate successor. The outstanding feature of his combination was the recall of Georges Bonnet as Finance Minister. In order to get rid of this dangerous adversary, Blum, during his tenure, had appointed him Ambassador to the United States. But now Bonnet and his wife made a triumphant return to France, their heads buzzing with grandiose plans for the future.

Blum became Vice-Premier in the Chautemps Government, Daladier kept the War Office, and Yvon Delbos Foreign Affairs. The same old game of reshuffling the cards began again.

During the Chautemps interlude, French democracy fell back into its well-known rut. No new reforms were projected; no initiative was taken in the field of foreign affairs. The dictators were feverishly accelerating their preparations, deploying their forces for the dramatic moves which were to highlight the year to come. But Camille Chautemps continued his small intrigues, his petty parliamentary combinations, and his short-lived expedients.

The Chautemps interim was an anti-climax for France. But not elsewhere. In September Mussolini paid a visit to Berlin. Italy joined the Anti-Comintern Pact with a flourish. Hitler made his first public bid for the rich soil and abundant resources of the Ukraine. The applause of the French Right mounted to a deafening roar of approval.

That same month an explosion wrecked the headquarters of the French Employers' Federation near the Champs-Elysées in Paris. Here, finally, was the "Communist plot"—"the Crime of the People's Front"—for which the Right was impatiently waiting. A violent press campaign was launched against the People's Front in general and the Communists in particular. The Nazi papers supported it with especial satisfaction. The stage seemed set for the final drive against the Left forces.

The Right had a blue-print for its plans: first, a series of blasts and bombings; then riots would be fomented during the October cantonal elections. These would be followed by disturbances and anti-Semitic excesses in French North Africa. By the middle of November rumors of an impending Communist *coup d'état* would be launched. Finally in December, with public opinion worked up to fever pitch, the "Committee for Secret Revolutionary Action" (abbreviated CSAR) would enter upon the scene. They would drive the Chautemps Ministers out of office and replace them with a dictatorial junta.

At the outset events faithfully followed the blueprint. Had it not been for one of those surprises in which political life in France has always been so rich, December 1937 might have seen the nation in turmoil. Curiously enough, it was Colonel de la Rocque, head of the "Croix de Feu," who warned the Government.

During the past year his organization had made decided headway throughout the country at the expense of all the other Right parties. Political circles freely predicted that in the next elections De la Rocque would emerge as the leader of the political Right, with about a hundred seats in the Chamber. More a military man than a politician, stiff and unbending in his manner, called a roughneck by many "nice people," the Colonel had alienated a number of powerful figures. He had called former Premier Tardieu a political corpse; he had attacked Pierre-Étienne Flandin; he was unsparing of invectives against many of the Rightist Deputies. He had purchased one of the larger Paris newspapers, *Le Petit Journal,* with a circulation of several hundred thousand. To the other reactionary newspapers this, of course, was an unforgivable sin. They joined the camp of De la Rocque's adversaries with alacrity. The proprietors and editors of *Le Jour, Le Matin, Le Journal* and

Le Petit Parisien constituted a solid phalanx arrayed against the Colonel. All Paris whispered that the money to buy *Le Petit Journal*, a tidy sum of nine million francs, had been put up by Pierre Laval, who considered the Colonel's organization the biggest and best-disciplined which could be placed in the field against the Popular Front.

The fight against De la Rocque was first waged by Duke Pozzo di Borgo, a Corsican with a fierce lust for power. He asserted in an article that for years the Colonel received subsidies from the secret funds of the Foreign Office. At the trial for slander which followed, this assertion was confirmed by Tardieu who seethed with desire for revenge on De la Rocque and Laval. He himself, admitted Tardieu, had handed over money. He had utilized the Colonel as a mercenary against the Left menace, as well as a personal publicity agent for himself. The same was true, according to Tardieu's testimony in the Lyon Court, of Laval who had paid De la Rocque for demonstrations of "popular enthusiasm" in his favor. Tardieu explained: "I thought it well to oppose the powerful forces for disorder with the forces of order. I had to meet possible action by 400,000 to 500,000 Communists. I got extremely good service from the 'Croix de Feu.' They kept order whenever and wherever I asked for it."

Several days after the trial a middle-aged man turned

Chautemps: Anti-Climax

up at the private apartment of one of Chautemps' Cabinet Ministers. He refused to disclose his name and exhibited an air of mystery. When he left, the Minister held in his hands a file with complete details of the plans of the so-called "Committee for Secret Revolutionary Action." The unknown visitor had been sent by De la Rocque.

When the evidence was presented to him, Chautemps was forced to agree to take immediate action against this menace.

The next day almost five hundred search warrants were issued. The police raided hundreds of private homes, offices and stores. They returned with amazing booty: 500 machine guns, 65 sub-machine guns, about 30 anti-tank and anti-aircraft guns, two tons of high explosives, not to mention many rifles and thousands of rounds of ammunition. Secret forts and pillboxes were discovered under garages and on secluded country estates. Powerful radio sending and receiving sets and secret telephone wires were also seized.

The arms were of German, Italian, Franco-Spanish and British manufacture. The list of the arrests made an impressive roll-call. It ranged from General Duseigneur, once chief of the Air Force Staff, and from landowner Count Hubert Pastré to civil servants, antique dealers, Army officers, mechanics and chauffeurs. The secret organization was modeled along military lines, with a commanding General Staff and four intelligence departments at its disposal. It was divided into divisions, brigades and battalions. A plan for complete mobilization of effectives had been drawn up. Maps of Paris and key provincial cities were found, together with card-indexed information on Army officers and regiments. A list of leading politicians slated to be arrested had been prepared. Special plans were devised for the immediate seizure of Leftist newspapers and organizations, Government buildings, and private apartments of Cabinet members.

The Republican régime was to be overthrown and replaced by a dictatorship, with an eventual restoration of the monarchy in view. The directorate nominated to rule France included Marshal Pétain, General Weygand, Jean Chiappe and Jacques Doriot. The latter had left the Communist Party in 1934 and founded the *Parti Populaire Français*. He was a powerful orator with a bull-like voice. For a certain period the French fascists were intrigued with his possibilities as a leader of the masses. The Left repeatedly accused him of receiving financial support from Berlin. Doriot never dared to bring a single libel suit against his accusers.

A former Cabinet Minister once confided to me that the Sûreté Nationale (the French Secret Police) was in possession of documents proving that Doriot was in the

Chautemps: Anti-Climax

pay of Berlin and that he had used Nazi funds to buy a large estate in Belgium.

Other documents brought to light showed that the CSAR conspirators were lavishly subsidized by several French industrial magnates and by a foreign country. Neither the names of the industrialists nor that of the foreign country were disclosed. But it was scarcely a secret to the public: the finger of suspicion pointed straight at the Nazis, at the armaments magnate Schneider and the tire king Michelin.

Because the conspirators covered themselves with hoods at their secret meetings, they were called *"Cagoulards"* or "hooded men."

The Cabinet meeting in which the plot was discussed was a stormy one. Blum, Dormoy and Pierre Cot demanded that the whole story of the criminal plot be revealed to the country. They insisted that every link between the "hooded men" and the Nazis be made public, and that the proof of Pétain and Weygand's connection with the ring be made possible. The majority of the Cabinet and the President of the Republic were adamantly opposed to so drastic an exposure. Bonnet and Chautemps threatened to resign if the venerable Pétain were compromised and dragged through the mud of scandal.

Blum, Dormoy and Cot yielded to the pressure.

The demands of many Leftists that all fascist organizations be disbanded were ignored. Dormoy assured the Chamber of Deputies: "There is no need to invoke emergency laws. The laws of the Republic are sufficient to guarantee the security of the republican régime."

For months the Right newspapers carried on a campaign for the liberation of General Duseigneur, Count Pastré and Deloncle. These "Cagoulards" were later freed. They were never brought to trial. Their friends fêted them at a victory reception.

In December, Chautemps and Delbos visited London, where they conferred with Prime Minister Chamberlain, Eden and Lord Halifax. After the meeting, a communiqué was issued which blandly asserted that "the policy of non-intervention in Spain has been fully justified."

Thereupon, Yvon Delbos set out on a tour of eastern and southeastern Europe. It was a pale, ineffectual copy of Barthou's tour of 1934. Behind Barthou's journey there had been a conception: Hitler must and could be stopped by a powerful coalition. Behind the present trip was the haunting fear that France's vacillations plus Hitler's successive triumphs might have frightened away French allies. But it was backed by no strong desire to formulate a policy that could stop Hitler. Delbos

Chautemps: Anti-Climax

granted Warsaw new loans for armaments as an inducement. The Polish Foreign Minister, Colonel Beck, took the loans—and continued his pro-Hitler dalliance. Rumania also received French credits for war supplies. King Carol grabbed them, but they did not banish his suspicions that Hitler's projected invasion of Austria, then whispered about in a crescendo of gossip in all the chancelleries, would encounter no opposition from the Western democracies.

In Belgrade, Delbos witnessed a wildly enthusiastic reception. Tens of thousands of Jugoslavs cheered him with cries of "Long live France! Long live democracy!" —but the police brutally dispersed the crowds. One person was killed, several seriously wounded. *Le Temps,* which generally reflected the views of the Quai d'Orsay, wrote an article criticizing these demonstrators and praising the pro-French sentiments of Jugoslav Premier Stoyadinovitch. And he, more than any other, was responsible for dragging Jugoslavia into the orbit of the Axis!

Upon his arrival in Prague, Delbos was informed that the French police had uncovered a plot to assassinate him during his visit to Czechoslovakia. The French press received official instructions to hush up the revelations.

The reception of Delbos in Prague was a mixture of public enthusiasm and official anxiety. For many months the Nazi newspapers had been carrying articles about the mistreatment of the Sudeten Germans. The teacher of physical culture, Konrad Henlein, had won the majority of the Sudeten people for his "Sudeten-German Party," organized along Nazi lines.

In a private conversation with Delbos, Eduard Beneš, President of the Czechoslovak Republic, expressed his deep misgivings about the Nazis' plans. He opened a file compiled by the Czechoslovak Secret Police. It showed that the Nazi preparations for the annexation of Austria were nearing completion. Beneš added: "Our turn is next—after Austria. What is France going to do about it?"

Delbos suggested that compromises be made with Henlein: "You must deprive Hitler of every pretext for causing trouble."

Shortly thereafter, a Czechoslovakian Minister informed a French journalist that President Beneš "was shocked by the lack of understanding of Hitler's psychology displayed by Delbos."

While officially expressing satisfaction with the results of his trip, Delbos told the Foreign Affairs Committee of the Chamber that quite the contrary was true. He hoped that France "would not one day have to choose between Britain and her southeastern allies." This phrase gave rise to much speculation. Had the English thrown out hints during the Chautemps-Delbos visit to

Chautemps: Anti-Climax

London which even indicated the possibility of such a choice?

It was at this same meeting that former Premier Flandin vigorously advocated a policy of retrenchment by which France, behind the Maginot Line and with her eyes fixed on her colonial empire, could calmly face all eventualities in Europe. "The destiny of France," he orated, "lies in her Empire." As if the French Empire would not stand or fall with the position of France on the continent of Europe!

Another conference of leading French industrialists and bankers was called. They informed Chautemps that the presence of Socialists in his Cabinet was undermining confidence in the nation's currency. They aimed especially to "get" Interior Minister Dormoy who possessed all the startling documentary evidence implicating the backers of the "Cagoulards." As if to underline their advice, they organized a new "flight of capital." Chautemps took the hint. At a session of the Chamber where new financial measures were under discussion, he suddenly unleashed a violent attack against the Communists, hoping this would force a withdrawal of the Socialists from the Cabinet. Their resignation was only the prelude to the retirement of the entire Ministry in the middle of January 1938. The trick had worked like a charm.

At length Chautemps returned as Premier. This time

he headed a purely Radical-Socialist team, which included no Socialists.

By the end of January 1938 the Government was warned by its Berlin Ambassador that Germany would move against Austria in the next few weeks. The German Foreign Minister, Baron von Neurath, personally informed François Poncet to this effect.

The menace to Austria hung like a sword over Europe. With his keen sense of dramatic suspense, Hitler omitted his customary January 30 speech commemorating the anniversary of his nomination as Chancellor of the Reich. News filtered out of Germany alluding to differences between Hitler and his generals. The world was kept guessing as to which would emerge the victor.

Hitler discharged the pro-Nazi War Minister Colonel-General von Blomberg and the anti-Nazi Army Chief Colonel-General von Fritsch. In addition, he named the one-time champagne salesman, Joachim von Ribbentrop, Foreign Minister. General von Keitel, unknown outside Germany and later described as an "office general," was appointed Chief of the High Command; and General von Brauchitsch, considered the most gifted of the German Army leaders after von Fritsch, was made head of the Army.

The world was still guessing about this drastic shake-up when a new bombshell exploded. The thin, austere Chancellor of Austria, Kurt von Schuschnigg, was summoned to Hitler's villa in Berchtesgaden, where he was forced to endure in silence a two-hour tirade by the Führer. Several times Hitler called in his military advisers from an adjoining anteroom to impress on the hapless Schuschnigg that every preparation had been made for an attack on Austria. The Austrian Chancellor was stunned. Under this nerve-racking pressure he agreed to reconstruct his Cabinet and to make Hitler's henchman, Dr. Arthur Seyss-Inquart, Vice-Chancellor. The name of Seyss-Inquart was soon destined to become synonymous with traitor.

After this ominous visit Schuschnigg sought advice and help from Austria's traditional well-wisher, Mussolini. But no telephone communications could be put through to the Duce.

From that moment on, events raced forward at breakneck speed. First from England, then from France Hitler received reassurances that his move against Austria would be unopposed. In a speech before the House of Commons Prime Minister Chamberlain practically gave the go-ahead signal to Hitler to proceed against Austria. The utterance is a matter of historical record which will forever plague that disastrous man from Birmingham: "If I am right, as I am confident I am, in saying that the League as constituted today is unable to provide collective security for anybody, then I say that we must not try to delude ourselves, and, still worse, we must not try to delude small weak nations into thinking that they will be protected by the League against aggression and acting accordingly, when we know that nothing of the kind can be expected."

The French echo came in a speech by the "neo-realist" as Flandin was now called. Addressing the Chamber of Deputies he sneered: "The peace of Versailles is on its death-bed. . . . A policy based on the League of Nations, collective security and mutual assistance is outdated and old-fashioned." He begged the Chamber to "stop assuming a heroic pose, because Austria is 'co-ordinated.'" "Today we are sheltered behind the Maginot Line," he concluded. "If we are attacked, we will be strong enough to hold out until the freedom-loving countries of Europe rush to our assistance, as they did in 1914."

A young Radical-Socialist Deputy, André Albert, put his finger on the festering sore of French politics when he declared that the changed attitude of many former French nationalists could only be explained by the fact that "they have fallen into Hitler's snare, and are ready to support his anti-Comintern crusade."

Alongside Flandin's perfidious utterances, the Foreign Minister's speech was pale and hollow, certainly not calculated to impress Hitler in the least. Delbos asserted that "the independence of Austria was essential to the balance of power in Europe." He added: "It is true that our obligations to Czechoslovakia will, if it comes to the test, be faithfully observed." Chautemps declared: "France will not fail its alliance with Czechoslovakia." The distinction made between Austria and Czechoslovakia could hardly be called discouraging to Hitler.

Exactly two days before Hitler entered Austria, Camille Chautemps simply ran away. He demanded plenary powers of the Chamber. During the debate, he suddenly walked out of the hall. Some of his Cabinet colleagues were so taken aback that they did not understand what he meant. He had to make a sign to them to follow him. For the second time since Hitler came to power, without waiting for a vote, Chautemps resigned. He dumped the responsibility for the critical situation into the lap of his successor.

On March 12, when Hitler invaded Austria, France was again without a Government.

Léon Blum received Chautemps' shocking heritage. It took him four days to form a Cabinet. His idea was a broad national government, reaching from Maurice Thorez, leader of the Communists, to Louis Marin, head of the Right-wing Republicans. He was forced to abandon his project because the Right flatly refused to collaborate. Addressing a group of Deputies of the Right on the day Hitler drove triumphantly into the

Austrian town of Linz, Blum implored them to join the Government together with the Communists. "In case of war," he pointed out, "you are going to mobilize the Communists just like anybody else. And, after all, the Communists represent 1,500,000 laborers, farmers and small tradesmen. You have no right to expel them. You will need them when you want to speed up production of armaments. You will need their help just as you will need the help of the C.G.T. . . . What are you afraid of? Do you fear that they will weigh heavily on foreign policy? Remember then that as head of the Government I preserved my entire independence on the Spanish issue. Some among you have said that the presence of Communists in the French Government would have a bad effect abroad. That is a vicious and abominable argument, for France cannot accept any veto from a foreign power."

A few hours previously Edouard Daladier, addressing a meeting of the Radical-Socialist parliamentary faction, demanded: "On the day of general mobilization are you going to send the Communists into the Army or into concentration camps?"

Only five out of the 230-odd Rightist Deputies supported Blum's proposal. As Emile Buré, a nationalist editor, ironically wrote in *L'ordre*: "Down with Barthou! Down with Delcassé! Forward to the ideological crusade, even though we perish from it!"

Chautemps: Anti-Climax

The second Blum Cabinet was composed of Socialists and Radicals. Daladier was Vice-Premier and Defense Minister, Paul-Boncour was at the Foreign Office. Neither Chautemps, Bonnet nor Delbos figured in the combination.

While Blum was in office a second time, a new drive by General Franco made rapid advances. The Insurgent troops succeeded in cutting the Loyalist territory in two by slashing to the Mediterranean. Spanish Prime Minister Juan Negrin flew to Paris to make a desperate appeal to Blum for help. His plea fell on deaf ears. No substantial help was forthcoming from the French side. The control over the French-Spanish frontier was slightly relaxed, so as to permit some of the Russian supplies held up in French ports to get through. It was enough to halt Franco's drive on the Ebro River. But not enough to turn the tide.

The second Blum Government lasted three weeks. Its executioner was again the arrogant lord of the Senate, Joseph Caillaux. The Senate rejected the Cabinet's demand for plenary powers. Once more the Chamber voted confidence in the Government; once more Léon Blum refused to take up the gage of battle.

By now it was obvious that the "200 Families" had attained their first objective: the Popular Front was definitely disrupted.

10

MUNICH

EDOUARD DALADIER, who succeeded Léon Blum, has been responsible for some of the blackest pages in French history. While he was at the head of the Government, the independent Republic of Czechoslovakia was throttled, the Spanish Republic was murdered, and the terrible defeat of France was prepared.

The Cabinet he presented bore an uncanny resemblance to the one of February 6, 1934, when Daladier and his colleagues, panic-stricken during the fascist riots, had made a precipitate exit. Here they were again. Wily Camille Chautemps, "the champion parliamentary acrobat of France," was Vice-Premier; lean, sallow Georges Bonnet was Minister of Foreign Affairs; the weary, cranky *roué*, Albert Sarraut, was Minister of the Interior; the colorless Mayor of Reims, Marchandeau, was Finance Minister; Daladier's protégé and former under secretary, Guy La Chambre, tall, dark, elegant, was Air Minister; another of Daladier's fledglings, Raymond Patenôtre, a millionaire, was Minister of National Economy. Not to speak of the eternal Minister of Agriculture, sly little Henri Queuille. "It's like an old family album," jeered Flandin. That was his way of covering up his discomfiture at having been left out of the combination.

The only newcomers to this third Daladier Cabinet were Paul Reynaud who, as Justice Minister, hoped to succeed Daladier; ambitious Ludovic-Oscar Frossard, Minister of Labor, who nourished similar dreams of succession; and the man with the card-index mind, Georges Mandel, who took over the Ministry of Colonies.

This Cabinet was regarded with intense suspicion by the Left and greeted with anticipatory pleasure by the Right. Four years before, *Gringoire* had called Daladier "the man with the face of an evil priest who has wallowed in blood." And *Le Jour* had reviled him as "a sinister subaltern ready to sell and resell his soul." Now both papers purred welcomes to the "sincere Minister of National Defense, who has done so much for the security of France."

The Right realized that sooner or later this Cabinet would have to turn to it for support, thus becoming its prisoner. A change of majority in the Chamber was in the offing. The Radicals were again poised for a fall to the Right. The coming event cast its shadow before. The Chamber gave an all but unanimous vote of confidence to Daladier: 577 to 1. As one well-versed publicist put it: "Nobody was satisfied with the Government, so everybody voted for it."

The *Dépêche de Toulouse*, Sarraut's extremely influential provincial paper, etched a bleak picture of the state of the nation at that moment. It moaned: "We are literally encircled and reduced to the barest possibilities of strategic defense. We are on the defensive—on our land frontiers, on sea and in our colonies."

The Ministerial declaration, bathed in insipid generalities, gave no concrete sign of recognizing this tragic situation. "The Government"—it proceeded like a litany—"will not allow threats to cast a shadow over our frontiers, our lines of communication and our colonies. It will not permit foreign influences or unrest caused by undesirable aliens to interfere with its complete freedom of action." The first phrase was a bow to the Left, the second a bow to the Right. As for "undesirable aliens," this did not refer to the Nazis brazenly circulating in Paris to sap French morale. It meant those Frenchmen who insisted on aiding Loyalist Spain!

And then Georges Bonnet settled down to work.

A very speedy and expert job he did too. Bonnet always believed in the magic of well-padded "envelopes" distributed to the right people. So he began a steady stream of subsidies to the newspapers and politicians. Behind him loomed one of the most powerful banks in France, Lazard Frères. Whenever his departmental secret funds ran low, Lazard Frères would lend a helping hand.

Daladier was no less adroit than Bonnet in his manipulation of the press and public opinion. Often he permitted rumors to circulate that he was in disagreement with his Foreign Minister. He played his hand so masterfully that he even fooled such a wary old fox as his Minister of Colonies, Georges Mandel.

Time and again Mandel repeated to me that Daladier was much better than Bonnet; that he was for a policy of resistance, and that his long-nosed Foreign Minister would soon be sent into the wilderness. Like so many others, he too was deceived by Daladier.

Almost simultaneously with the formation of the Daladier Cabinet, the journals of the Right launched their campaign against Czechoslovakia. *Gringoire* ran the headline: "Do you want to die for Czechoslovakia?" It made a big stir. The campaign reached its first peak when *Le Temps* ran an article by Professor Joseph Barthélemy. The Professor's thesis was that the mutual assistance treaty between France and Czechoslovakia was no longer operative because of Hitler's denunciation of the Locarno treaty with which the French-Czechoslovak pact was linked. Herriot called it "a stab in the back of Beneš." Of course, when Stefan Osusky, Czechoslovakian Minister to Paris, paid a hurried visit to Bonnet, he was assured that the Government repudiated the article and would loyally and unhesitatingly carry out its obligations to Czechoslovakia.

The day after this encounter I saw Minister Osusky

and warned him not to place too much confidence in Bonnet's word. I was not the only one. Some of my journalist colleagues, who feared for Czechoslovakia, went so far as to tell the Czech envoy that Bonnet would double-cross him. But the self-assured Osusky left these warnings from various quarters unheeded. Up to the very last moment, even after he was cautioned by Cabinet Ministers, he was certain that Daladier and Bonnet were going to fulfill their treaty obligations.

Across the Channel, Chamberlain and Halifax were busy appeasing the Duce. On April 16 an agreement was signed between England and Italy. This was tantamount to a recognition of the conquest of Abyssinia and an official British blessing on Italian intervention in Spain. The accord stipulated that Italy must withdraw her "volunteers" at the close of the Spanish War. The agreement was something of a blow to France as well. She had confidently expected that the Anglo-Italian agreement would be made dependent on a similar pact being signed between France and Italy. At the end of April the French Cabinet met prior to the departure of Daladier and Bonnet for conversations with the British.

There was an unpleasant altercation at the meeting, and it closed on a note of distinctly bad feeling. Mandel, backed by several other Ministers, insisted that no commitments be made in London which would be contrary to France's treaty obligations, meaning the Franco-Czech and the Franco-Soviet pacts. Bonnet played the injured innocent. Nothing of the kind, he chided, was in his mind. Besides, any such decision by the Cabinet would hinder the departing Ministers' freedom of movement. But Mandel was obdurate, and finally Daladier and Bonnet were instructed in line with his proposals.

Before leaving for London, Daladier called in Minister Osusky and again assured him that France would honor her obligations.

Then the two men whose names are indissolubly linked to the fateful period of appeasement met in London. Daladier and Chamberlain differ greatly in many respects. The thin cadaverous Birmingham merchant with the gouty foot and the hawk-like beak, and the burly baker's son with the melancholy face to which he vainly strives to impart a Napoleonic scowl—what a contrast! The one, son of the meteoric Joseph Chamberlain and half-brother of a Foreign Minister before whom all doors automatically opened; the other a petty schoolteacher who had to worm his way through the devious labyrinth of French policy. Yet there is a strange resemblance in the characters of the two men. Both are vain, intolerant, unable to brook contradictions. Both believed in the miracle of direct conversations with the fascist dictators. Both believed they were indispensable for the continued preservation of the then present social order. Both lacked imagination. Both were horrified at the thought that the world might change—Chamberlain because he was part and parcel of Britain's ruling strata; Daladier because, with the instinct of the "little man" who has made good, he clung to the few privileges separating him from the lower classes.

Hence when these two men met, accompanied by their Foreign Ministers Halifax and Bonnet, they had no trouble in arriving at an understanding. At this very first meeting the policy which eventually led the two men to Munich was shaped. Of course, not in every detail. And perhaps without foreseeing how far they would have to travel in the next few months. There were numerous minor points on which Daladier and Chamberlain did not see eye to eye. These were conditioned by several elements: the different geographic positions, economic interests and internal problems of their respective countries. Chamberlain had an assured majority from the dominating party in his Parliament; Daladier had to rely on a coalition of votes from various parties which, in turn, were at variance on many issues. But these were non-essentials. The two Ministers were basically in agreement on the central problem: namely, the necessity of coming to terms with the dictators because of their belief that this was indispensable for the maintenance of the present order in Europe. It was this common outlook which caused them to set out together on the road to Munich. If they did not correctly appreciate all the consequences of their policy and all the concessions they would have to make, they were at any rate prepared to go a long way to meet the dictators. Once *en route*, they had to stumble wretchedly from milestone to milestone.

At this historic encounter in London, Chamberlain persuaded Daladier and Bonnet that the victory of General Franco was only a matter of days or weeks. So they joined forces to stifle the Spanish Loyalists' appeal for help at the impending meeting of the League of Nations.

Moreover, it was in London that the preposterous idea of mediation between the sovereign Czechoslovak Government and the Hitler-puppet Henlein was born. It arose from the Ministers' feeling that they could cope with Hitler's demands only if he did not attack Czechoslovakia. In the event of aggression, they feared that public opinion in their own countries would force them to participate in the conflict. So their main problem was to prevent Hitler from attacking Czechoslovakia, not in order to save that hardy democratic nation, but in order to destroy it. Their task was to contrive to prevent an attack, to give Hitler the fruits of victory without a war.

It was in London, too, that Daladier consented to continue the policy of his predecessors toward Soviet Russia. This meant a refusal to sanction conversations between the French and Russian General Staffs.

In return for their acceptance of Chamberlain's proposals, the French Ministers were promised that conversations between the French and British General Staffs would be extended. Much to the annoyance of the British, the Bonnet-inspired French papers claimed that a virtual military alliance had been effected. But Bonnet and Daladier had to inflate the agreement to get their Cabinet to swallow its more dubious portions.

The policy adopted in London dominated the foreign relations of France and Great Britain for the next year.

Back in Paris, Bonnet explained to the journalists in his clique that at the proper psychological moment a mediator would be sent to Czechoslovakia.

Immediately after the conclusion of these talks, the first pressure on the Czechoslovakian Cabinet was applied. The French envoy De Lacroix and the British Minister Newton visited Czechoslovakian Premier Dr. Hodza and urged him to start negotiations with Hitler's agent Henlein. The latter, encouraged by the attitude of the British and French, had formulated the Sudeten demands in an eight-point speech at Karlsbad. He demanded nothing less than the right to organize the

Munich

German section of Czechoslovakia into an autonomous territory on familiar Nazi lines.

In May the League of Nations Council heard an urgent appeal from Loyalist Spain. Its modern airy hall was literally packed with spectators. Foreign Minister Alvarez del Vayo presented the case for the Spanish Republic. The majority of the thirteen Foreign Ministers and delegates to whom he addressed himself did not even make a pretense of listening. Republican Spain demanded that Article 16 of the Covenant, providing for collective aid against aggression, be applied.

The cold voice of Lord Halifax announced that Great Britain would not associate herself with the proposal of the Spanish delegate. Georges Bonnet, wearing his customary double-breasted dark-blue suit, concurred in substance with Halifax's verdict. He spoke with disgusting suavity and even more disgusting regrets. The desperate, losing fight went on for three sittings. It was a scene of pathos and tragedy. Then the resolution which Señor del Vayo had presented to the Council was put to a vote. The "No's" of Lord Halifax and Georges Bonnet fell in the dead silence like quick slaps. The physical tension of the listeners was almost unbearable. Only the Soviet Foreign Commissar, Maxim Litvinov, supported the Loyalist cause.

Next to me a young woman representing a Swiss

newspaper began to cry. Señor del Vayo and his assistant left the room deathly pale but sternly erect. I dashed for the telephones to flash the news to my home office.

In the lobby of his hotel Bonnet, embarrassed and ill at ease, attempted to explain to a few journalists that he could not have acted otherwise, but that France would not allow Spain to fall prey to Hitler and Mussolini. Somebody shouted, "You've killed Spain!" Bonnet blanched and hurriedly turned on his heel.

A few days later he received a foretaste of totalitarian gratitude. In a speech at Genoa the Duce bluntly declared that France and Italy were "on opposite sides of the barricade." He was referring patently to Spain. Those commentators in France who had so often foretold the inevitable deterioration of Italo-German relations were also rudely awakened. The Duce asserted no less bluntly that from the Italian mobilization on the Brenner Pass in 1934 to March 1938 "much water has flowed beneath the bridges of the Tiber, the Danube, the Spree, the Thames and even the Seine. Everything diplomatic and political which passed under the name of Stresa is dead and buried, and as far as we are concerned, will never be resuscitated."

If the Duce had buried the Stresa Front, certain French circles had not. Although Mussolini's speech rendered his admirers in Paris speechless for a spell, they quickly recovered and resumed their plotting. Even Hitler's visit to Rome, where he was received like a triumphal conqueror and where the two dictators demonstrated the solidity of the Rome-Berlin Axis, did not dampen the Paris Mussolini-ites. Hope springs eternal. . . .

A new event intervened to focus attention on Nazi Germany. Hitler massed a huge army on the German-Czech frontier. An attack on Czechoslovakia appeared imminent. On May 21, 1938 the Czechoslovakian Government ordered partial mobilization. Would guns supplant diplomats?

I went to the French Foreign Office where I was received by a high official. He informed me of the latest telegrams from the French Ambassador in Berlin. Their contents confirmed the news of Germany's elaborate preparations on the Czech border. The very latest dispatch announced that the British Ambassador had ordered the personnel of the Embassy to make ostensible preparations to leave the country.

For the next few hours peace hung in the balance. Hitler, in the face of such unexpected resistance, backed down. The attack against Czechoslovakia was temporarily off.

Hitler yielded on this occasion in spite of the fact

that the attitude of Poland, Rumania and Jugoslavia abetted his plans. The Polish Ambassador to France, summoned by Bonnet, declared categorically that the Poles would not support the French should the latter go to war to defend Czechoslovakia, and that under no circumstances would Poland permit the passage of Soviet troops. The Jugoslav Minister left no doubt that Premier Stoyadinovitch was exceedingly proud of the freshly signed Italian-Jugloslav agreement. France could count on no help from that quarter. The statement of the Rumanian Minister, though less emphatic than those of his Polish and Jugoslav colleagues, was nevertheless full of reservations and objections. France could not count on Rumania either. The lesson of Vienna was too fresh in the memory of the small States. Naturally Bonnet went to great pains to have the discouraging news spread. So Hitler undoubtedly knew all about Bonnet's conversations with the three envoys— and yet he did not attack. Why?

Winston Churchill stated: "If war is averted, as I believe it will be, it will be due to a rudimentary and emergency form of collective security." Indeed, something of that kind seemed to emerge on May 21. The Czechs mobilized and made it plain that they would resist. The sensational preparations for departure made by the British Ambassador in Berlin led Hitler to believe that the British and the French would come to the aid of Czechoslovakia. There was no doubt in his mind

Munich

that the Soviet Union would fulfill its obligations under the Czech-Soviet treaty of mutual assistance. And there were other reasons which induced him to hesitate. The German Army did not yet feel strong enough to risk a general conflict. Far from it. The line of fortifications on the Franco-German border, later called the Westwall, was only in its blue-print stages. Against all these odds Hitler did not dare to attack.

The twenty-first of May could have been a turning point in European history, but because of Daladier and Bonnet it remained an accident, a flurry without consequences. Two days later the Nazi papers attacked the "war-mongers" who spread "lies that Germany had mobilized." And soon Daladier and Bonnet adopted the same argument.

To a few parliamentarians who visited him, Daladier declared with short-tempered irritation that on May 21 Beneš's irresponsibility had brought Europe to the verge of war. Not only had Beneš mobilized, growled Daladier, although the Germans had not done so, but he had also refused to accede to Henlein's demands which, after all, were acceptable.

Such tactics as these could not fail to have repercussions in Czechoslovakia. On June 10 the Czech Government accepted the Henlein demands as a basis for negotiations. Slowly, implacably, the door was opening for the official Nazi entry into the last democracy in central Europe.

Having dealt Czech morale a rude blow, Bonnet and Daladier turned back again to Spain. At the beginning of June, Bonnet had a long conference with former Premier Flandin. Then on June 11 Flandin made a very significant pronouncement. Asserting roundly that the war in Spain was "the greatest menace to the peace of France and that an anti-Franco policy is contrary to the interests of France and dictated by Moscow," he cried: "The French people will not allow the Popular Front, after having accumulated so many ruins in two years, to add that of war."

Two days later Daladier ordered the French-Spanish frontier to be hermetically sealed. Republican Spain suffered a virtual blockade. Afterward Daladier appeared before the executive committee of his party to announce: "We shall stick to the method of non-intervention, because we want the destiny of Spain to be settled by the Spaniards themselves."

In a new attempt to stem the Insurgent tide, the Spanish Republican troops crossed the Ebro in a well-prepared offensive. A Radical Deputy claimed that when Georges Bonnet heard of this striking Republican success, he was almost sick with rage.

For a few days in July, Spain and Czechoslovakia were crowded off the headlines by quite another—and more peaceful—event. Paris awaited the visit of the King and Queen of England. The City of Light put on its most ceremonial array. The city was dressed in flags and bathed in a sea of color. Hundreds of thousands of spectators, half-curious and half-proud, massed to express to the visitors the true sentiments of Paris. The Minister of Interior, Albert Sarraut, was less concerned with popular enthusiasm than with safety measures. The poor man had not forgotten the murders in Marseilles. So now he ordered thousands of seizures and temporary detentions, especially among the German and Italian anti-fascist refugees. When King George and Queen Elizabeth rode through the brilliantly decorated streets of Paris they could see soldiers and Gardes Mobiles by the tens of thousands, and the good people of Paris by the hundreds of thousands. But the people could not see them! Their view was blocked completely by a solid wall of armed guards.

Parades, social functions and glittering receptions followed. The most elaborate affair was at the Quai d'Orsay where Mme. Odette Bonnet saw one of her dreams come true: she played hostess to the Royal couple. But behind this shimmering curtain of festivities the world of realities plied its course. That week Daladier and Bonnet met Chamberlain and Halifax and decided on the man who was to go to Prague as mediator between the sovereign Czech Government and an opposition group directed unmistakably from the outside. The British Ministers hit on the name of Lord Walter Runciman. He was known for his pro-German views. During the first World War he had been a member of the liberal Asquith Government. A wealthy industrialist himself, Lord Runciman had extensive connections with Germany's magnates. These were some of the attributes which probably led Chamberlain to choose him.

Lord Runciman arrived in Prague on August 4. The initiative in the Czechoslovakian question had passed completely into the hands of the British; the Franco-Czech alliance was overshadowed by Lord Runciman's task. Lord Runciman's mission was viewed with deep concern by the few French journalists who fought against the appeasement trend. As one of them expressed it: "If Lord Runciman is not extremely careful, he may easily open the dikes to the rapid absorption of central Europe by Germany."

The tension heightened. Hitler ordered the mobilization of more than one and a half million men—to be kept with the colors for at least twelve weeks. About half a million Germans were literally torn from their dwellings and transported overnight to the western border of France. They were needed to accelerate the construction of the Westwall or "Siegfried Line." The Nazi press ostentatiously publicized this mobilization and the feverish work being done on the fortifications. The war of nerves was in full swing. What was France's answer? Mobilization? No—a speech by Daladier.

On August 21 the Premier spoke over the radio. His broadcast gave no comfort to the Czechs. There was not a word in the address to bolster up their morale in their terrible plight. But there *was* a broad hint to Hitler that the French Premier was ready to go to any lengths to meet him. The crucial words were: "Like all war veterans, I am ready to do anything to prevent the destruction of European civilization." These words were not precisely calculated to stop the threat of aggression.

This radio speech marked a turning point in French internal policy as well. It was Daladier's final break with the Left. He told of how business was suffering in the country, how the middle classes were suffering, and then, turning to labor, he categorically asserted: "France must get back to work."

He explained what he meant by this cryptic phrase —the removal of the bulwark of France's recent social reforms, the forty-hour week. This achievement, precious to French labor, would have to be set aside. France would have to work forty-eight hours a week and still more, if necessary. Overtime, he emphasized, cannot be paid "at the present prohibitive rates" and cannot depend "on idle formalities."

Daladier was Vice-Premier when the Blum Cabinet introduced the forty-hour week. Now he joined the chorus of French reactionaries who howled that the social legislation of the Popular Front had caused irreparable damage to French production. He accepted the pet theory of big business that if capital was to contribute to the swift rearming of France, it should be assured of a higher rate of profit. He left out of account the sabotage of production by big business. A very detailed and impressive memorandum was drawn up by the Trade Union Federation, illustrating how the employers sought to prove that nationalization of the arms factories had diminished their productivity. When the armaments business came under State control, most of the former owners and managers were kept on as heads of their factories. They made no serious efforts to speed production. Daladier found no words of criticism for them. Not a murmur about the muddle and disorganization, particularly in the aircraft factories where the constant changes in design kept the workers idle for days and weeks at a time. Not a hint of the stealthy attacks by the "200 Families" against the franc. And not a breath about their connivance with the dictators.

Daladier was well aware that some three million people in France, including many skilled workers, were unemployed. If anybody was to be put back to work, they should have been. They would have welcomed nothing better than an end to the demoralizing effects of forced idleness. Instead, Daladier decreed a lengthening of the working hours.

He evidently decided to separate himself from his allies on the Left who had hoisted him back into power. For him the Popular Front was a convenient vehicle for his political comeback. Now he insisted on being the master. He did not relish being reminded of the program he had sworn to defend, of the obligations he had assumed. For him a program was a scrap of paper. But political power—that was something else again. He had once hoped that the Popular Front would make him and his party the strongest factors in French political life. When Blum and the Socialists came out on top, he bore it with an outward show of loyalty. But inside he harbored deep, ungovernable resentment.

During the first months of his Premiership, Daladier realized that the political situation furnished him with powerful trump-cards. The Right was looking for a man who could successfully oppose the People's Front and stifle its rebirth. The reception he received from their newspapers indicated that they were ready to accept him as the "man of the hour." True, they hoped to make him their prisoner. But he, in turn, hoped to make them his. They needed him, he felt, just as much as he needed them. They would not pester him with daily pinpricks about the programs and promises he had formulated years ago. Bygones were bygones. They would let him go on, provided only he struck against the Left. In the present set-up they did not have a single man who could do the job. He, Daladier, could.

Inwardly he had always been closer to them than to the Left. Force of circumstance had made him a prominent man of the Left and scapegoat of the Right. As early as his first tenure of office in 1933 he had attempted to rid himself of the Socialists and come to terms with the Right. The situation had not been ripe for it. Now it was. He could join the forces for which he had always felt an attraction. Now he could make the Radicals fall to the Right—and without playing second fiddle. For the first time in its history the Radical-Socialist Party could turn coat and still stay on top.

Many Radical politicians felt the same way as Daladier. They had had enough of the Popular Front. Nazi propaganda, seconded by the appeasement elements in France, had made enormous headway in the top circles of the Radical-Socialist Party. As a matter of fact, their present leaders were the most ardent of the appeasers.

That Daladier consummated the rupture with the Left and that he chose a moment of extreme international tension to alienate French labor, seems to bear out the contention that he had already made up his mind to surrender to Hitler's demands. A general who expects to lead his army into battle does not tell his troops on the eve of the conflict that he is going to cut their rations and pay. That is practically what Daladier did in his radio speech. Dr. Goebbels grasped the full import of Daladier's words. He is reported to have told the Führer after the French Premier's broadcast: "After that speech I don't see how he can stand up against us."

Through a subsequent indiscretion it became known why Daladier had decided to deliver this address. It had transpired at a meeting with Joseph Caillaux, Anatole de Monzie, and Martinaud-Déplat, a former Radical Deputy. Caillaux explained to him at great length that the present situation of the country was a guarantee that France would not be drawn into a war, even one in defense of allied Czechoslovakia. Caillaux was categorical: Frenchmen would not fight for the Czechs, hence it was imperative to come to terms with Hitler. He added that the present juncture must not only be used to clarify Franco-German relations, but also, as he put it, "to put the French house in order." The prevailing tension seemed to him a suitable moment to abolish the social legislation of the Popular Front which the Senate detested.

Daladier was at first reluctant to accept Caillaux's

proposals. He thought an attack on the forty-hour week might antagonize labor too strongly and might lead to trouble, which in the present situation appeared highly undesirable. But finally he agreed, entrusting Martinaud-Déplat to prepare the draft of the radio speech.

The address stirred the French people profoundly. They felt themselves stabbed from behind. Excitement ran so high that the Ministers of Labor and Public Works resigned. Daladier replaced them with two men from the same party, the Union Socialiste Républicaine. The new Minister of Labor was Charles Pomaret, whose charming wife helped him make considerable advances in his career. The Minister of Public Works was the brilliant, successful and unscrupulous lawyer, Anatole de Monzie. He was a friend of Laval, an admirer of Mussolini, an unswerving enemy of the Czechs, and one of the wiliest schemers in French politics. His inclusion in the Cabinet was a program in itself. He strengthened the appeasement group decidedly.

Then Georges Bonnet made a cunning move. On September 4, at Pointe de Grave, a monument was unveiled to the American troops who landed in France in 1917.

Preceding Bonnet, the American Ambassador Mr. Bullitt asserted: "If war comes to Europe once again, nobody can predict whether the United States will be involved or not." And then Bonnet made a pronouncement which created considerable excitement in the United States. Referring to American-French friendship, he ventured: "The one friend is irresistibly compelled to rush to the aid of the other friend who is in danger." It was a daring thing for a French Foreign Minister to say; especially for a man like Georges Bonnet who had spared no efforts to belittle the help France could expect from the United States in case of war. Why, then, did he utter it? Paul Reynaud, shocked by the unfavorable American reaction to the speech, maintained that he did so in order to provoke an official American denial. He would then be able to brandish it to discourage the "war-mongers" among his colleagues. Another Cabinet Minister expressed a similar conviction to me.

Bonnet also volunteered the statement, in the same talk, that France would faithfully carry out her obligations to Czechoslovakia. He did so under sharp pressure from Georges Mandel, who threatened to resign if the Foreign Minister did not include such a pledge in his address. It was the seventh official declaration, since Daladier took office, of France's "loyalty to her treaty obligations."

On September 5 the Maginot Line was manned. About 80,000 specialists were called to the colors.

The next day the combined effect of Bonnet's declarations and these military measures was shattered by an article written by Émile Roche which appeared in his paper, *La République*. Roche wrote: "If Czechs and Germans cannot live together within the framework of the centralized Czech State, then they must be separated." The tie-up between Roche, chairman of the Radical-Socialist Party of the Northern Département, and Daladier and Bonnet was a known fact. As a matter of fact, without assistance from the secret funds of the two politicians, the paper could never have been kept alive. It was one of those so-called "confidential papers," read exclusively in political circles because it was regarded as an unofficial mouthpiece of the Premier.

Chamberlain's mouthpiece in England, the *London Times*, made a similar statement on September 7.

On September 8 the annual Nazi Party Congress in Nuremberg opened. The Quai d'Orsay was in receipt of several warnings that on September 13, the day of Hitler's key speech, the assault on Czechoslovakia would begin. That, as I have previously stated, was the very thing Daladier and Chamberlain were striving at any price to prevent. They would be able to come to terms with Hitler only if no attack were forthcoming. If Hitler struck, public indignation in Great Britain and France would probably force the two governments to take action. So on September 11, Neville Chamberlain leaped

Munich

into the breach. He issued a statement, reading: "Great Britain could not remain aloof if there were a general conflict in which the integrity of France was threatened. ... It is of the utmost importance that Germany should make no mistake about it; she cannot with impunity carry out a rapid and successful military campaign against Czechoslovakia without the fear of intervention by France and even Great Britain."

This declaration won a few valuable days of respite, enough for Georges Bonnet to finish his work of demoralization.

First of all, the notion that Soviet Russia was ready to stand by the Czechs had to be destroyed. Bonnet hurried off to Geneva for a talk with Litvinov. The Soviet Foreign Commissar proposed a joint *démarche* by Britain, France and the U.S.S.R. in favor of the Czechs, and the application of Article 11 of the Covenant of the League of Nations. The proposal remained unanswered, unaccepted.

On September 12, back from his trip to Geneva, Bonnet warned the Cabinet that Soviet Russia was by no means prepared to fulfill its obligations; that Litvinov took refuge in a clause of the Czech-Soviet treaty which required consent of the League of Nations for Russian aid; that Rumania was not disposed to allow the passage of Soviet troops.

At that same meeting Bonnet also dwelt on the poor

condition of the Red Army. He placed before his colleagues "reliable" information to prove that the Red Army was unable to wage war. The source of this information was the Japanese military attaché.

Bonnet's assertions about the Russian evasion were characterized by the Soviet Ambassador to Paris, Jacob Suritz, as downright lies. This he stated to a French Cabinet Minister who approached him, adding that Litvinov had affirmed without reservations that Russia was ready to help, if France would do so too. Litvinov had asked for a vote in the League of Nations, but only in order to overcome possible Rumanian opposition to the passage of the Red Army across its territory.

In a statement made much later in Chicago, President Beneš of Czechoslovakia explained that the Russians had offered help even if the French refused to collaborate.

The next day, September 13, Hitler was to deliver his speech in Nuremberg. Outwardly it was the big event of the day. The world held its breath awaiting the Führer's outburst. But in reality something more momentous occurred that day. In Paris, at the meeting of the French Cabinet, Georges Bonnet succeeded in swinging a majority of the Ministers to a policy of surrender to Hitler. He did so by placing before them what he called the résumé of a memorandum prepared by General Gamelin on the state of the French armed forces.

Munich

According to this résumé, the French Army was so inferior, especially in the air, to the Germans that it could not risk an armed conflict. The logical conclusion was that the French military situation was hopeless. Asked whether the résumé did not deal with only one side of the picture, Bonnet replied that it dealt "with all the essential points" in Gamelin's report.

Naturally it created a profound impression on the Cabinet. Only six Ministers opposed Bonnet's defeatist attitude. The majority followed his lead. Daladier did nothing to soften the shock of Bonnet's report. President Lebrun supported the Foreign Minister wholeheartedly.

That same day other strange things happened. Daladier saw the British Ambassador twice, Bonnet saw him once. Bonnet told Sir Eric Phipps that France was in no position to fight. As a confirmation he let him read the famous résumé.

That same day a Parisian bank, known to have close connections with Bonnet, issued orders to its agents to buy up pounds sterling.

That same evening Daladier communicated with Chamberlain by telephone, proposing that the British Prime Minister seek direct contact with the Führer.

On September 14 it was announced that Prime Minister Chamberlain would fly to Berchtesgaden to meet Hitler.

On September 15 Hitler in Berchtesgaden demanded of Chamberlain that a plebiscite be held in all predominately German Czechoslovakian districts on the question of Anschluss of these territories with the Reich. Chamberlain promised to bring him an agreement to this demand within a week.

In a speech delivered two days before, Hitler had declared that Beneš must come to terms with Henlein within the framework of the Czech State. Now, in the face of such weak-kneed surrender, he raised his price. On September 18 Mussolini publicly declared that in the event of a conflict "the side of Italy was chosen."

That same day at a conference in London, Chamberlain, Halifax, Daladier and Bonnet agreed that all Czechoslovakian districts with more than 50% of Germans should be handed over to Hitler—without a plebiscite. It was even more than Hitler had asked for.

The day after the London meeting, Emile Roche, Daladier's spokesman, said in *La République*: "If the Czechs reject the London plan, it will be their own lookout. There is no treaty that we know of which would compel us to intervene." And Léon Blum wrote in the Socialist organ *Populaire*: "War has probably been averted. But it has been averted in such conditions . . . that I cannot feel any joy, and am merely filled with mixed feelings of cowardly relief and shame."

The French Cabinet met and accepted London's decisions. But at the insistence of Mandel and Reynaud, it was decided that no pressure was to be brought to bear on the Czech Government. After the Cabinet meeting Bonnet summoned the Czech envoy. An hour later when Stefan Osusky left the Quai d'Orsay, he was a shattered, broken man. "Here you see the condemned man. He has been sentenced without even being heard," were his words to the waiting newspaper men. It was a deeply tragic sight.

Here is how "no pressure" was brought to bear on the Czechs:

On September 19 the London decisions were communicated in an official note to the Czech Government. The French people did not learn the full extent of these proposals until a week later.

On September 20 the Czech Government rejected the London proposals. That evening British Minister Newton informed the Czech Government in Prague that "if it persisted in the rejection, the British Government would disinterest itself in her fate." French Minister de Lacroix was in firm accord with this attitude.

On September 21, at two o'clock in the morning, President Beneš was awakened by the two envoys for their fifth *démarche* in twenty-four hours. They were in a hurry because the week accorded for Chamberlain's reply to Hitler was almost up. They brought an ultimatum: "If war breaks out because of the Czech Government's negative attitude, France will not take action, and in such an event Czechoslovakia will be held responsible for having provoked a war. If the Czechs join forces with the Russians, the war may become an antibolshevist crusade from which it will be very difficult for the French and British Governments to dissociate themselves."

The content of this ultimatum, as here given, was revealed after Munich by the Czech Propaganda Minister.

After having asked the envoys to put their declarations in writing, Beneš summoned the Czech Cabinet. Faced with the ultimatum from their French ally, the Czechoslovakian Government accepted the London proposals.

On the same day Bonnet reported to the French Cabinet that the Czechs had agreed without pressure to the Franco-British proposals. Even as he spoke, demonstrators marched through the streets of Prague shouting: "Down with France!" French decorations and medals were piled up in a heap in front of the French Legation. The head of the French military mission, General Faucher, resigned. He sent back his military decorations and joined the Czech Army.

Several Cabinet Ministers—Reynaud and Mandel among them—tendered their resignations to Daladier, leaving it to him to make the proper announcements when he saw fit.

The reactionary French press exulted in the Government's decision with a frenzy of enthusiasm. Editorials praising Georges Bonnet crowded the columns of these papers. The organ of the Left-wing Radical-Socialists, *L'Oeuvre,* which for a long time had opposed the "fall of the Radicals to the Right," had joined the appeasers from the outset of the Czech crisis. Its editor, Jean Piot, printed a long article hailing Georges Bonnet as the savior of peace. That evening, at a café where he had been drinking, Piot confided to a few colleagues that he was paid 20,000 francs for this article.

On September 22 Chamberlain flew to Godesberg to keep his appointment with Hitler.

The "Battle of Godesberg," as it was called in the pro-appeasement papers, lasted for two days. Confronted with new and more drastic demands from the Nazi leader, Chamberlain had to make at least a show of resistance.

Our correspondent phoned us from Godesberg that the conversations were bogging down; that Chamberlain was not going to give in. But he also told us that there was talk of a new conference, in which France and Italy were to participate.

The longer the Godesberg discussions dragged on, the higher the political temperature in Paris mounted. Attempts were made to unseat the Cabinet. Some of the Ministers who had handed Daladier their resignations were making overtures to the President of the Senate, white-bearded old Jules Jeanneney. Herriot, President of the Chamber, was also approached to form a new Cabinet. Blum and his former Foreign Minister, Yvon Delbos, went to the extent of throwing out feelers to the extreme Rightist former Premier, André Tardieu. Czech Minister Osusky received visits from a number of parliamentarians and Ministers. They implored him to persuade Czechoslovakia to stand firm.

By the next day the Daladier Cabinet seemed doomed. The Communists asked for Parliament to be convened. If the Chamber were forced into an open vote, it appeared certain that a majority would not—or could not—associate itself with the intrigues of Daladier and Bonnet. At this crucial moment Albert Chichéry, parliamentary leader of the Radical-Socialists, saved the situation for the Government. He induced a majority of the Radical-Socialist Deputies to oppose the reconvening of Parliament.

Two versions were circulated explaining why Chichéry's stratagem proved successful. One was that Bonnet simply bought off some of the wavering Radicals and instructed them to take a stand against any convocation of the Chamber. The other was that Daladier threatened to dissolve it, following which he would go to the country on the electoral issue: "Peace or War." He would endorse and support with the secret funds only those Radical-Socialists who upheld him. However,

Munich

under pressure from the General Staff, partial mobilization was decreed in France, calling between 600,000 and 700,000 men to the colors.

Lord Halifax, meanwhile, had informed the Czechs that he could no longer assume responsibility for keeping them from mobilizing.

On September 24 Chamberlain returned from Godesberg. It was rumored that he had not been able to come to an understanding with Hitler. War seemed to draw nearer.

That same day the exodus from Paris began. Tens of thousands, mainly well-to-do people, left the capital in a hurry. My telephone rang incessantly. Friends and acquaintances were saying good-bye. Early in the afternoon my editor discussed with the staff plans for evacuation of the paper if war should come. The Government was supposed to be going to Clermont-Ferrand or to Tours. The business manager made arrangements with a near-by provincial printing plant to get out our paper. The big newspapers were said to be following the Government's lead.

It looked pretty dismal. On the same day Bonnet mapped his strategy for a counter-offensive. As Flandin has since revealed, both men had agreed upon a plan. Flandin would make an appeal to the French people for peace. So would André Delmas, head of the influential Teachers Union. Delmas guaranteed to persuade his executive committee to issue a strong anti-war manifesto, which would be posted all over the country. The funds for publicizing Flandin's appeal were advanced by Bonnet.

On September 25, the French Cabinet met to discuss the attitude Daladier and Bonnet should take in London, where they had again been summoned by Chamberlain. It was decided that the Ministers should adhere to the first London proposals—cession of the Czechoslovakian districts containing more than 50% of Germans—and that they should insist that no more pressure be brought to bear on the Czechs. Bonnet was also instructed to urge the Poles to cease their hostile anti-Czech maneuvers.

Later Bonnet told one of the journalists accompanying him that should an emergency arise, Mussolini would be asked to step in and mediate. "I am sure there will be no war," insisted Bonnet. "There is no need for you to evacuate your family." The correspondent, a friend of mine, phoned me immediately. We were both considering sending our wives to the country.

On September 26 Hitler spoke at a big meeting in the Berlin Sportpalast. He lashed out at Beneš and the democracies with the utmost scorn and contempt. He briefly complimented Mr. Chamberlain. Then he made one of those promises which he always had on tap but which he never dreamed of keeping. "The Sudeten demand is my last territorial claim in Europe," he shouted.

"Once the Sudeten problem is settled, I am not interested in the remaining Czech State. I am even ready to guarantee its frontiers. We don't want any Czechs!"

On September 26, too, a communiqué was issued by the British Foreign Office. The key passage read: "The German claim that the transfer of the Sudeten areas has already been conceded by the French, British and Czechoslovak Governments. But if, in spite of all efforts made by the British Prime Minister, a German attack is made upon Czechoslovakia, the immediate result must be that France will be bound to come to her assistance and that Great Britain and Russia will certainly stand by France."

This was a statement of tremendous importance. It would bring home to the French people the real situation. A whispering campaign had been gaining ground that France would have to stand alone. But this unequivocal declaration made it plain that she could count on British and Russian help. If Hitler attacked Czechoslovakia, he might have to fight the French, Czech and Red Armies, and the British and French Fleets. Unless something were done by Bonnet, the French people would finally get a clear picture of the real proportions of the forces involved. Then they could not help but draw favorable conclusions for France.

So Bonnet's first task was to annul the probable effect of this communiqué on the French morale.

On September 27 the papers of the Right, on Bonnet's instructions, stated that the alleged communiqué from London was a *"fausse nouvelle."* The French Foreign Office, they continued, when asked replied that it knew nothing about it.

That same day a delegation of Rightist Deputies visited Daladier to inquire about the London statement. He showed them a note from Bonnet saying that the declaration "emanated from a civil servant of no importance in the London Foreign Office." The effects of Whitehall's pronouncement were muffled and killed.

Meanwhile, the *Agence Havas* reported from Germany that Hitler had ordered general mobilization for 2 P. M. September 28. Again the appeasement press howled. Again on Bonnet's instructions, they screeched that the item was an invention of agents of Moscow who wanted to drive the country to a war. They fell back on their old stand-by: the Quai d'Orsay reported having no confirmation of the news.

Sensational posters were stuck up throughout the country. They read in part: "Frenchmen, they are fooling you! The Popular Front wants to drag you into war and is spreading false news to make you believe that war is inevitable." The posters, signed by former Premier Flandin, protested against mobilization. A few hours later they were torn down.

Similarly posters of the Teachers Union appeared, declaring that "it was intolerable that for reasons of procedure or prestige the statesmen should break off negotiations."

From London, Chamberlain wired President Beneš that Hitler intended to invade Czechoslovakia on September 28. That evening the British Prime Minister delivered a radio speech.

We listened to this broadcast in my chief's office. When it was over, most of us had the feeling that Britain and France would give in. Two passages were particularly striking. One was: "How horrible, fantastic, incredible it is that we should be digging trenches and trying on gas-masks here, because of a quarrel in a faraway country between people of whom we know nothing."

That was the way many people in Britain and France felt. Chamberlain faithfully expressed the sentiments of a large section of the middle classes in both countries. But it seemed strange that a British Prime Minister would express such sentiments if he were really eager to bolster up the fighting spirit of his own country and in that of his Ally. It indicated, rather, that he was willing to bolster up the courage of those who did not want to fight.

The other notable passage was: "I would not hesitate to pay even a third visit to Germany if I thought it would do any good. But at this moment I can see nothing further I can usefully do in the way of mediation." The implication of this phrase might be that if somebody else could see something he could usefully do in the way of mediation—Mussolini for instance—then Chamberlain would certainly not hesitate to go to Germany again. It was a curiously ominous reminder of Bonnet's remark to my friend that Mussolini was going to step in at the last moment. For the past several days some of the Bonnet newspapers had predicted mediation by Mussolini.

In the early morning hours of September 28 the British Fleet was mobilized. I was informed of this mobilization over the telephone by a high official of the Quai d'Orsay. "So it's going to be war after all?" I inquired. He answered, "It looks that way."

"And what does Bonnet think?" I probed.

"Well, he's optimistic. Just now he's in his office with François Piétri and his Chef de Cabinet, Jules Henry."

Nothing good could come from the counsels of the Mussolini-admirer Piétri and the Bonnet-admirer Henry. I rang up several of my journalist friends. The result: odds of 75% to 25% that war was imminent. I jumped into a taxi and rode down to see one of the Ministers who was opposed to Bonnet's policy. He was still working in his office. Here was his opinion: "There's a majority in the Chamber for a policy of resistance. A solid majority! Daladier will have to follow it." He was

Munich

so convinced of this majority that he continued to speak of it for half an hour. This time, he assured me, Hitler was in for it.

"How about mediation by Mussolini?" I asked.

He answered forthwith. "Only if Hitler asks for it. Neither France nor Great Britain can ask the man to mediate who, ten days ago, declared that Italy's side is chosen in the event of a conflict."

"But the papers are full of stuff like that."

"Newspaper talk," he retorted with a peremptory gesture.

While we were conversing in those early hours of September 28, the telephone wires connecting Paris with Berlin and London were hot. Bonnet was sending new instructions to François Poncet in Berlin and to Charles Corbin in London. The former was instructed to make new and more far-reaching proposals to Hitler—proposals which virtually signified an acceptance of his Godesberg demands. Corbin in London was told to persuade the British, through their Ambassador in Rome, to approach Mussolini on mediation. Yet all this time a leading French Cabinet Minister was assuring me that it was impossible.

And in Berlin, Hitler had just heard from Chamberlain. "I still think that you can have what you ask for without war."

Now the flight from Paris reached its peak. All in all, over 250,000 people moved out of the capital.

On September 28 at noon war seemed inevitable. . . .

That same afternoon the capitulation of the democracies became official. Chamberlain announced in the House of Commons that, through the mediation of Mussolini, the British and French Prime Ministers were invited by Hitler to meet him in Munich.

A day later Daladier and Chamberlain flew to Munich to meet Hitler and Mussolini. That evening the Munich Agreement was signed, and the Sudeten areas of Czechoslovakia were handed over to Hitler. The inner and the outer pincer-movement against France had joined hands for the first time in the Bavarian capital.

Here the story of Munich ends, and the story of Prague begins.

11

MUNICHMEN AND ANTI-MUNICHMEN

THE outburst of public enthusiasm which greeted Daladier and Chamberlain in Munich showed the real sentiments of the German people. They too were frightened by the idea that twenty years after the first war, a new one was about to begin. But at the same time the victory of Munich encouraged the belief that Hitler could get away with anything. It suggested that the democracies were unable to put up any real resistance.

After Munich, Daladier and Chamberlain asserted that while the Godesberg conditions were those which a victor would impose on a victim, the Munich conditions placed Czechoslovakia on an equal footing with Germany for all future conversations resulting from the accord. How they figured that out, remains their secret. Before Munich, Czechoslovakia had a well-trained army and a formidable fortification line. She lost both of these on September 29. To speak of an independent Czechoslovakia after Munich was a tragic, unholy farce.

Nor did Daladier and Chamberlain treat this country as an independent sovereign State. She was not allowed to participate in the negotiations either in London or in Munich. When the verdict was finally communicated to the Czechs, it was done so in the most humiliating manner imaginable. A month later a friend brought me the description of this scene by one of the two Czechs who went to Munich: Dr. Hubert Masarik. I tried to have this account published in my paper, but my editor banned it. According to Dr. Masarik, he and his colleague Dr. Mastny were summoned late at night to meet Chamberlain and Daladier. The British Prime Minister briefly related the decisions to them, several times interrupting his speech with loud yawns. Daladier did not utter a syllable. Then the two statesmen disappeared. That was how the Czechs were notified that between October 1 and 10 the whole of Sudetenland, one-fourth of the national territory, including the entire Czech Maginot Line, would be occupied by Nazi troops.

Daladier returned to Paris the next day by airplane. He was reported to be taken aback when he glimpsed the throngs gathered around the aerodrome of Le Bourget. But then he heard cries of "Long live Daladier! Long live peace!" He assumed a dictator's pose, alighted from the plane, and strutted with Georges Bonnet to a waiting car. As the automobile drove through the city to the War Ministry, Daladier was standing à la Hitler. Bonnet, sitting next to him, was acknowledging the joyful greetings of the crowd with a thin-lipped smile.

Another story, which was circulated much later, was that Daladier had stood up quite well in Munich until lunch time. Then, having drunk heavily, he returned to the conference room and did not offer so much as a show of resistance. This tale came by a devious route from the British Foreign Office.

Daladier's rôle in the month leading up to Munich has been variously depicted. Some people have painted him as a true patriot who, after a severe inner struggle, finally agreed to the Munich Pact for the sake of France. But the truth is that on the most crucial occasions Daladier fully supported Bonnet's tactics. He did not once contradict the false statements of his Foreign Minister which had such catastrophic consequences.

When Bonnet presented the Ministerial Council with his résumé of the Gamelin memorandum, nobody was more qualified than Daladier, Minister of National Defense, to silence him and to lay the truth before the Cabinet. Daladier knew that the General Staff had arrived at conclusions opposite to those put forward by Bonnet.

He knew that Gamelin had underlined the following facts: (1) the Chief of the German General Staff, General Beck, resigned his post on September 3 because "he did not want to lead the Army into a catastrophe"; (2) the German Westwall was far from completion and, according to the French military attaché in Berlin, "as easy to dent as cottage cheese"; (3) the German Army had by no means finished its preparations, and it would take a year more of the most strenuous efforts before it could risk a war; (4) the French General Staff had quite a different opinion of the Red Army than the contemptuous estimate of the Japanese military attaché which Bonnet had quoted to the Cabinet and, on the contrary, considered the Russian airplanes and tanks the equal of those of Germany; (5) the splendidly equipped Czech Army of forty divisions, 1,000 airplanes and 1,500 tanks could resist for at least two to three months if left to fight alone.

All these things Daladier knew, yet he remained silent.

Daladier let Bonnet do the dirty work. Only after the ill-omened Foreign Minister's résumé had produced its damaging effect, only after it had been freely circulated in parliamentary circles and given to the British Ambassador—only then did Daladier attempt to save his face. Some ten days later he held a conversation with the General Secretary of the C. G. T., Léon Jouhaux. The trade union leader revealed subsequently in a public speech that the final phrase of the Gamelin report read: "In spite of all the difficulties, we must intervene."

Daladier played the same double game on the occasion of the British communiqué concerning the help France could expect from Great Britain and Soviet Russia in the event of war. When Rightist deputies questioned him, he barricaded himself behind a note from Bonnet which stated that "the communiqué emanated from a civil servant of no importance in the London Foreign Office." But when the harm was done, he divulged in a speech on October 4 that the declaration had been authorized by Prime Minister Chamberlain himself.

Indeed, the statement was written by Lord Halifax personally in the presence of Neville Chamberlain and Winston Churchill, at a conference at 10 Downing Street. Winston Churchill's son Randolph divulged this information in my presence in the House of Commons, to a group of British M. P.'s.

Edouard Daladier permitted Georges Bonnet and the appeasement press to deny the fact that Hitler was about to order general mobilization for September 28. Yet he knew that this information was true. After Munich, Bonnet, in a circular to French diplomats at their posts, wrote: "Marshal Goering declared on September 27 to Sir Nevile Henderson that "if the next day, the 28th, at 2 P.M., the Czechoslovak Government has not accepted the German Godesberg memorandum, mobilization measures will be taken at once and will be followed by action.'"

Daladier knew that his Foreign Minister was indulging in large-scale speculations on the money exchange, the success of which depended on a surrender to Hitler. The Secret Police had provided him with copies of all orders on the Bourse which Bonnet's bank had executed for itself and for him. Several Ministers, informed of these operations, had demanded the arrest of the head of the bank and the dismissal of Bonnet. Daladier had refused.

He knew about the conspiracy which was being plotted at the Quai d'Orsay. Several of his Ministers informed him on different occasions that Bonnet had met with a group of unofficial advisers with whom he mapped out the strategy of demoralization. Daladier was aware of the fact that the slogans for the campaign had been launched from the Quai d'Orsay. Bonnet's advisory staff consisted primarily of former Premier Flandin and Jean Mistler, Chairman of the Foreign Affairs Committee of the Chamber. Another member of the circle was the unimpressive but ambitious deputy from Corsica, François Piétri. The General Secretary of the Socialist Party, Paul Faure, a bitter foe of Léon Blum, attended meetings of the Bonnet group. Marcel Déat, who as Air Minister in the 1936 Sarraut Cabinet had played a fateful rôle, had the ear of the Foreign Minister. The deputy-lawyer Gaston Bergéry, a dangerous intrigant, was a frequent guest of this inner circle. Two prominent trade unionists belonged to it: René Belin, Assistant Secretary of the C. G. T., whose publication *Syndicats* was heavily subsidized by Bonnet, and André Delmas, leader of the Teachers Union.

These men could be seen at the Quai d'Orsay daily and hourly during this critical period. They furnished the appeasement newspapers with material against the so-called war-mongers—Georges Mandel, Jules Jeanneney, Edouard Herriot, the Britons Winston Churchill and Lloyd George. They exploited France's lack of air power against Goering's mighty air fleet; Jews against Catholics; pacifists against interventionists. They created a feeling of uncertainty in the country, forerunner to the undermining of morale. Georges Bonnet was portrayed as an angel of peace, while Georges Mandel was a sinister devil in the pay of the Jews, seeking to erect a Jewish-dominated France on the ruins of the Fatherland. Daladier was extolled as the "strong man" who wanted to save France from annihilation. Jules Jeanneney, President of the Senate, was said to be too senile to understand what he was doing. The mighty belly of Edouard Herriot was described as being full of the most sinister plans against France.

When during those hectic days Winston Churchill came to Paris, he was assailed as war-monger Number One. The rumor was spread that he had lost his capacity for straight thinking because of his overfondness for whiskey. Lloyd George was the old fool who had never forgotten that he had been forced to yield to Clemenceau, and who was thirsting for revenge against France. Such were the poisonous tales ejected like an inky fluid by Bonnet's advisory council.

They circulated the lie that President Beneš had asked Bonnet to put pressure on him so that he could force the Czech Cabinet to capitulate.

They wrote the text of Flandin's anti-mobilization poster.

They were the General Staff of the inner pincer movement which worked to destroy France. They were the most active among all of Hitler's agents inside France.

12

PRAGUE

AT MUNICH an avalanche was set in motion. Before two years were out, it would sweep over Europe and bury it.

It seemed for a brief spell that Daladier recognized the portents. In his first speech to the Chamber after Munich he declared: "It is possible, as has been written, that at Munich the face of the world was changed within a few hours." But then he continued to behave as though the world still bore its old face. Having dismissed Czechoslovakia with a few curt phrases, he announced to the Chamber that he was going to ask for new plenary powers.

He did not dare to put the Munich Pact to a direct vote. Many deputies would not have risked an open stand on it. So the Chamber voted on a motion for adjournment which implied agreement. Only 75 out of 618 Deputies saved the honor of France.

Plenary powers were voted by the Daladier Government's new majority, which now ranged from the Radicals clear over to the extreme Right. Daladier became manifestly their man.

If Daladier conceived of Munich as an end, he was

cruelly roused from his illusion. Axis speeches and articles reminded him that it was only the beginning. The "squeeze game" of the Axis was proceeding with the rôles appropriately distributed.

Virginio Gayda, Mussolini's mouthpiece, started the ball rolling with an article in the *Giornale d'Italia*: "The Czechoslovakian affair is only one point gained for peace. . . . Many other significant problems in the present situation force Italy and Germany to adopt a mistrustful and waiting attitude."

Then, beginning one week after Munich, Hitler made a series of speeches. What he said amounted to the threat that he would not tolerate what he termed the "war-mongers" in the British and French Governments. He especially singled out Churchill, Eden and Duff Cooper. He reminded the French and British Munichmen that "there still were less privileged German brothers living outside the Greater German Reich." And he again raised the demand for colonies.

The answer in Paris to these harbingers of a new crisis was a continuation of the stale old political game of cabals and intrigues. Bonnet thought the moment propitious for a new bid for the Premiership. Mme. Bonnet's yearning for this post for her husband was so obvious and ungovernable that a Deputy jokingly proposed that Bonnet be accorded the title of "former Premier."

Bonnet was laboring for a Franco-German declaration which would recognize the existing frontiers. This, he felt certain, would augment his prestige to such an extent that he would then be able to demand the Premiership. In the months following Munich, he dispensed colossal sums from the secret funds for personal publicity. Almost everywhere in the French press pages were devoted to editorials commending him. Stories of "popular" demonstrations in his honor appeared daily.

The Nazis knew about Bonnet's ambitions and exploited them for their own ends. A Deputy told me about a conversation with Count Welczeck, in which the German Ambassador confided to him that Bonnet had boasted in great detail about his political plans. The Deputy added that he felt humiliated to hear of Bonnet's struttings from such a source.

Another bidder for Daladier's position was Pierre-Étienne Flandin. His ambitions also played a rôle in the Nazi calculations. However, he temporarily lost ground in the race when it became known that he had sent a telegram of congratulations to Hitler after Munich. This forced him to hug the background for a while. The Socialist Deputy Grumbach read Hitler's answer to Flandin before the Foreign Affairs Committee: "I have constantly," Hitler's telegram ran, "followed your activity in the past year with great interest and sympathy." Daladier, irked at Flandin's competition, placed the text of Hitler's answer into Grumbach's hands.

No sooner had they voted for him than the members

of the new majority put the screws on Daladier. He had hoped to outmaneuver the Right. Now they showed him where he stood. In the course of a highly charged conversation, Caillaux presented him with an ultimatum. He demanded that Daladier send an Ambassador to Italy, where the post was vacant, had been vacant for over a year. He further pressed the Premier to make the promises of his August radio speech a reality by abolishing the forty-hour week. He demanded that Finance Minister Marchandeau—who was under suspicion for entertaining the notion of planned economy and exchange control—be tossed to the wolves. He finally demanded the dissolution of the Communist Party. Caillaux's intervention was followed by a demand from a group of Right-wing Deputies who stated their case in unequivocal language. Big business, too, fixed its guns in position. A few billion francs fled the country to remind Daladier of the fate of those of his predecessors who had not yielded.

Daladier took the hint. The Ambassador to Berlin, François Poncet, was nominated Ambassador to Rome. He was replaced by Robert Coulondre, until then French envoy in Soviet Russia. A diplomat of minor rank, Naggiar, went to Moscow Bonnet seized the occasion of this diplomatic shifting to place the Press Office of the Quai d'Orsay in the hands of a nonentity, Bressy, whose sister-in-law was on intimate terms with a Nazi diplomat.

At the annual Radical-Socialist convention in October Daladier spoke bitterly against the Communists. A motion passed by the assembly declared the People's Front officially dead. A huge fire in a Marseilles department store, costing the lives of many people, served as the ghastly background for this Radical gathering.

On his return to Paris, Daladier reshuffled his Cabinet. The unfortunate Finance Minister Marchandeau, who did not know what it was all about, went to the Justice Ministry. Aspiring little Paul Reynaud became Finance Minister. His friend, Countess Hélène de Portes, predicted this reshuffle to me four days before it occurred.

After Munich, Nazi propaganda worked with redoubled energy in French political circles, drawing-rooms and editorial offices. The "France-Allemagne Committee," where Vice-Premier Camille Chautemps hobnobbed with Otto Abetz, flooded the country with beautifully printed magazines lauding Franco-German friendship. The Paris kiosks received an influx of coarse anti-Semitic literature. Mme. Bonnet was heard making cheap anti-Semitic remarks not only in snobbish salons but also at her hair-dresser's and while shopping. Doriot's minions sold an inexpensive, specially expurgated French edition of *Mein Kampf*. The title page showed that it was printed in Germany. The

"Anti-Comintern" office in Geneva circulated tons of pamphlets against the Franco-Soviet Pact.

Seasoning his lies with half-truths, denials, contradictions and bribes, Bonnet fed his press with material castigating the so-called war-mongers. The most incredible and fantastic inventions were printed, so long as they were aimed at the pitiable remnants of Czechoslovakia, at Republican Spain or Soviet Russia. The Right press did not pause to examine either their credibility or their source. The campaign of *"fausses nouvelles"* became a daily feature of the appeasement press. President Jeanneney of the Senate coined a phrase in French which could be translated in two ways: that Bonnet was the greatest denier of news or that he was the greatest liar. In Parliament, Bonnet's lies were a frequent topic of lobby gossip. One Deputy, referring to an old French proverb which affirms that the nose grows with lies, invariably would greet me with the words: "Georges' nose has grown again."

Bonnet, angered by personal attacks against him in the anti-appeasement press and furious at the unfriendly attitude of most of the foreign correspondents, cast about for revenge. He asked the Minister of Interior to expel three leading British correspondents, one of them being Cadet of the *London Times*. Cadet's guilt lay in the fact that in one of his articles he hinted at Bonnet's technique of lies. Minister Sarraut refused to grant the request for fear of diplomatic complications. So the fascist weekly *Gringoire*, liberally supplied with data from the Quai d'Orsay, fired one broadside after another at the foreign journalists.

Then Laval made his bid. At the Senate Committee for Foreign Affairs he demanded that the Franco-Soviet Pact of Mutual Assistance, which he had negotiated, be denounced. He was vomiting forth, as someone phrased it, his own child. He dwelt fondly on Hitler's designs against the Soviet Ukraine which, he averred, France could only welcome. Encouraged by the Quai d'Orsay, the journal *Le Matin*, soon followed by many other papers, described with great gusto Hitler's preparations for a Ukrainian campaign. The tiny capital of the Carpatho-Ukraine, which at that time still belonged to Czechoslovakia, was crowded with French special correspondents. Their stories were profuse in details of Nazi activities in that remote region which was to serve as a jumping-off base for the attack on the Soviet Ukraine. Listening to them, one thought a German-Soviet war was just around the corner.

A shot fired in the German Embassy in Paris shifted the interest from internal problems for a few days at least. A Jewish youth from Poland, Herschel Grynspan, killed the German diplomat Herr von Rath. When in retaliation Hitler unloosed a wild Nazi pogrom against the Jews, the civilized world reacted with an outburst of shocked fury. Only the French Rightist press played the pogroms down. Bonnet expressly asked them to do so. He did not want to spoil his plans for the Franco-German declaration.

In this atmosphere of nervousness and uneasiness, the new Finance Minister, Paul Reynaud, promulgated his emergency decrees. They shoved a heavier burden on the shoulders of the people. Income taxes and indirect taxes were greatly increased. Cigarettes, bus and subway fares, postage and telephone rates became more expensive. The forty-hour week was virtually abolished. Overtime was made compulsory. One million and a half railwaymen and State and municipal servants were threatened by a so-called "Committee of the Axe." At least one hundred thousand wage-earners were faced with the loss of jobs.

Labor received the news with enhanced irritation. It accepted Munich with very bad grace. It felt unable to swallow the betrayal of Czechoslovakia after that of Spain. As one leading trade unionist put it: "Compared with this Munich butchery, the Hoare-Laval plan looks like a piece of delicate surgery." And now the decrees virtually abolishing the forty-hour week and reaching deep into the pockets of the people, produced an attitude of hostile bewilderment and anger. Strikes broke

Prague

out. There was talk of a general strike. Léon Jouhaux uttered these prophetic words: "An attempt is now being made to prepare the worst humiliation of all—to divide you internally and thus to prepare the conditions for your complete decline. France, once the light and the conscience of humanity, will sink into darkness and will become the servant of the dictatorships."

To coördinate the Axis "squeeze game," Ribbentrop went to Rome. Here the tactics for the prosecution of the Italian demands were discussed. Another subject under discussion was the offensive which General Franco was about to launch, with Italian "volunteers" and German *matériel*. A third topic was the gentleman's agreement between London and Rome. On his return to Germany, Ribbentrop asserted in a speech that "slowly but surely the old world is breaking down."

But Bonnet was not discouraged. He announced that the Franco-German negotiations were successfully terminated and that Hitler's Foreign Minister would come to Paris to sign a joint Franco-German declaration. That was eleven days after the pogroms in Germany which so profoundly shocked the conscience of the world.

The next day Chamberlain and Lord Halifax came to Paris. They were greeted by a hostile public demonstration and by a round of official festivities. The British Ministers were about to visit Rome. They discussed with their French colleagues the concessions to be offered to the Duce, especially the official recognition of the Franco régime in Spain which "they considered the first condition for an appeasement in the Mediterranean."

The Duce gave a totalitarian answer to these appeasement conversations. Two days after Rome announced the impending visit of the British Ministers, the Italian Chamber of Deputies witnessed a violent outburst of anti-French sentiment. During a speech by Count Ciano, the fascist Deputies sprang up with shouts of "Djibuti—Corsica—Nice!" Pale, rigid, the French Ambassador François Poncet witnessed this staged demand for French territory, which was accompanied by benevolent smiles from the Government bench. François Poncet did not leave his diplomatic loge.

Bonnet hastily summoned the diplomatic correspondents. He implored them not to attach undue weight to this incident. It did not, he claimed, represent the official Italian attitude. That evening some of his satellites toured the Paris editorial offices to make sure that the news would be played down. With a few honorable exceptions, the papers followed Bonnet's lead.

That same November 30, police guards and troops

Prague

were mobilized in Paris. A twenty-four-hour general strike was on. It was only lukewarmly supported by those unions under pro-Munich leadership. In violation of all precedents, the strike was announced four days in advance. This gave the Government time for drastic counter-measures. All striking civil servants were threatened with immediate dismissal. So were the railwaymen. The union leaders did not include the public utilities in Paris in their plans for a walk-out.

That evening Daladier spoke over the radio. It was the speech of a victor. Sanctions were immediately taken against the strikers. Thousands were fired. Hundreds were arrested and sentenced in summary fashion.

Early in December, Paris opened its gates to one of the leading spirits of the Nazi Fifth Column. Joachim von Ribbentrop slipped quietly into the French capital. He feared demonstrations, but the signing of the Franco-German declaration recognizing the mutual frontiers as definitive was staged with much pomp. This new "scrap of paper" was blazoned in movie shots, radio broadcasts and newspaper articles.

For the first time in the history of France an official Government function was organized on a racial basis. The Jewish Cabinet Ministers Georges Mandel and Jean Zay were not invited to the dinner party for Herr von Ribbentrop. The wife of the Naval Minister, Campinchi, stayed away in sign of protest. So did Jeanneney and Herriot.

In his last dispatch from Berlin François Poncet, who negotiated the Franco-German declaration, quoted a phrase of Goebbels' to the effect that "nobody wins in the lottery who doesn't at least risk buying a ticket."

Daladier and Bonnet purchased a lottery ticket: a Hitler promise. They paid a stiff price for it: the French alliance with Czechoslovakia and Soviet Russia. They drew a blank.

Ribbentrop was accompanied by Otto Abetz, a specialist in Franco-German affairs and, as was later revealed, one of the heads of Nazi espionage and bribery in France. Abetz narrated one story with particular gusto: how, for a moment during the Munich crisis, Hitler had raged when he feared he might encounter resistance that the German Army was not ready to face. He related that Hitler in his despair had agreed with the Duce that the latter should propose mediation in order to save the Führer's face. So Mussolini would have jumped into the breach anyhow, even if Chamberlain and Bonnet had not proposed him. But then the position of the Anglo-French leaders at Munich would have been much stronger.

Ribbentrop has since maintained that in the Paris conversations Bonnet gave Germany a free hand in its "drive to the East." It is difficult to know which of the two to believe. At any rate, a few days after the talks Bonnet addressed the Chamber Foreign Affairs Committee. He said he expected further German conquests in the East. He was asked whether France would fulfil her obligations under the Franco-Polish and Franco-Soviet pacts, if these countries were attacked. Bonnet replied that he did not believe either of the two countries was capable of defending itself against Nazi Germany. He added that further German moves in the East would not alter France's strategic position. It was clear enough. Not only Berlin, but also Moscow carefully noted his observations.

Gradually, in spite of efforts made to gloss over them, the anti-French demonstrations in Italy became known in France. They provoked great resentment among the people. Even big business circles, usually in sympathy with Mussolini's methods, found these claims on French possessions extremely distasteful. Their idea had always been to buy off the dictators by allowing them to gobble up small nations, despite the strategic dangers such a policy implied. But they regarded these demands for French territory, coming so shortly after Munich, as a breach of a tacit agreement. So they stiffened. The Suez Canal Company, at its annual meeting, adopted an intransigent position on Italy's fond eyeing of the Canal. This elicited from Mandel the following quip:

"Now we can feel safe. The Suez Company is going to save the honor of France—with dividends as usual, of course!"

The anti-Munich Ministers demanded that an official stand be taken against the Italian provocations. So now the Chamber witnessed a strange sight: firm asseverations from Bonnet, "the man who had hoisted the white flag over the peace treaties." He passed over in silence the fact that Italy had denounced the Rome Accord signed by Laval in January 1935. Instead, he assured the Deputies that "not an inch of French territory would be ceded." The Deputies smiled grimly at a new joke making the rounds: "It seems that Bonnet has been bought by the French Government!"

Daladier was more than ever in a Napoleonic mood after crushing the general strike. Now he decided on a tour of France's North African possessions. This was to serve a double purpose: it would indicate France's answer to Italian claims, and it would strengthen the ties between the mother country and the colonies. One other motive was in his mind. A triumphal tour would shatter Bonnet's fond aspirations to be Premier. As Daladier's secretary told me, "This trip, if it is the success we expect, will take the wind out of Bonnet's sails for a long time to come."

For decades the principal center of the Empire had been French North Africa. There were other rich and far-flung colonies: Indo-China in the Far East with its rice and mineral wealth; the great, remote island of Madagascar off South Africa; strategic islands in the South Pacific; a few possessions in the New World; the important mandated territories of Syria and Lebanon in the Near East. But the main base of the Empire was in North Africa. Algeria, Tunisia and French Morocco —as well as the Mediterranean island of Corsica—acted as vast reserve storehouses for grain and wine.

French North Africa was also a reservoir for troops. It was by calling on big native levies that the French military leaders hoped to lessen the numerical disparity between France and Germany caused by the former's lower birth rate.

This explains, too, why basic French naval strategy hinged on keeping open the communication lines across the Mediterranean to North Africa. In that region of the world the most menacing rival was Italy with her grandiose dreams of empire.

Daladier's tour took him to Corsica, Tunisia and Algeria, where tremendous popular demonstrations for democratic France took place. The Premier made many speeches in the course of his journey. He repeated France's firm decision to maintain the integrity of the French Empire. "We shall resist," he cried, "any attack, direct or indirect, by force or by guile, with a determination and an energy which nothing in the world can stop."

Even as he spoke, an indirect attack against France on a large scale was in full swing. Franco troops, Italian legionaries and Nazi tanks were driving against Barcelona. The situation of the Spanish Republicans was desperate.

They possessed, as later official accounts showed, barely 30,000 rifles to use in the front lines. Their ammunition stores were empty. Their aviation was outnumbered ten to one. The Spanish Republic sent desperate pleas to Paris. Soviet armaments and munitions, two shiploads full, were lying at anchor for weeks in a French Atlantic seaport, waiting for permission to be shipped across the French-Spanish border. Bonnet said, "No." Daladier said, "No." Franco drove on.

The nearer he came to Barcelona, the more the excitement in Paris mounted. Even deputies who had previously opposed the Republicans were now in favor of sending aid. The plight of the retreating armies, the spectacle of the civilians who had withstood famine and bombardment for so many months, was heartrending. But Neville Chamberlain, back from Rome where he had received a frosty reception, sent his ambassador to Daladier and Bonnet to remind them to keep the French-Spanish frontier closed. So Daladier and Bonnet, in spite of the rising tide of anger of the Left, turned down the plea of the Spanish Foreign Minister who had come to Paris. The Russian munitions had to wait until several days before the fall of Barcelona. Then permission was granted to send them through. They arrived too late, of course. Franco's troops found the untouched boxes lying at the railway station at Barcelona.

Barcelona fell at the end of January 1939. Two weeks later Franco troops made their appearance at the French frontier. Hundreds of thousands of soldiers and civilians from Republican Spain fled to France. There they were placed in camps. They suffered neglect, inclement weather and undernourishment. Henri de Kérillis wrote at the time that the disorganization in the refugee camps showed the shocking incompetence of the French civil and military authorities. The Right newspapers answered by campaigning against the "blackmail with pity" and by demanding that those "criminals" be delivered to Franco.

A new page was added to France's humiliation. Senator Léon Bérard, Laval's candidate for the coming presidential elections, went twice to Burgos to negotiate the recognition of Franco by France. He was not received by the General. For days he cooled his heels waiting for an appointment with Franco's Foreign Minister. France had to promise the gold which the

Spanish Republicans had deposited and all the arms they had laid down at the French frontier, before Franco deigned to accept recognition. The Chamber accorded it by a meager vote of 323 to 264, with about twenty abstentions. More than thirty Deputies of Daladier's own party voted against him.

An emissary went to Rome. He was Paul Baudouin, a friend of Laval and a director of the Bank of Indo-China. Baudouin, as head of a Franco-Italian company enjoying a monopoly of salt exploitation in Italian East Africa, was a frequent visitor to the Italian capital. He had connections with the most important people in Italian political circles. His business interests and political preferences made him an eager partisan of a *rapprochement* with Italy. What he offered in Rome could only be surmised: shares in the Suez Company, a new status for the Italians in Tunisia and, perhaps, the port of Djibuti, terminus of the only railway in Abyssinia. For some time now the story had been spread that Djibuti could not be defended. High officials at the Quai d'Orsay told me that they suspected Bonnet was hatching a Djibuti deal.

The Count de Brinon went to Berlin. His mission was to persuade Ribbentrop to mediate between Italy and France. He failed. But his trip nearly brought about the resignation of Robert Coulondre, who felt humiliated by De Brinon's frequent confidential missions.

In March, Madrid fell to Franco. Thereupon, the

Daladier Government radiated optimism. So did Whitehall. Hitler, it was said, would require a long time to digest Austria and Sudetenland, both of which he had swallowed in 1938. Having recognized Franco, it was argued, the democracies would then be in a position to effectively bar any increase of Nazi and Italian influence in Spain, and even to lessen it. Marshal Pétain, Ambassador to Madrid, was regarded as a strong asset in this game. The gentleman's agreement between Great Britain and Italy predicated on a Franco victory, would now begin to function. And France, profiting from the "purified" European atmosphere, would also come to an understanding with Mussolini.

Whoever tried to warn against such unwarranted optimism was assailed as a war-monger. *Le Jour* demanded that "those scoundrels" who saw dark clouds in the skies, like Pertinax and Geneviève Tabouis, should be handcuffed.

The optimism continued to grow, in spite of news from Berlin that a new Hitler coup was in the offing. Early in March, Neville Chamberlain issued a statement in which he declared that all signs pointed to a tranquil political future and an easing of the economic situation in Europe. His voice in France was Pierre-Étienne Flandin, who on March 12 declared: "Echoes reaching us from London these last days are much more optimistic concerning the international situation. It is a fact that the prophets who worked so hard and are still working to alarm public opinion in France now see their sinister predictions given the lie one by one." One of Bonnet's mouthpieces wrote a violent article on March 14 against all those who predicted that Hitler was going to move again.

On the evening of that day, the President of the rump Republic of Czechoslovakia, Emil Hacha, was compelled to face an enraged Hitler. Together with Ribbentrop and Goering, the Führer broke down Hacha's resistance in a several hours' grilling. The sick old man was kept conscious only by means of injections. The Nazis, thinking of everything, placed the medicine in an adjoining room. Hacha, shattered and helpless, finally signed a prepared "agreement," placing Bohemia and Moravia under Hitler's protection.

On March 15, 1939, five and a half months after Munich, Hitler entered Prague. Standing by a window of the old Hradschin Castle, once a residence of the Bohemian kings, he looked down on the lovely old city. In their homes that night, the Czechs wept.

This sensation was quickly followed by others. As a minor dish Hitler swallowed Memel, which he forced the Lithuanians to cede. On Good Friday Mussolini invaded Albania and annexed it to the new Roman Empire. As the Chinese Ambassador in London remarked: "The air is black with the wings of chickens coming home to roost."

13

THE APPROACH OF WAR

THE CONQUEST of Czechoslovakia changed the balance of power in Europe. But if the rest of Europe was haunted by a nightmare, Hitler was haunted by one too —that of a war on two fronts.

What he feared most was a real understanding, a binding alliance between the Western democracies and Soviet Russia. That was why he had striven so energetically to demolish the Franco-Soviet Pact. That was why his agents in France attacked it as the only genuine obstacle to a Franco-German friendship.

Hitler's soldiers occupied Prague, but the German officers billeted there asserted that soon they would be on the move again. Toward Poland? Behind Poland loomed the enormous shadow of Soviet Rusia. What if the democracies, recognizing the danger, finally broke through the thicket of Hitler propaganda and approached the Russians for a clear-cut alliance?

In one of the reports from Berlin which Bonnet has never published, it was stated that after the fall of Prague Hitler followed the development of negotiations between the Western powers and Soviet Russia like an aviator scanning weather-bureau reports. He understood.

The question was whether the democracies would understand as well. Would they continue appeasement or would they abandon it?

It has been said that after Prague, Daladier and Chamberlain changed their minds; that they then abandoned the policy of appeasement. I find this hard to believe. The stubborn Chamberlain, with his conservative background and his outlook of a Birmingham merchant, is hardly liable to burst the confines of his own world. A narrow resentful provincial like Edouard Daladier does not learn easily. Both men lacked the greatness which is the stuff of real statesmen, the readiness to admit errors. Daladier was not at all prepared to concede that he had made mistakes in the past.

The policy of appeasement was not dictated by sentimentality. It was not the result of a state of mind which abhorred war so profoundly that any sacrifice seemed preferable to it. No, this policy flowed from a purely political conception which has been aptly expressed by the French fascist paper *Combat*: "The Right-wing parties had the impression that in the event of war not only would the disaster be immense, not only was a defeat or a devastation of France possible, but more than that a defeat of Germany would mean the crumbling of the authoritarian systems which constitute the principal rampart against Communism and perhaps the Bolshevization of Europe."

The Approach of War

After the fall of Prague, Chamberlain and Daladier might have been shocked and rendered indignant by Hitler's ruthless strokes. They might have been furious because of what they regarded as a personal affront to them by the dictators. But just as a father might be angry when his child exhibits ugly traits of character yet still continue to regard it as his child, so the fathers of appeasement clung faithfully to their baby. As a matter of fact, a Russian proposal was made three days after the fall of Prague for a conference between France, Great Britain, Russia, Poland, Rumania and Turkey to discuss means of resisting further aggressions. However, it was rejected as "premature."

Chamberlain made his position clear in answer to a question concerning the Russian offer when he stated that the "Government was not anxious to set up in Europe opposing blocs of countries with different ideas about their forms of internal government." Daladier eagerly joined in. "Have I any need to add," he said, "that the close and profound agreement with Great Britain has never had greater strength than today?"

Encouraged by the fate of the Russian proposals, the Nazis contemplated a swift move into Danzig. By the end of March information leaked out of Berlin, Warsaw and Danzig that a Nazi *putsch* was imminent. Then the rumors died down, dissipated by the threat of Polish mobilization measures. The Nazis apparently were still hoping to add one more unopposed conquest to their record.

But the threat to Danzig, fraught with the peril of war, hardened public opinion, especially in England. Something had to be done. The obvious thing to do was to enter into negotiations with the Russians, and to put forward precise proposals. That was not done. Instead, a mutual-assistance pact against aggression was signed with the Poles. Russia was not consulted. In April the democracies, through the mouth of Mr. Chamberlain, gave two more unilateral guarantees: to Greece and to Rumania.

That same month a Franco-British proposal was made to Russia to guarantee aid to Poland in the same way as the democracies had done. The Russian answer came within two days: a proposal for a downright triple alliance between France, Great Britain and Russia.

The month of May brought many warnings to France that if an agreement with Russia was sought, this was the time to conclude it. Soviet Foreign Commissar Litvinov, for years a leading figure in Geneva, resigned. Vyacheslav Molotov, Soviet Premier, took over his portfolio. Robert Coulondre, French Ambassador to Berlin, reported that a member of Hitler's "inner circle" had, during a conversation with a diplomat, lifted a corner on Germany's attitude toward Russia. Since Bonnet showed no intention of reacting to this warning, one of the high officials on his staff informed a few Deputies, who in turn brought pressure to bear on Daladier. So finally, on May 9, the Russian proposal was answered—more than three weeks after it was made.

The reply was a slight modification of the first Franco-British suggestion. Russia should guarantee Poland, but not engage in combat before the democracies made their declarations of war. The Soviet Ambassador, confronted with this counter-proposal, waxed sarcastic: "In these days when a peace declaration doesn't mean peace, a declaration of war wouldn't necessarily mean war."

Again the Russians wasted no time in replying. They waited only five days; they reiterated their demand for a clear-cut alliance.

Two weeks elapsed before the democracies made up their minds. During this period the Germans and Italians completed negotiations for a military pact between themselves. Coulondre sent another warning from Berlin. This one was much more sharply worded. According to his current report, Ribbentrop was obsessed with the idea of a *rapprochement* between Germany and the U.S.S.R. "Ribbentrop's hopes," Coulondre wrote, "may have been strengthened during these last few days by the difficulties encountered in the course of the Anglo-Soviet conversations."

On May 27 instructions were finally sent to the French and British Ambassadors in Moscow to enter into negotiations for a triple alliance with the Russians.

That same day a military alliance between Nazi Germany and fascist Italy—"The Pact of Steel"—was signed. The negotiations for it lasted exactly twenty days.

Inside France confusion grew by leaps and bounds. The French Socialist convention revealed a deep split in the Party on every issue except one: relations with Russia. The united front between the two parties was severed. The General Secretary, Paul Faure, one of Bonnet's advisers, warned against an alliance with Russia. "If the Axis powers feel encircled," he said, "they will go to war."

Marcel Déat, another of Bonnet's confederates, began a press campaign against any commitments for Danzig.

Meanwhile the talks in Moscow hit a snag. The Russians demanded that indirect aggression be included among the clauses which would set the proposed alliance in motion. The democracies refused.

Instead, an official of the London Foreign Office, William Strang, was dispatched to Moscow to assist the British Ambassador in the conversations. The choice was not a happy one. The Russians suspected that Strang was hostile to an agreement. They remembered his collaboration with Lord Runciman during the latter's mission in Czechoslovakia.

Coulondre sent another plea from Berlin to hasten the Moscow pact. He remarked that "before definitely making up his mind in one direction, Ribbentrop is awaiting the result of the negotiations between the Western powers and Russia." The keenness with which the Moscow news was followed in Berlin was also confirmed by a June dispatch to the *London Times*: "If the negotiations should fail, the Reich will no doubt attempt to secure the Russian front by means of an economic *rapprochement*, as well as by political assurances." This correspondent foresaw exactly what happened two months later. The French press was counseled by the Quai d'Orsay not to quote from his article.

At this point, considerable speculation was caused by an article written by Zdhanov, one of Stalin's confidential advisers, who expressed his disagreement with those of his associates who believed that the British and French were really desirous of offering genuine resistance to aggression. In his view, what the democracies wanted was a one-sided pact which would merely bind the Russians to help them and would give no promise of mutual aid—a pact which no country with self-respect could sign.

Worried by Zdhanov's article, several French Ministers pressed for the dispatch to Moscow of a Cabinet member with full authority. In London, Chamberlain was urged in the same direction. The Russian Ambassador, Ivan Maisky, hinted to Lord Halifax that the latter's presence in Moscow would be welcome, and would greatly facilitate negotiations. Chamberlain stubbornly refused to send Halifax.

The month of June closed on a somewhat more reassuring note.

Hitler's chief agent in France, Otto Abetz, was expelled. A clever, cultured man and a glib conversationalist, he was married to a French woman and was the lion of many a Parisian smart set. Countess Hélène de Portes, Paul Reynaud's lady friend, and the Marquise de Crussols, Daladier's friend, numbered him among their guests.

He had huge sums of money at his disposal. He bought newspaper men, editors, and publicity directors. He bought politicians. In a report from Berlin, buried in Bonnet's files, it was stated that Abetz, in an expansive mood, once boasted having more than a dozen French parliamentarians in his back pocket.

News more concrete than ever arrived at the Quai d'Orsay concerning a turn in Russo-German relations. This communication was from the Consul-General in

Hamburg who wrote: "According to economic circles generally well informed, if an agreement is not signed shortly between London, Paris and Moscow, the Soviet Government will be ready to sign a five-year non-aggression pact with the Reich."

In the third week of July news leaked out concerning discussions between Hitler's traveling salesman, Dr. Wohlthat, and the British Minister for Overseas Trade, Robert Hudson. These conversations dealt with a kind of economic appeasement, including a loan to Germany of between half a billion and a billion pounds sterling.

On his return from Russia, the French Ambassador, Naggiar, told a Deputy that this news had had a terrific effect on Moscow. The Russians proposed that the democracies send a military mission with full powers to conclude a military agreement. They hoped that such talks would also facilitate a solution of the political problem. After some hesitation, the British finally consented to this proposal on July 25. Again they chose officers of minor importance. In the words of the British Minister for Economic Warfare, Hugh Dalton: "The Russians expected Gamelin and Gort and complained that people had been sent without proper credentials, people who were not fit to talk on equal terms with Voroshilov." Lloyd George also attacked the British Government for its handling of the Russian affair.

"They have," he said, "no sense of proportion or of the gravity of the whole situation. The world is trembling on the brink of a great precipice and liberty is challenged."

It took sixteen days for the military mission to reach the Russian capital. By this time the tension between Poland and Germany had attained new heights. The Nazi attack was prophesied first for August 15, then for the 23rd or 24th. The annual Nazi Nuremberg Convention was postponed. Military preparations continued unabated.

At first it was reported that the Anglo-French talks in Moscow were running smoothly. But when the problem of how Russian aid for Poland could be made effective was discussed, a new and final stalemate arose over the participation of Soviet forces in the defense of Poland. But, as a high official of the Quai d'Orsay phrased it, the Poles said they could take care of the German attack by themselves.

On August 23 the Russian-German non-aggression pact was signed.

The French people, unaware of the repeated warnings from their own diplomats in Germany, were taken by surprise.

The final week of August was full of contradictory

The Approach of War

moves and counter-moves as war loomed nearer. Bonnet instructed the French Ambassador in Warsaw to impress upon the Polish Government "that it should refrain from any military reaction in the event of a proclamation by the Danzig Senate of the Free City's rejoining the Reich." This signified that France had decided to let Hitler have Danzig.

Optimistic news was followed by pessimistic, and vice versa, like a volatile barometer. Hitler was reported ready for a compromise. Sir Nevile Henderson flew from Berlin to London and returned to his post with a new proposal. Robert Coulondre visited the Führer several times. Daladier exchanged letters with Hitler, writing that France would fight on the side of the Poles if the latter were attacked.

Millions of Frenchmen were called to the colors. Hundreds of thousands left Paris. Then, at the end of August, news came that the Poles and Germans would enter into direct negotiations. A Minister told me with relief, "Tonight we may sleep calmly."

Suddenly the German radio stifled this optimism by reading a memorandum containing the Nazi conditions for a settlement with Poland. It added ominously that the request of the Nazi Government that the Poles send a plenipotentiary with full powers to negotiate had not been fulfilled. Therefore, the conditions were no longer valid.

"Do you think they will strike tonight?" I inquired at the Quai d'Orsay.

"The Minister thinks it is just one more Nazi bluff," was the reply.

The next morning I was aroused by the news that the Nazi troops had crossed the Polish frontier.

A Cabinet council sat for a long time that day. A Minister informed me that Bonnet was authorized to accept the invitation of the Duce for a conference on September 5. No conditions were attached to this acceptance. The British Cabinet likewise accepted, but demanded that the Germans withdraw their troops from Poland. There was a several hours' controversy between London and Paris before the French Government finally aligned itself with the British.

General mobilization was ordered. The cafés were packed to capacity. So was the subway, and the buses. No taxis were available . . . and there was no news! Just rumors.

On September 2, Parliament gathered to hear Daladier speak. Everybody knew that it was to be war. Daladier's words left no doubt about it.

The Nazi troops in Poland drove on. The first reports about terrible air bombardments came through.

Sunday, September 3, was the last day of peace. The

The Approach of War

French Ambassador visited Ribbentrop and declared that France would be at war with Germany at five o'clock in the afternoon if the Nazi troops were not withdrawn from Poland. The British ultimatum expired at 11 o'clock.

The watch crept forward at a snail's pace. It took an eternity before the hands reached the 5. France was at war!

Would the Nazi planes come tonight? I am sure the question was asked in every private dwelling that evening. A police patrol stopped me near the Place de l'Opéra and asked me for my papers. The sergeant swore irreverently: "Those bastards will come tonight!"

The blackout was depressing. Air-raid wardens chased up and down the streets blowing their whistles whenever they saw a streak of light behind a curtain. In our street we had a warden who was an enthusiastic whistler. He gave us many a headache during the war.

There was almost no work at the office. Censorship was instituted.

Meanwhile, the Nazi troops drove still deeper into Poland.

14

FROM SITZKRIEG TO BLITZKRIEG

THE MOBILIZATION went off like clockwork—at least so the authorities told us. What they forgot to add was that it took, according to plan, almost fifty days before mobilization was completed. Hitler overran Poland in half that time.

There is no one general formula for the manner in which war must be waged. If Germany followed the idea of the *blitzkrieg*, it was not only because the German General Staff was guided by an ungovernable desire for attack. The concept of the *blitzkrieg* was born in Italy and adopted by Germany because the chances for both nations lay in a quick decision. Germany's geographic position, its agricultural productivity, its dependence on foreign raw materials made it imperative to concentrate on a few, swift, deadly blows.

The situation of France was different. Outnumbered two to one, confronting a foe with a powerful military tradition, France's predicament demanded that this inferiority in man-power and industrial potentiality be offset by alliances with other peoples equally interested in prohibiting the Nazis from dominating the Continent. If France failed in this, she went to war with heavy odds against her. She could overcome them only if she could

From Sitzkrieg to Blitzkrieg

delay the decision long enough for the blockade to begin to tell on German morale.

This was the idea which gave birth to the Maginot Line. Since these fortifications have proved of no great value in the war it has become almost axiomatic to assert that France was defeated because of her misguided faith in this Line. I think that this interpretation does not do justice to the truth. The idea of the Maginot Line in itself may have been correct. What was fatal was the "Maginot spirit" to which it gave birth.

By that I mean that the French General Staff, in its calculations, depended more on the concrete pillboxes and blockhouses of the Line than on the men who were there to defend it. It is said that the French General Staff prepared in 1940 for a resumption of the war of 1914. If this be so, it is correct above all in the sense that French military strategy did not take into consideration the enormous changes which have transpired in the past twenty years.

Not that the French General Staff was unaware of the new techniques which modern warfare required. It might have underestimated—probably it did underestimate—the rôle of the airplane and the tank. But that is not sufficient to explain the crushing defeat. Where the French generals, and with them the political leaders, failed completely was in their gauging of the social factor.

A modern war with its vast technical possibilities can

be lost before it starts. That is the real, underlying lesson of the Battle of France.

When France entered the war, she was split from top to bottom. She was divided because of the war itself, and because of the circumstances leading up to it. An outstanding military theoretician of Nazi Germany has written that in war one question has to be avoided under all circumstances: "Why the war?" But almost the whole French people insisted on an answer to this query when hostilities began. Those who believed it necessary to sacrifice a faithful ally like Czechoslovakia—one small country, many small countries, in order to save peace—asked now: "Why should we fight for Poland?" Others who foresaw that this sacrifice of small and friendly nations would lead to war, and whose worst predictions were now realized, wondered: "Why didn't we fight for Czechoslovakia?" These questions could be read in almost every eye—of the soldier leaving to join his regiment, of the mother and wife and sister waving a tearful good-bye until the train vanished in the distance.

Nobody expected outbursts of enthusiasm. The newspapers maintained that the silence with which the war was greeted was a sign of dignified decision. It meant, they claimed, that the French were resolved to put an end to an impossible situation—*il faut en finir*. But it was not that. It was with gloom in their hearts that

Frenchmen went to war. At best people were resigned to suffering its consequences. They were not convinced that it was necessary to wage it.

The politicians on whose shoulders fell the task of convincing the people were incapable of coping with such a staggering burden. How could it be otherwise? They were the same men who had affixed their signatures to the Munich document. They were the same men who, by their sins of omission and commission, had shattered the morale of the people. The Government said: "Unity is the crying need of the hour." But it was itself divided. The newspapers filled their front pages with praise of the wonderful courage which the French people were showing. But on page two, they continued their old quarrels and grudges and polemics.

How could there have been unity? Unity cannot be achieved by words. It centers around an idea, a necessity. The people did not feel any of these things in this war. Fight for democracy? The slogan lost its attractiveness for one part of the populace when democracy not so long ago was linked with betrayal and dishonor.

Fight against Hitlerism? The watchword was not attractive to another portion for whom Hitler was the bulwark against bolshevism. The enemy, they thought, was not across the Rhine.

Nazi propaganda knew the magic of this idea. It had worked shrewdly with it before the war. It did so during the war. A powerful Fifth Column, entrenched in some of the loftiest posts in the State apparatus, was its standard-bearer. When the war began Hitler had already penetrated to the heart of France. The French bastion was undermined from within before it was taken from without.

France fought against Germany for ten months. For eight and a half of them the French people saw and waged a *sitzkrieg*. French nerves were exposed to a constant drumfire of propaganda, while no effective counter-barrage from the French side was in evidence. For one and a half months Hitler made his *blitzkrieg* on France. The decision was already reached in the first fortnight of this lightning assault. When the Germans broke through at Sedan and arrived at the Channel the campaign in France was over. Twice within seventy years the fate of France was sealed at the same place. Sedan has become the symbol of the misfortune of France. After the Sedan of 1870 the Third French Republic was created; at Sedan in 1940 it was killed.

The ten months of the campaign in France may be divided into five periods. They follow each other remorselessly like the acts of a Greek tragedy. I think it is

From Sitzkrieg to Blitzkrieg

best to deal with these five sections in order, before presenting the general conclusions to be drawn from them.

The first period extends from the outbreak of the war to the fall of Warsaw. It lasted twenty-seven days in the month of September.

During this interval Hitler offered a most friendly countenance to France. "I do not war against the French. I am not going to attack," he stated in his Reichstag speech marking Germany's entry into hostilities. So his radio stations and his agents in France repeated it incessantly.

I remember chatting with a journalist's wife whose husband was one of the war correspondents with the French Army. She repeated verbatim to me the main passages in Hitler's speech. The newsdealer from whom I used to buy my papers told me: "As far as we are concerned, the Germans have been very nice to us."

During the first four weeks of the war France quickly became accustomed to the restrictions involved. The blackouts changed the City of Light into a city of darkness. The first air-raid alarms passed without any untoward consequences. Our neighbor, a young girl working at the Ministry of Colonies, became hysterical when the sirens sounded for the first time. But most of the women in our apartment house stood stiffly against the wall with their gas masks on their faces. By the third alarm the sirens were taken as a matter of course. Nobody grew frightened or panicky. In the beginning we all dragged our gas masks with us with the same pride with which one wears a war decoration. Gradually they were disappearing from the streets.

The French Army advanced cautiously across a No Man's Land and a tangle of mine fields in the Saar territory. Herds of pigs were sent ahead of the army to cause the mines to explode. It was reported that this advance forced Hitler to withdraw six divisions from the Polish front to his Westwall. There was no need for them to enter into action. Save for a few minor scouting episodes, there was not a single encounter between the French and German armies worth mentioning. In this period, too, the first British troops arrived in France. It was high time. Fifth Columnists exploited their absence among the soldiers. Grumblings and murmurs of "Where are the English?" were heard in many quarters.

Daladier, of course, reshuffled his Cabinet. At long last, much too late, Georges Bonnet was evicted from the Foreign Office. Daladier added that portfolio to his own. Bonnet went to the Ministry of Justice, where he shielded Hitler agents from prosecution.

By the middle of September my editor received reliable information that Bonnet had created a substantial fund earmarked to support the campaign for an understanding with Hitler. Two groups of politicians were prominent in guiding this movement. About fifteen deputies centered around Gaston Bergéry and Marcel Déat. Some thirty more parliamentarians formed a second clique around former Premier Laval and Adrien Marquet, Deputy and Mayor of Bordeaux. Bonnet acted as a kind of liaison officer between these two groups. He and Laval advanced most of the money necessary for the intrigues.

The first two meetings of the Supreme War Council took place in this opening period of the war. Chamberlain, accompanied by some of his Ministers, met Daladier "somewhere in France." Their discussions turned around the desperate plea of the Poles for help, around the speed-up in British conscription and the policy to be adopted toward Italy and Russia. The two Prime Ministers decided that no airplanes should be sent to Poland because they would not avail to turn the tide, and that the French Army should try to continue its pressure on the Westwall in order to draw Nazi troops from the East—but without taking any risks. Chamberlain explained the difficulties he faced in extending conscription because of the lack of trained officers and equipment for the new troops. An agreement was reached regarding a new approach to Italy in order to separate her from Germany. Mussolini would be offered the port of Djibuti, territorial concessions in British Somaliland, more shares and more directorates on the Suez Canal Board; broader rights for the Italians in Tunis, and huge credits. The Supreme Council also decided to coördinate the activities of the French and British armies in the Near East, and to get them ready for a possible conflict with the Soviet Union. General Weygand had just been named Commander of the French forces in Syria.

In the middle of September the Red Army occupied eastern Poland. Thereupon, the Russian Ambassador in Paris informed Daladier that Soviet Russia wanted to remain neutral.

While the Polish campaign drew to a close, Daladier held conferences with the General Staff and with his Minister of the Interior Albert Sarraut to decide on measures to be taken against the Communists. A member of Daladier's staff told me that at one of these conferences Daladier engaged in a stormy argument with General Gamelin. The General Staff opposed the banning of the Communist Party. The General feared that, with approximately every tenth man in the army a Communist, such an act would create wide discontent even among many workers who had no Communistic sympathies whatsoever. He was afraid of the effect on the morale of his troops, but finally bowed to Daladier's will. Sarraut backed up the Premier in the exchange of views. The Communist Party was outlawed.

After a heroic defense, Warsaw fell. That same day French troops began to withdraw from the sectors in the

From Sitzkrieg to Blitzkrieg

No Man's Land to which they had advanced. They retired to the Maginot Line.

The first period of the war ended.

The next phase extended over October and November to the beginning of the Russo-Finnish War. The offensive of the Hitlerites inside France was now becoming more daring and ubiquitous. It left deep corroding traces on the morale of the French people.

The main argument of Nazi propaganda changed to: "Why continue this war? Poland is finished. Bolshevism has taken a giant step forward in Europe. It has occupied half of Poland and placed garrisons in the three Baltic States. If it is not stopped now, it may soon be too late. The only man to stop its onward rush is Hitler. Therefore, an understanding with him becomes all the more essential."

During these months the French newspapers, with the exception of the few which had opposed Munich, began openly to treat the Russians as Public Enemy Number One. Hitler was relegated to a secondary position. A British M.P. attending a meeting in Paris told me: "Reading the French press one has the impression that France is at war with Russia and merely on very unfriendly terms with the Nazis."

Early in October Hitler delivered a Reichstag speech

containing, as he put it, his final peace offer. A few days later we received a small leaflet by mail at the newspaper office. Obviously printed in Germany, it reproduced the highlights of Hitler's speech. These leaflets must have been distributed by the thousands throughout France. The police discovered afterward that these pamphlets were smuggled into France via Switzerland with the help of a group of "Croix de Feu" men living on the French-Swiss border near Geneva.

In October the French-British-Turkish mutual-assistance pact was finally signed.

On the domestic front new decrees were put into effect. They extended the working week to 72 hours, levying a 15% tax on incomes and a 40% tax on all overtime payments. These measures caused considerable restlessness in the factories, particularly because no new tax on profits from armaments was introduced.

Marcel Déat, who signed a leaflet demanding immediate and unconditional peace, was questioned by an examining magistrate and released. A short while after, the charges against him were dropped.

A member of the Socialist Executive Committee, Professor Zoretti, circulated a revealing letter in the lobbies of Parliament and in various editorial offices. He was expelled from the Socialist Party because he had asked

From Sitzkrieg to Blitzkrieg 325

a Swiss Socialist to intervene with the Socialist International for a peace talk. Zoretti divulged that Paul Faure was associated with him in this move; that Faure was collaborating closely with Laval; and that the intervention of these two politicians had prevented the entry of Blum as Vice-Premier and Herriot as Foreign Minister in the Daladier Cabinet when it was reshuffled. These revelations were not without a certain grim humor, since Zoretti also quoted anti-Semitic utterances made by Paul Faure against Léon Blum.

Faure and Laval continued to advise Daladier.

A shake-up in Mussolini's Cabinet was hailed in the French press as a sign that the Duce was eager to eliminate all pro-German influences from his Government. Two papers which attempted to express the contrary opinion—and, as subsequent events have proved, the truthful one—were savagely censored and warned that they would be banned.

The month of November began with high excitement. Rumors were rife that the Nazis were about to invade Holland and Belgium. Early one morning, at about five o'clock, I was aroused by a call from the Foreign Office saying that the invasion had begun. It was a false alarm. According to the Quai d'Orsay the Generals had prevented Hitler from marching. In my opinion, the rumor of the impending attack on the Low Countries was launched by Goebbels as a factor in the "war of nerves." Similar rumors circulated constantly, keeping the military and political leaders in a nerve-racking state of anticipation. When Hitler's real attacks were launched, unfortunately they always came as a surprise.

The news of the explosion in the Munich Beer Hall of a time-bomb which missed Hitler by twenty minutes, became known in Paris. It was generally regarded as a symptom that the situation inside Germany had gone from bad to worse. The official theory was that the Gestapo arranged this murderous attempt by itself, either to restore Hitler's popularity with the German people or to prove the indispensability of the Gestapo. The story of the attempt had a somewhat comic aftermath. Two different groups of German émigrés boasted of having organized it. They reported on their preparations for the plot with a wealth of details from two so-called German underground radio stations, operated by the French Propaganda Office in Paris. Their elaborate fantasies were soon taken off the air.

A day after the explosion in Munich, two agents of the British Secret Service were kidnapped by the Nazis from the Dutch border town of Venloo. The Nazis maintained that the two Englishmen were involved in the bombing plot. The British Government, on the other hand, revealed that they had gone to the Dutch-German frontier to receive German peace proposals. A high

From Sitzkrieg to Blitzkrieg 327

official of the Dutch Secret Service, who often came to Paris, told me that the two men were bearing a personal letter from Lord Halifax to Goering. About this time the French and British Governments nursed the hope that a combination of Goering, Dr. Schacht and several prominent German industrialists, all opposed to the German-Soviet Pact, would overthrow Hitler and come to terms with the Allies.

Internally, relations between Premier Daladier and Finance Minister Reynaud were strained to the breaking point, owing to Reynaud's mounting influence. The tiny agile "watchdog of the Treasury" was generally dubbed "the Dauphin" in parliamentary circles, because it was commonly believed that he would shortly inherit Daladier's mantle. To put a stop to the "draft Reynaud for Premier" movement, which was gaining in Parliament, Daladier sent him to London for important economic proposals with the British. Reynaud's discussions with Chancellor of the Exchequer Sir John Simon only resulted in an understanding couched in vague generalities. Reynaud's failure was utilized by Daladier to check his boosters for a while.

Naturally, the jealousy between these two men gravely influenced the course of Cabinet affairs. Once when two British Ministers came to Paris, Daladier did not invite Reynaud to the luncheon which he gave for them. The Britons had to visit Reynaud in his own office—but they went there prior to the Daladier luncheon. That flung the Premier into such a fit of rage that he nearly called off the lunch.

Parliament began to show the strain of the war of nerves. The inactivity of the French Army was viewed with deep concern by one group. Another exploited it as an additional reason for the necessity of peace. At the Senate Foreign Affairs Committee, Laval made one of his sorties. He attacked the Government for not trying hard enough to come to terms with Mussolini. His friend Paul Baudouin returned empty-handed from Rome. Laval, supported by a majority of his colleagues, demanded severance of diplomatic relations with Russia. In this he found allies in *Le Temps, Le Journal des Débats, Le Matin,* and others. The campaign was conducted with furious vigor and mounted to a stormy crescendo when the Russo-Finnish war began.

The next three months were almost completely dominated by this event. The third period of the War was characterized by a most violent anti-Soviet campaign.

Shortly after the conflict in Finland began, French and British diplomacy set to work in Geneva. Russia was expelled from the League. Warning voices like that of Kérillis, who adjured them "not to add a hundred and seventy million Russians to the eighty million Germans

France already has on her neck," were completely drowned out by the clamor for a declaration of war on Russia.

The most fantastic reports about the chaos in the Red Army were circulated in the press. The two parliamentary groups of Bergéry and Laval, toiling for peace with Hitler, pressed Daladier to go to war against Russia. The danger that the two conflicts, the Franco-German and the Russo-Finnish would then merge, these groups insisted, was in reality an advantage for France. They calculated that a fusion of the two wars would permit a large-scale anti-bolshevik crusade. This might entice Italy and Spain to the side of the Allies and probably would cause most of the European neutrals and the United States to enter the conflict on the French side.

General Weygand was summoned to Paris to discuss the Near Eastern preparations. Another French General was sent to Finland as military adviser. Airplanes and tanks were made ready for shipment to Helsinki. For three months the belief was fostered in French public opinion that the Finns could win the war against Soviet Russia, or could at least resist for a year.

In the Chamber, however, a crisis was nearly caused by the shocking muddle of the censorship and by Daladier's arrogant treatment of the politicians. It was narrowly averted when the Premier assured Parliament that he did not mean to strip it of all its rights. On the strength of these promises, a war budget of 259,000,000,000 francs was voted.

At the end of the year a British division relieved some French troops in the Maginot fortifications. The British soldiers got a turkey dinner for Christmas. This caused an uproar in the French lines because the poilu disliked intensely being paid less and fed worse than the Tommy. A French infantryman received approximately two and a half cents a day, a British fifty-eight cents.

At the turn of the year, the French High Command issued the comforting statement that the Maginot Line had been tripled and extended along the Belgian frontier to the sea.

The new year began with a shake-up in the British Government. War Minister Hore-Belisha was replaced by Oliver Stanley. A colonel at the French War Office told me that the French General Staff was not at all displeased by the dismissal of Hore-Belisha. He had committed the unpardonable sin of eliminating some of the old generals. "You see," the colonel murmured, "our generals don't like the idea of being displaced by younger ones either."

In political circles a storm was brewing against the French High Command. The complaint was that Gamelin was not energetic enough in his conduct of the war. He was criticized for being too cautious and

From Sitzkrieg to Blitzkrieg

for opposing any offensive action. The name of General Noguès, Governor-General of Morocco, was put forward as a possible successor. Then a new alarm over Belgium and Holland saved Gamelin. But bad blood continued in the Chamber. The lobbies were openly hostile to Daladier. The demand for a secret session of Parliament enlisted more and more supporters. "If Daladier goes before a secret meeting of the Senate," Jeanneney told me, "he will not receive a hundred votes."

The circles around Bergéry and Laval began to urge that Marshal Pétain be made Premier to supplant Daladier. "The great soldier alone," they insisted, "can get France out of this terrible mess." Daladier, they claimed, was too flabby and yielding with the Communists and the British.

But Daladier prepared his counter-offensive. First he had a special committee set up in the Chamber to deal with the Communist question. The committee proposed the elimination of all Communists from public office.

Finally, Daladier arranged another meeting of the Allied Supreme War Council. The French and the British decided to intervene in Finland against the Soviet Union, if the Finns publicly demanded it. An army of 50,000 men gathered in a French port to be sent to Finland.

Having thus prepared the ground, Daladier appeared before Parliament in a secret session—the first of the war. It lasted thirty-one hours. It ended with an open vote of confidence of 535 to 0, endorsed by all the parties in the Chamber.

The offensive of the appeasers now took on renewed life. The largest morning paper in France, *Le Petit Parisien,* was swinging back into the appeasement camp, hinting at possibilities of coming to an understanding with the Nazis. A conference of Socialist Party provincial secretaries proved that the party machine was behind the appeaser Paul Faure.

Public opinion was more or less prepared for Finnish reverses toward the end of the campaign. However, the peace announcement between Russia and Finland, after the breakthrough of the Mannerheim Line, came as a big surprise to most of the country. The papers had predicted too often a continuance of Finnish resistance. Daladier was forced to call a new secret session of the Chamber.

He emerged a beaten man. Three hundred deputies of various parties abstained from voting for him. Only 239 supported him.

The third period of the French war ended with Daladier's resignation. To save his Government, Daladier had brought the nation to the brink of war with Soviet Russia. He had secretly sent airplanes and tanks to

From Sitzkrieg to Blitzkrieg 333

Finland, the absence of which was badly felt shortly thereafter on the French front. He had deepened the rift separating the French people.

His successor was Paul Reynaud.

The "Mickey Mouse of the French Parliament" had waited long for his hour to strike. A lawyer abounding in talents, a skilled parliamentarian, he had participated in many Cabinets.

He came from a wealthy family which had made its money out of department stores in Latin America. Small, agile and dapper, he first gives the impression of an impetuous man who acts quickly. He always seems to be in a hurry. "To act swiftly," he once said, "is the secret of success."

Little men often prove decisive. Reynaud compensated for his shortness by the zeal of his ambition. He is knowledgable enough not to have to put on airs. No doubt, his travels have taught him much. He has been around the world several times. He has visited every country which in the past few years has played a decisive rôle in world politics. He speaks English and Spanish fluently.

His career has been an easy succession of triumphs. The first time he took the floor at a lawyer's conference he was elected executive secretary of the Paris bar.

In the Chamber he represented the Paris Stock Exchange district. He was considered an able technician in financial matters. He sat in Parliament on the benches of the moderates—that is to say, on the Right. His political career was assured when a Clemenceau quip about him was made known: "He must bite well, that little mosquito."

His rich talents were limited by the fact that he was only an able technician. Nobody could analyze a problem and dwell on all its salient features better than he. But he was nothing but a technician. The people wanted a person in whom they could trust and believe. Not a dry, even if eloquent, calculator. Not somebody who saw only the technical points of a program, but one who saw its human and social aspects as well. That is what Paul Reynaud lacked. When he framed his emergency decrees after Munich, when he levied crushing taxes on the low-income brackets during the war, he saw only the need of balancing his budget. He forgot the needs of the man who had to pay. He understood perfectly the vital importance of mechanization in modern warfare. For years he fought to develop a better mechanized army for France. But what he overlooked was the man who has to sit in the tank, to drive the truck, to fire the gun. His knowledge of human nature did not extend much beyond the Stock Exchange and the drawing-rooms of Paris. If he knew history better than the history-professor Edouard Daladier, he shared with the latter an essential ignorance of the elements which move the wheels of history.

His relations with women overshadow his entire life. For almost twenty years he was a friend of Countess Hélène de Portes. She exercised considerable influence on him. During the war she had such a hold on him that the policy of France suffered from it.

Countess de Portes was the daughter of a civil engineer of Marseilles. One of her girlhood friends told me that in spite of her seemingly unattractive appearance, she always held a powerful attraction for men. When she met Reynaud she already knew life thoroughly. Her marriage with the Count de Portes, which took place after she became intimate with Reynaud, gave her entrée to Parisian society and to big business circles. In Paris it was claimed that this set shaped her political views. It was further rumored for years that she was a lobbyist for several big business interests.

One of her friends was Paul Baudouin. Baudouin was a friend of Laval and an admirer of Mussolini. It was the Countess de Portes who paved the way for the political collaboration of the two Pauls—Reynaud and Baudouin.

The fourth period of the war began with the formation of the Reynaud Cabinet. It was not a brilliant

Government that he presented to the Chamber, but rather a collection of mediocrities, some taken over from the Daladier combination, others from former Cabinets. The novel features were the ousting of Georges Bonnet and the entry of several Socialists. The Interior Minister was a nondescript Radical-Socialist, Senator Henri Roy.

Parliament manifested resentful hostility to the new Government. The Right was opposed to it because it included Socialists, the Radicals because of the downfall of their leader Daladier, which they attributed in part to Reynaud's intrigues. The new Premier had to take in Daladier as Minister of National Defense, in order to survive. But the two were not on speaking terms. Neither were their lady friends, the Countess de Portes and the Marquise de Crussols.

Marie Louise de Crussols d'Uzès had hold on Daladier similar to that of the Countess on Reynaud. Daladier lost his wife in the early thirties. Shortly afterward he entered into friendly relations with the Marquise. She comes from a wealthy family which made a fortune in canning sardines along the Breton coast. She acquired nobility by marrying the grandson of the dowager Duchess d'Uzès.

The Marquise, vivid and attractive, kept a lively political salon for years. It was the rendezvous of diplomats, Deputies and representatives of high finance. It was there that Daladier, the man of the 6th of February, made his peace with big business.

Reynaud escaped defeat in Parliament by a one-vote majority. He had a redoubtable quadrumvirate against him: Laval, whose influence was mounting rapidly in the Senate; Malvy, a former Minister whom Clemenceau had sentenced for high treason; George Bonnet, and Paul Faure.

When Reynaud formed his Cabinet, the more quiet days of the war were almost over. By the middle of March, Mussolini and Hitler met at the Brenner Pass. The Reynaud Government soon had to face the practical effects of the decisions taken by the two dictators.

As the new master of the Quai d'Orsay, Reynaud had to deal with an incident provoked by Daladier. The latter had demanded of Moscow that the Soviet Ambassador be recalled. The envoy had transmitted a resolution of the Russian colony in Paris by wire condemning "the French war-mongers for their frenzy against the Soviet Union." Jacob Suritz departed. When the climax of the French drama came, there was neither a French ambassador in Moscow nor a Russian envoy in Paris. But all the while emissaries were scurrying to and from Mussolini.

A few days before Hitler invaded Denmark and Norway, Reynaud spoke on the radio. He defended the war against the charge that it was "phony." He did not then know how right he was. He claimed, moreover, that France had forged the weapon for victory and was going to use it. How wrong he was!

With the invasion of the Scandinavian countries, events began to move swiftly. It looked at first as if Hitler had met his match in the British Fleet. It appeared that his troops might be cut off from the mainland. Churchill boasted: "Hitler has made the worst blunder since Napoleon." Reynaud swung a hostile Senate to his support in a speech replete with optimism. He rendered a dramatic account of the sinking of scores of Nazi ships in Norwegian waters. A British-French expeditionary force landed in Norway. But by the end of April the Allied War Council had to withdraw the troops. It was a staggering blow to French morale. Only in the vicinity of the Arctic port of Narvik did French Alpine troops, Poles and Britons continue to fight against Austrian mountaineers. Again Hitler achieved an impressive victory. It soon had a telling effect on the sentiments of the small neutral nations.

It was at the beginning of May that Chamberlain ventured to say: "Hitler has missed the bus." Three days later Nazi parachutists landed in Belgium and Holland. The fifth, the tragic period of the French war, had begun.

The telephone rang insistently in the very early morning hours. I was informed of Hitler's new move. I dashed to the Premier's office where his secretary told me that he was just phoning London. Reynaud, on his way to his secretary's office, flung at me: "The French troops are on the march!"

Had the great decision come? Or was Hitler only after Dutch naval and air bases? Paul Reynaud thought, as he told me that same evening, that Hitler was staking all on the throw. If such was his opinion the measures he had taken were not propitious for a successful French counter-move. He enlarged his Cabinet to include Louis Marin, an old Lorrainer, head of the Right-wing Republicans, and Jean Ybarnégaray, Vice-President of the "Croix de Feu." To meet Hitler, Reynaud took a Hitlerite into his Government.

The events are still vivid before my eyes. In one minute Paris changed. It was electrified, but not by optimism. Rather by a curious mixture of fear, premonition of evil things, and relief that the intolerable stalemate was finally broken.

In London, Winston Churchill supplanted Neville Chamberlain.

Five days after the initial attack, Hitler's troops marched upon French soil. For the second time in twenty-five years France was invaded.

On the day the breakthrough came at Sedan, we were awaiting news in the office. The official dispatches were optimistic. Private information was not as cheerful, but even then was far from revealing the extent of the catastrophe. I made the rounds of the Ministries. "General impression very grave, but we'll manage somehow."

The Dutch gave up. The Belgian-French-British Armies were retreating. Reynaud changed his Cabinet. He called in Pétain, the friend of Franco, as Vice-Premier. He sent Daladier to the Foreign Office and took over the National Defense Ministry. He appointed the fascist General Weygand Generalissimo, and Paul Baudouin Under-Secretary of State. Georges Mandel, "Clemenceau's policeman," took over the Ministry of the Interior.

That was Reynaud's answer to the arrival of the Nazis at the Channel. The Allied Armies were severed. They were never able to join again. In the French Cabinet a powerful Fifth Column, summoned by Reynaud himself, began its underground work. Or rather continued it.

At the first Cabinet Council, described to me by a terror-stricken Minister, Marshal Pétain pleaded for an immediate ending of the war. Weygand declared he was called in two weeks too late. No chance to hold out, he repeated several times. Both men belonged to the group which preferred to see Hitler rather than the Popular Front in Paris.

Blow after blow rained on France—at ever shorter intervals. Air alarms sounded in Paris. A stream of refugees—Dutch, Belgian, French—poured through the capital. Floods of rumors, generated we knew not where, spread like wildfire. One day they began burning the files of the Foreign Office on the street at the Quai d'Orsay, because the High Command had telephoned that a Nazi armored column would be in Paris within a few hours. It did not come then. Hitler was fighting the Battle of Flanders first.

Paris was declared part of the Army zone. Buses were commandeered. Strict orders for curfew were issued. The café terraces were empty. Thousands of Austrian and German refugees were herded into the sports stadiums. "Fifth Column! Fight the Fifth Column!" the newspapers shrieked. It was thought that Mandel was finally purging the Parisian salons and editorial offices of Hitler agents. He banned *Je Suis Partout*, a Nazi-inspired paper, and made a few arrests. But by the end of May *L'Ordre* complained: "There are many thousands of Communists in prison and only a few Hitler agents."

Three French Armies, the British Expeditionary Force, the remnants of the shattered Belgian Army corps retreated to the Channel. Boulogne fell, then Calais.

But France did not yet reach the end of her misery. Leopold, King of the Belgians, surrendered to Hitler. For more than a week hundreds of thousands of relatives waited agonizingly for news from Flanders. Had their sons and husbands and dear ones been evacuated?

A savage air raid on Paris came almost as a relief.

Many Parisians could not bear the thought that millions of Frenchmen were suffering while they were safe. The raid killed 260; hundreds were wounded.

Paris emptied. Hundreds of thousands of human beings left. We prepared to leave the city. The Government was leaving too.

The Battle of Flanders ended. Less than half of the French Armies could be evacuated. The others fell into Hitler's hands.

The Battle of France began.

For two days it seemed as though the front might hold. But then the British gave way on the left flank. The retreat to Paris started.

The Reynaud Cabinet was again reshuffled. Daladier was ousted. Paul Baudouin went to the Quai d'Orsay.

The Government fled Paris.

Mussolini declared war on France, just when it was practically over.

I went to Tours.

Paris was expecting the Nazis at any moment.

A nation which has lost a war looks for the responsible parties. It does not always fasten on the guilty.

While I write these lines, Pétain and Laval have set up a Court in the sleepy little market town of Riom to try those "who are guilty of the change from the state

From Sitzkrieg to Blitzkrieg

of peace to the state of war." History will not recognize a verdict pronounced by these men. The Pétain Government is nothing but a creature of the Nazis. And as such it acts.

France went into the war against terrific odds. Laval had wrecked collective security. Blum's non-intervention policy had split the forces capable and willing to resist a Hitler aggression. Daladier and Bonnet had sold one ally, Czechoslovakia, down the river. They had demolished the mutual-assistance treaty with Soviet Russia. At Munich the war was almost lost for France. The situation could have been reversed only if the popular forces in France had been convinced that there would be no more retreats after Munich; that there would be no attempts to destroy the social legislation of the Popular Front; that the French Government genuinely desired to collaborate with all the anti-fascist governments. Instead, the Daladier-Bonnet Government continued and intensified its anti-labor policy after Munich. This demoralized the country. Paul Reynaud's contribution was to saddle the "little man" with an economic burden too heavy to carry.

So, at the outbreak of hostilities, France was split, demoralized by the betrayals it had witnessed. It had no confidence in the leadership.

Because his tools sat in the highest seats of office, Hitler knew every move which the French or British

Government, or the Allied Supreme War Council, decided to make. When the Supreme Council decided to put a British division in the front line, Hitler knew about it two hours later.

When King George VI of Great Britain visited the front, the German broadcasters described his moves before the French and British press.

When Reynaud and Daladier quarreled, the German radio knew all about it.

Of course, the Nazi broadcasters faked a good many reports about dissensions in the French Cabinets. Nevertheless, it was shocking to learn how well-informed they really were.

Sabotage was not the work of a few Hitler agents alone. A large section of big business participated. So did high officials in the State administration and the Army.

The first flaws in France's technical armor were already revealed at the very outset of the conflict. The winter of 1939-40 was one of the most rigorous in a century of European history. But the French Army lacked blankets. Why? It was simply a complete lack of organization.

So was the shortage of shoes. In the outposts of the Maginot Line, French soldiers were forced to face rain

From Sitzkrieg to Blitzkrieg 345

and sleet and bitter frost wearing lightweight summer shoes. They wrote home asking for heavier ones. One of these letters was published by a newspaper, with an accompanying appeal to send footwear to the soldiers. The paper was attacked by other publications because it "disclosed secrets to the enemy."

In the second month of war, a worker at the Bloch airplane factory told me that they were producing less planes than before the war because of the lack of raw materials. In reality, French airplane production again reached the pre-war level only in 1940.

The Army suggested that planes be purchased in the United States. The Air Minister refused to place large orders, because the French manufacturers insisted that the money be spent in France. Huge orders for tanks and airplanes, placed shortly after the outbreak of the war, might have changed its entire course, and certainly would have altered its tempo.

Underground airplane hangars and factories were built at a snail's pace that seems incredible even for normal peacetime conditions. It was not sabotage by the workers. It was the result of instructions being altered all the time, of materials arriving late.

Nazi propaganda raged throughout France. French propaganda was either in the hands of a man like Giraudoux who shared Hitler's racial ideas, or in the hands of Frossard, a confirmed Munichman who inaugurated his stay at the Propaganda Ministry with a series of radio talks attacking Russia. In fact, the French radio programs generally were so dull that nobody wanted to listen to them. Foreign-language propaganda was entrusted to people who had either lost contact with their country of origin, or did not understand the first principles of modern propaganda.

The censorship kept the French people uninformed or miserably misinformed. Its head, Martinaud-Déplat, was a former Radical-Socialist Deputy who, in 1936, broke Popular Front discipline at the elections. At the run-off ballot he maintained his candidacy with the support of the Right against the Communists. He was then defeated. He was a personal friend of Daladier and a Munichman whole-heartedly on the side of appeasement. He staffed his office mostly with retired or former officers, some of them members of the royalist-fascist *Action Française*. These men persecuted every newspaper which had opposed Munich. No genuine news about Italy was allowed. When, toward the end of 1939, Count Ciano made a vehement attack against France, the French press was forbidden to carry the address. But the most roseate and totally unrealistic speculations about Mussolini's attitude were welcomed. So were the most fantastic accounts, purportedly from inside Germany, depicting the Reich as on the verge of collapse from mass famine. The familiar pictures of 1914, showing a German soldier easily induced to desert for a loaf of bread, came back into vogue. When the Franco press in Spain indulged in unsavory invective against France, the French papers were not permitted to report it.

Speeches of British Cabinet Ministers and parliamentarians were censored. So was the second official British *Blue Book*. It appeared on the kiosks for one day; then the French authorities swooped down and seized it. It was a week before it was again permitted to be sold publicly.

Corruption in Parliament and the press played a significant rôle in France's downfall.

Once, before an examining committee, Daladier testified that "eighty per cent of the French press is subsidized either by Government or private sources." Of the twenty-five-odd daily papers published in Paris, four— *Le Temps, Le Journal des Débats, L'Information* and *La Journée Industrielle*—were openly owned by big industrialists. Ten of the others received important financial support from the "200 Families"; three were in the hands of a paper manufacturer, Jean Prouvost, whom Reynaud later appointed Minister of Information. The Socialist organ *Le Populaire* was subsidized by Reynaud when Paul Faure, in order to get rid of Blum, induced the provincial Socialist sections to discontinue their support. The rest of the papers, the so-called "confidential sheets"—so called because of their extremely small circulation—lived from hand to mouth. They begged in order to keep alive, as an editor of one of them told me. Only two of the dailies published in Paris during the war were outspokenly anti-Munich: *L'Époque* and *L'Ordre*.

The official institution of "secret funds" in the Government budget gave a constitutional blessing to corruption. The "envelopes" were made ready at the beginning of every month at the Quai d'Orsay and other Ministries, to be called for either by the business managers or the journalists of the various papers. When censorship was established the "kept" press hated it. The reason was, in the words of one business manager, "Ministers who can suppress attacks by means of the censorship will not pay." Once, by chance, I was in the office of an important news agency at the time Daladier took over the Foreign Office from Bonnet. The burning question of the hour was not "What kind of a policy is he going to follow?" but "Qui va toucher?" The phrase might best be translated: "Who's going to get a rake-off?"

One of Bonnet's spokesmen, expressing the Minister's views in an influential evening paper, was before the Munich crisis editor of a news-letter subsidized by the Czechs. In this sheet he took an anti-Munich stand. He managed to ride two horses going in opposite directions for quite a time.

A former Deputy with connections at the Quai

d'Orsay made a digest of the foreign press every morning for Georges Bonnet. He received 5,000 francs monthly for this service. Then he took a carbon copy, went over to the Finance Ministry, dictated the same press digest for Reynaud, and received 4,000 francs monthly for his pains. After lunch he worked for a foreign journalist to whom he sold bits of information he had picked up at the Foreign Office and the Finance Ministry. In the evening he edited a news-letter subsidized by the Premier's office.

Corruption in Parliament was just as flagrant. Clemenceau once tartly remarked: "French parliamentarians do nothing but: *'toucher et coucher!'* "

An old habitué of the Chamber explained to me the following hierarchy among the *"corruptees."*

The lowest ranks consisted of former Deputies who did most of the lobbying. Then came young parliamentarians trying their first wings in the political arena, usually in the employment of minor firms. Then the well-established lawyer Deputies working for big business. On the top rung were former Ministers, now chairmen or board members of wealthy firms.

During the war, some of the Deputies made a nice income by helping to exempt people from military service. My informant estimated that of the 618 Deputies, at least 300 were on somebody's payroll.

The military Intelligence Service, the so-called

Deuxième Bureau, was a nest of corruption. Not only has it been established that some of its agents were working for the Nazis, but that some of its officials in Paris used their position for blackmail and shady deals. I know of three cases of refugees being forced to pay huge sums to a high officer in the Intelligence Service, in order to receive their naturalization papers. The *Deuxième Bureau* did a thriving business in false passports. Ministers were informed often enough of especially glaring cases of corruption in that department. They were unable or unwilling to do anything about them. The *Deuxième Bureau* seemed all-powerful. During the war, it failed to function.

The secret police, or Sûreté Nationale, was part of the political machine. Most of its officials collaborated with Deputies and politicians. During the war about fifteen men of the Sûreté were discovered collaborating with the Gestapo.

The French Army did not, of course, live in a vacuum. It was also infested with this vermin of corruption which marked the waning years of the Third Republic. High officers were eager for jobs with large corporations. They served as liaison agents for big contracts.

General Maurice Gustave Gamelin, who headed the French Army from 1935 on, must have been aware of the demoralization in the officers' corps. The majority of officers sympathized with the dictators and did not even take the trouble to conceal their sentiments. Gamelin did nothing to purge the Army of even its most suspect elements. He attained his post of supreme command by chance. General Georges was slated to succeed Weygand in 1935. But since Georges had been gravely wounded during the murders at Marseilles in 1934, Gamelin was chosen instead. His career showed no traits of brilliance, no flashes of genius. Generals require a legend. It was hard to weave one for Gamelin. He was the most unimpressive of French Generals. He served on Joffre's General Staff. He lived on the glory of having drawn up Joffre's famous order of the day on the eve of the Battle of the Marne.

But this much must be said in favor of Gamelin: never, unlike such of his fellow officers as Pétain and Weygand, did he plot against the Republic. But that virtue does not suffice to make a commander-in-chief. As head of the Army he was one of those responsible for the gaps and lags in armaments. Had he, as befitted his duty, served warning in time, remedies might have been procured. He was responsible for the terrible neglect of the Little Maginot Line, which was to have extended from the main Maginot Line to the Channel. The Little Line bore a great name, but consisted of a series of shoddy field fortifications. That was all.

Last of all, General Gamelin bears responsibility for the French Army's most fateful move: the march into Belgium. Imperative considerations dictated that the French Army remain in its prepared positions. If it moved out of line, it must meet an enemy possessing overwhelming superiority in mechanical and technical equipment and in airplanes, in a territory where there were no fortifications. Any advance into Belgium exposed the French Army to a flank attack through the Belgian Ardennes Forest region.

It has been reported that the British Ministers urged this advance. The old argument as to which were to be defended, the Channel ports or the Paris area, flared up in the most critical hour of the war. Gamelin, against the advice of an overwhelming majority of his Staff, decided to dispatch troops to Belgium.

General André Corap's Eighth Army was the pivot of the French advance. It advanced at such a speed that it covered ten miles in three days. It had not yet arrived at the positions it was supposed to reach when the German mechanized units broke through. Twenty per cent of Corap's Army was saved, the rest perished or fell prisoner to the Nazis. The gap left by this catastrophe—was it treachery or a colossal blunder?—could never be filled.

From numerous reports I have heard, it appears evident that many of the superior officers were not equal to their tasks. They went into the war against their own convictions; they did not believe it was the right war to fight. A large proportion of the reserve officers belonged to the "Croix de Feu" and other fascist organizations. They looked upon the Nazis with undisguised admiration. They were not the proper men to lead soldiers either in attack or defense. In fact, they were not trusted by the men under them.

When the first defeats came the officers' corps immediately showed signs of decomposition. When the Battle of France turned out badly, some of the officers quit their units and evacuated their families from Paris.

France was not beaten by Hitler. It was destroyed from within by a Fifth Column with the most powerful connections in the Government, big business, the State administration and the Army.

On board the ship which bore me from France, I met one of the wealthiest and most influential grain brokers in the country. At the outbreak of hostilities he sought and found refuge in the Army Supplies Department. Then he established a sub-department of the Supplies division at his private home in Paris. Then in May he bought his way out of the Army. Through lavish bribes, he managed to get himself sent on a mission to Argentina. We talked at great length about the tragedy which had befallen France. I asked him the questions I had put to myself so often: "Why did it happen? How did it happen?"

He answered: "Because France had too many men like me." This cynical admission is the best explanation I have heard.